# SAP® Project System Handbook

Kieron N. Dowling

Mc
Graw
Hill

New York   Chicago   San Francisco
Lisbon   London   Madrid   Mexico City
Milan   New Delhi   San Juan
Seoul   Singapore   Sydney   Toronto

**The McGraw·Hill Companies**

**Library of Congress Cataloging-in-Publication Data**

Dowling, Kieron N.
  SAP(r) project system handbook / Kieron N. Dowling.
    p. cm.
  ISBN 978-0-07-154450-4 (alk. paper)
  1. SAP R/3. 2. Project management—Computer programs. I. Title.

  HF5548.4.R2D69 2008
  658.4′04028553—dc22

                                        2008005194

McGraw-Hill books are available at special quantity discounts to use as premiums and sales promotions, or for use in corporate training programs. To contact a representative, please visit the Contact Us pages at www.mhprofessional.com.

### SAP® Project System Handbook

1234567890  DOC DOC  0198

ISBN    978-0-07-154450-4
MHID    0-07-154450-X

**Sponsoring Editor**
  Wendy Rinaldi

**Editorial Supervisor**
  Janet Walden

**Project Manager**
  Aparna Shukla,
  International Typesetting
  and Composition

**Acquisitions Coordinator**
  Mandy Canales

**Copy Editor**
  Jan Jue

**Proofreader**
  Manish Tiwari

**Indexer**
  Kevin Broccoli

**Production Supervisor**
  Jean Bodeaux

**Composition**
  International Typesetting
  and Composition

**Illustration**
  International Typesetting
  and Composition

**Art Director, Cover**
  Jeff Weeks

**Cover Designer**
  Pattie Lee

Dedicated with love to my children: Damien, Fiona, and Tia.

# Contents at a Glance

v

# Contents

# Acknowledgments

S AP, naturally. Who have rekindled the professional lives of many a gifted dinosaur after the gradual decline of the mainframe! Thanks to Rettitiswarane Velayoudam for his contribution to the section on Project Progress under Tips and Tricks. I would also like to thank the staff of McGraw-Hill whose professional approach has made this possible.

# CHAPTER 1

# Introduction

This guide provides a concise reference to the most important aspects of the SAP R/3 PS module. *Project System* (PS) equates to anything that is project-oriented and has a life cycle. Apart from providing detailed background information about the features of PS, this guide includes useful reference information such as Transaction Codes, Report lists, Tables, and Fields—vital when you're offline and need to refresh your memory.

One of the hardest things to communicate to those trying to implement business requirements in PS is the various methods by which things can be done. Questions range from "How does PS work?" to "How can I distribute my planned costs over five years all in one go?" to "Why can't I see my Planned Costs?" Reading this book should lead you in the right direction. It has been developed with a top-down approach, starting with the big picture and "drilling down" to detail as you progress.

## Project System: An Overview of PS

In business, just about everything can be viewed as a Project. The decision to use PS depends on the degree of complexity and functionality desired. SAP R/3 has other modules that offer objects capable of emulating a project—Production Planning, Sales & Distribution, Controlling with Internal Orders, and Customer Services, to name a few. But none has the depth of structure, integration, and complexity available in PS.

What exactly is PS? It is a repository for planning, collecting, and generating costs and revenue via a structure that truly represents what you are doing over a period of time. How simple is that? As simple or complex as you want it to be.

If it has a start, a middle, and an end—it's probably a project.

Everything associated with a project revolves around what SAP terms *Work Breakdown Structures* (WBSs) and *Networks*. These are the objects that do all the work and carry information about what the project will do. They can trigger events, schedule work, and generate demands for materials and services required to carry out the project.

The SAP R/3 manual defines *Projects* variously:

"[G]enerally complex, unique, having a high degree of risk, having precise goals, are limited in duration, are cost and capacity intensive, are subject to quality control and have strategic importance to the company carrying out the project."

"Projects can be structured according to how the project is organized and the process involved in carrying out the project."

"Projects are generally used as cost and revenue collectors."

## From Start to Finish

There are myriad examples where the preceding may not apply because of the nature of how a project can be structured.

For example, a project could be created as a single element without any associated structure whatsoever; in this case, it's simple because none of the "progressive" elements of project management apply. You might just want to record all the costs associated with the recruitment of a person into the company or with buying a mobile phone (there are, of course, other ways of doing this in R/3).

On the other hand, you might build a highly complex structure that reflects every single task associated with the building of an offshore platform, including the various services, creation of assets, billing of customers, and so on. Needless to say, all possible functionality would have to be utilized, including cost/revenue planning, budgeting, resource/capacity planning, activity control, milestones, Gantt charting, manufacturing, capitalisation, earned value, and so forth.

As seen in Figure 1-1, an SAP R/3 Project might "progress" from Definition through to Settlement.

You **Define** what you want to do from a business perspective, **Develop** a strategy that's represented by a structure, **Plan** your costs and revenues, and schedule when events must occur, approve the **Budget** and distribute it throughout your structure, release the project and **Execute** day-to-day confirmations, frequently **Evaluate** progress by reporting, **Settle** it to its intended receiver, and **Close** it off.

## Organization

From an Organizational standpoint, PS has many tentacles, which demonstrates how integrated it is. The fundamental elements of any business are driven by its organizational chart—information such as Company, Profit Center, Plant, Business Area. This "Master Data" provides the basis upon which reporting is performed. The organizational chart also keeps the elements of a project "honest," meaning that the relationship between these organizational values is respected.

Figure 1-2 contains a diagram of the various Organizational references each of the Project Objects may have associated with them.

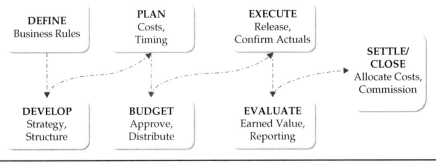

**FIGURE 1-1**   From start to finish.

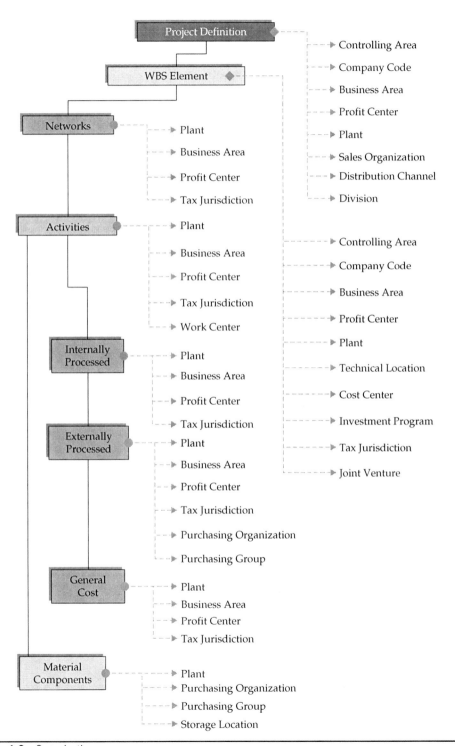

**FIGURE 1-2**   Organization

## Integration

Here we have an overview of the primary integration points for PS—there are others, such as Fixed Assets and Human Resources, but they do not play as substantial a part as the ones shown in Figure 1-3.

**Controlling (CO)**   Substantial integration exists between PS and CO. This is because PS relies on so many objects that belong to CO for Integrated Cost Planning, Settlement, Results

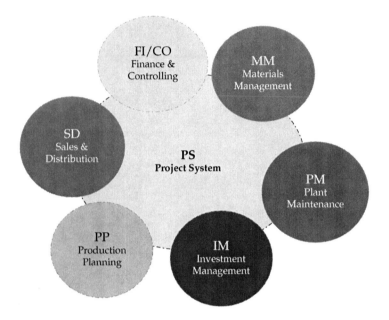

| Finance & Controlling | Project/WBS Number, Network, Controlling Area, Company Code, Business Area, Cost Center, Cost Element, Work Center, Activity Type, Profit Center, Results Analysis Key, Object Class, Internal Order, Account Number, Jurisdiction Code |
|---|---|
| Materials Management | Project/WBS Number, Network, Plant, Material Number, Material Group, MRP Controller, Vendor, BOM |
| Sales & Distribution | Project/WBS Number, Network, Partner, Sales Organization, Distribution Channel, Division, Sales Order BOM |
| Plant Maintenance | Project/WBS Number, Network, PM Orders |
| Production Planning | Project/WBS Number, Network, BOM |
| Investment Management | Project/WBS Number, Network, Investment Programs, Measure |

**Figure 1-3**   Integration

Analysis, Resource Planning, and any reporting that involves Cost Elements. Controlling Area is the most obvious connection, without which PS could not function. In Workforce Planning via Work Centers/Activity Types, there is integration with Human Resources (HR) to register personnel who are assigned to projects.

**Materials Management (MM)**    Based on Materials and BOMs, PS has the ability to create Reservations, Purchase Requisitions, and Purchase Orders via Easy Cost Planning Execution Services and Networks in general. This powerful integration makes PS a key player in the logistics cycle, including the ability to handle Services via Service Masters and Contracts. Further, the ability of Networks to work with Catalogues takes PS into SRM (Supply Relationship Management), where the Internet plays a large part in sourcing materials and services. Additionally, PS can help manage the MRP (Material Requirements Planning) cycle with its MRP Grouping functionality. PS is the "owner" of the ProMan facility, which tracks and helps manage all the Procurement document flows.

**Sales and Distribution (SD)**    PS has a fairly straightforward integration with SD via Order Numbers. All SD Orders (Quotations, Sales Orders, Consignment Orders, etc.) can be assigned to a project for the purpose of planning revenue, creating Billing Plans, and posting costs. DIP (Dynamic Item Processor) Profiles assist in the process of simulating and automatically creating Sales Documents, plus providing a means to bill customers based on activity within a project (Resource-Related Billing). Additionally, Assembly Processing provides the means for a Sales Order or Quotation to automatically generate a Project using Configurable Materials.

**Finance (FI)**    As PS is primarily a Cost Planner and Cost Collector and therefore a slave to FI/CO, its primary objects (WBS and Network) rely on actual expenditure to manage Account Determination, which is really the Chart of Accounts. Ultimately, all costs end up somewhere in Finance. Cash-flow management is also a feature that PS can be used for, via Funding Areas in Treasury.

**Production Planning (PP)**    Though not a major player in the PS side of integration, it is via MM that PP is informed of Production Orders using special settings in the Material Master.

**Plant Maintenance (PM)**    At the heart of this integration is Maintenance Orders, which, like most external orders, can connect to PS for Planning and Settlement purposes. Generally, Maintenance and Service Orders apply to Capital (Asset) or Customer-based projects, where equipment serviced onsite can be managed in a Project.

**Investment Management (IM)**    Quite a substantial amount of integration is involved here. IM seamlessly integrates with PS to manage Assets Under Construction (AUCs). Cost Planning can be managed in PS, sent to Investment Programs, and returned to the project as a managed Budget. AUCs are automatically generated when a project is released, so there is a relatively important connection to Fixed Assets.

# Summary

SAP PS has many strings to its bow and it depends on you to decide which elements to include in your design. In the next chapter, we take a look at a typical scenario and include the elements you might use.

# Scenarios

As you can imagine, many thousands of scenarios could be applied to an implementation. The one that follows is for a typical Sales-oriented project. You can take the individual elements and piece then together as you wish.

## A Typical Scenario

Following is a scenario involving most of the popular features of PS, from initial structuring to close-out. This chapter suggests what a project might look like in a normal situation.

It is a generic view and only serves to give you a bird's-eye view of a typical project scenario. To best describe most events that could take place within the PS module, our scenario emulates the basics of a project.

Here, the process is demonstrated in a linear fashion so you can appreciate what can be achieved and refer to the handbook for further detail.

### A Typical Working Scenario

Imagine we are going to construct a very simple Boat. In reality, there would be many structural elements to our Boat, but we only need to concentrate on the most important events, as you can see in Figure 2-1.

Each of the events in Figure 2-1 will have some or all of the following activities influencing them.

---

**NOTE** *Project OBJECTS are the various elements that carry vital data that make up a project:*
- *Project Definition*
- *Work Breakdown Structures*
- *Network Header*
- *Network Activities*
- *Activity Elements*
- *Milestones*

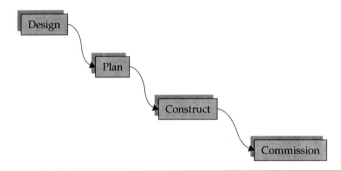

FIGURE 2-1 High-level steps

## Elements in the Scenario

| Element | | Purpose |
|---------|---|---------|
| Project Structure | | To provide a structure that represents the main events |
| Customer Order | | To record the Sales Order and connect it to a project |
| Network | | To detail what tasks are needed |
| Materials | | To requisition or reserve the raw materials needed to carry out the project |
| Labour | | To identify Human Resources needed to carry out the project |
| Schedule | | To plan when tasks will take place |

| Element | | Purpose |
|---------|---|---------|
| Milestones | | To identify key events |
| Planned Costs | | To plan how much the project will cost to carry out |
| Budget | | To control and limit expenditure |
| Workforce Planning | | To be specific about who will carry out the work |
| Status | | To control business functions |
| Actuals | | To record what actually happened as it occurs |
| Settlement | | To pass project costs to a receiver |

### The Project Structure

Suggested Transactions: **CJ20N**

In the first instance, a structure of events must be created. This structure is called a Work Breakdown Structure (WBS). Each WBS is connected to the one below it, but they can be placed beside one another to form a matrix, as shown in Elements in the Scenario. Collectively, they are called "Operative Projects." A WBS can be copied from what is termed a "Template" or "Standard Project" or from another Operative Project. The whole structure is "owned" by the Project Definition (just a "crown" that sits at the top of the tree).

Firstly, you create the Project Definition. Then, each WBS is created independently and given a Level Number, which determines where in the hierarchy it is placed.

Each WBS carries lots of information, such as Organization, Dates, Special Settings, Project Type, Who is responsible, and so on (see Figure 2-2). All of this is discussed in plenty of detail later.

*Think of a WBS as a Cost Collector.*

---

**TIP**  *When a project is manually created, it initially has a status of CRTD (Created). This means it cannot have any real costs and revenues posted against it.*

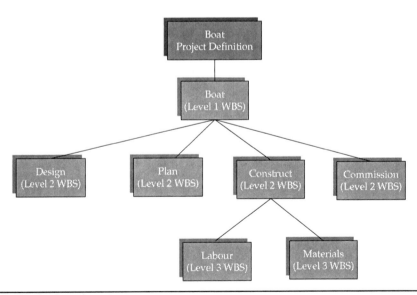

FIGURE 2-2   The basic project structure

### The Customer Order

Suggested Transactions: **CJ20N, VA01**

This is an optional integration point. If the business is using SD (Sales and Distribution), we can create a Sales Order that may have been derived from a Quotation. Each line item of a Sales Order is linked to a Billing element of our project. It may be that our Sales Order is a simple "one-liner"—in which case, it is linked to the Level 1 WBS. The act of optionally making this link issues a "Revenue Plan" for the project. Of course, if the Sales Order was a "four-liner," you could link each line to each Level 2 Billing WBS. It depends on where you want the Revenue to belong, because certain elements of your WBS may just carry internal costs. Note that you can only link a Sales Order line item to a WBS that is flagged as "Billing" (see Figure 2-3).

---

***TIP*** *Sales Orders can automatically create Projects (called "Assembly Processing") or Projects can automatically create Sales Orders (called "Simulated Sales Pricing").*

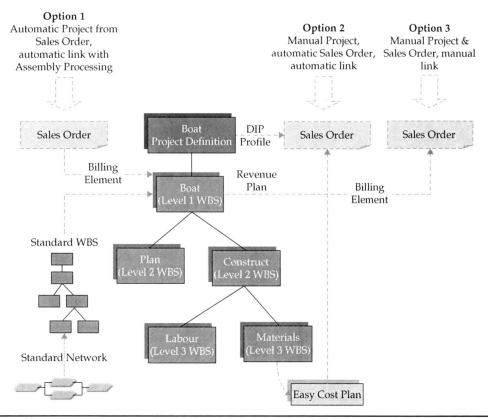

**FIGURE 2-3**   The project structure for Billing

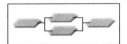

### The Network

Suggested Transactions: **CJ20N, CN01, CN21, CJ27, CJ2D**

Networks are connected to WBS Elements. They are a collection of Activities that can split up to represent such elements as Labour and Materials. Activities can be combined, in fact. But for this example, they are separate. Our project could have Activities linked to the lowest level of each WBS—that is, Design, Plan, Construct Labour, Construct Materials, and Commission: Activities contain Durations and Start-Finish dependencies, which is the basis for Project Scheduling. Operative Networks can be based on Standard Networks (Templates). See Figure 2-4.

---

***TIP*** *Networks are so called because each Activity can have a relationship with another Activity. These are called "Start-Finish rules." You can control when events are triggered.*

---

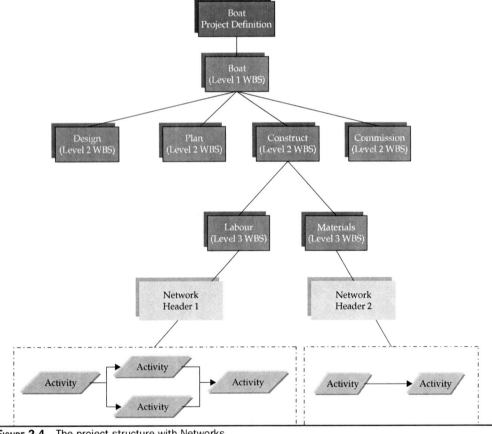

**FIGURE 2-4** The project structure with Networks

### The Materials

Suggested Transactions: **CJ20N, CJ27, CJ2D**

The place at which Materials will be ordered for our project is called Material Components, a subset of Network Activities. Here, you simply add the components you want to order. Each line of the order list can have either "Stock" or "Non-stock" materials ordered. In the case of Stock items, a Reservation will be generated to hold the stock (this is not a Commitment). In the case of Non-stock, a Purchase Requisition will be generated (which will result in a Purchase Order and therefore a Commitment). Further control of how the material is managed from a Material Requirements Planning (MRP) perspective can be specified in the Procurement Type, which considers things like long lead-time strategies.

In all cases, however, nothing significant will occur until the project has had its status changed to "Released." This is discussed more fully in Status Management.

When the Materials are entered, the cost of them (determined by the pricing policy of your business in the Control Key Parameters) and the overheads specified in your Costing Sheet are calculated and placed into the Plan Total for the Activity. These costs are used later, when we look at the Planned Costs. See Figure 2-5.

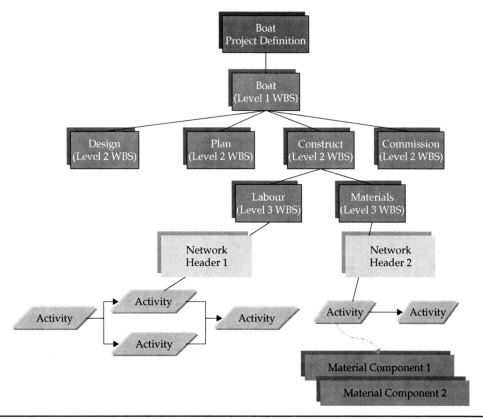

**Figure 2-5**  The project structure with Material Components

### The Labour

Suggested Transactions: **CJ20N, CJ27, CJ2D, CNR1, KP26**

Labour costs are usually determined by the Activity Type (not a hard and fast rule). You can also use Activity Types to represent things like medical tests or machining. Prices (Costs) per unit in an Activity Type (for example, per hour, per day) are maintained in the Controlling module of SAP (Planned Activity Prices) because they belong to Cost Centers. Activity Types in association with Network Activities are classed as "Internal Activities." The cost of using an Activity is determined by the length of time you use it in minutes, hours, days, weeks, and so on. The Work Center is used to determine the organization's capacity to perform the work. They are not necessarily used to represent utilisation of one resource—they can represent a group of people, a machine, or simply one person. Work Center/Activity Types are static fields within the Internal Activity (that is, there can only be one set per Activity). Additionally, Personnel can be assigned to Internal Networks to form the basis of Workforce Planning. (See "The Workforce.") As in Materials, Activity Types generate a planned cost, which updates the Order Plan Total (version 0). See Figure 2-6.

**FIGURE 2-6**  The project structure with Work Center/Activity Type

**The Schedule**

Suggested Transactions: **CJ20N, CJ27, CJ2D, VA01**

How you perform Date Scheduling in your projects depends on the method you want to adopt. In our case, we might simply apply the Forward Scheduling rule where the Activity Dates determine the WBS Dates. In other words, if you say that an Activity is due to be utilized on May 7 for ten days, then the associated WBS will inherit those dates (they don't have to if you don't want them to). But if you have another Activity under the same WBS, their combined date ranges can be moved up to the WBS. The combinations are many—even to the point where you may want to "Copy" the dates from your WBS down to your Activities. If, for instance, you tell SAP to Schedule your project, it will take actual events into consideration and change dates accordingly. This may affect whole project's critical path to the point where additional resources are required to complete the project on time, or maybe tell you that you will be late.

WBSs and Activities carry several dates: Scheduled Start/Finish, Latest Start, Latest Finish, Forecast, and so on. In a manufacturing environment, Backward Scheduling is used.

Finally, if you have many activities that are "linked" across WBSs, scheduling becomes even more complex. See Figure 2-7.

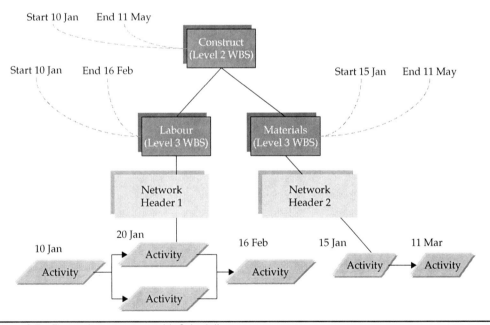

FIGURE 2-7    The project structure with Scheduling

### The Milestones

Suggested Transactions: **CN11, CJ20N, CJ27, CJ2D, CNMT**

These relatively simple objects can be attached to both WBSs and Activities. They can represent an event you want to remember, or they can have intelligence. In our case, we would use them to identify points in time when the customer must be issued with an Invoice, commonly referred to as *Milestone Billing*. This is done by specifying a percentage of the total account to be released for Billing. The Sales and Distribution term for this is *Billing Blocks* (meaning blocked for billing). When a Sales Order is linked to a WBS, it is capable of finding all the Milestones associated with it and creating a Billing Plan either in the Project or in the Sales Order. A Billing Plan is Blocked until it is opened for release when the milestone is given an Actual date, which is manually entered by the user.

Milestones can also get really clever and tell Activities to perform special functions—like "Release Activity number 10 when Activity number 9 is finished." Other functions of Milestones include Milestone Trend Analysis (MTA), a reporting tool that works with Project Versions. See Figure 2-8.

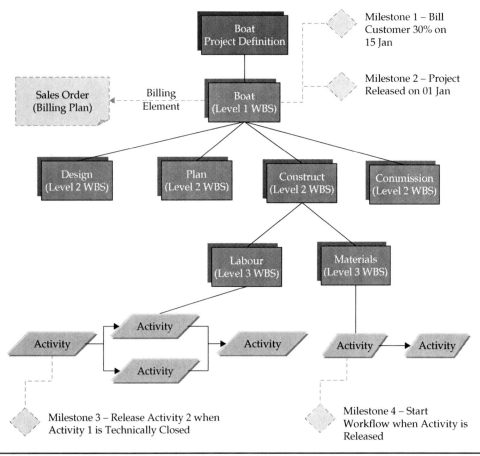

FIGURE 2-8 The project structure with Milestones

### The Planned Costs

Suggested Transactions: **CJ40, CJ20N, CJ27, CJ2D, CKCM**

Having already generated our planned costs via Materials and Activity Types, you can, if required, generate further planned costs using General Cost Activities, or if there are no Network Activities in your project, Easy Cost Planning will allow you to plan costs directly against a WBS Element using Activity Types, Cost Elements, or Materials.

This planning process can be simple or complex, depending on how you configured your Planning Profile: Structure or Detailed.

It may be that you did not want Activities at all—in which case you merely calculate your costs by Cost Element and transfer them to your Planned Costs for each WBS. You can, if you wish, maintain many "Plan Versions" and compare them for optimisation. Plan Version ZERO is the one PS always uses as its baseline plan, however.

PS permits Bottom-up, Top-down, or Open Planning (see Figure 2-9). See "Planning Profile" in Chapter 5 for more.

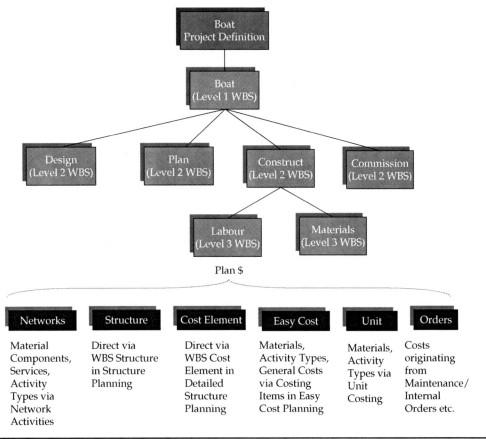

| Networks | Structure | Cost Element | Easy Cost | Unit | Orders |
|---|---|---|---|---|---|
| Material Components, Services, Activity Types via Network Activities | Direct via WBS Structure in Structure Planning | Direct via WBS Cost Element in Detailed Structure Planning | Materials, Activity Types, General Costs via Costing Items in Easy Cost Planning | Materials, Activity Types via Unit Costing | Costs originating from Maintenance/ Internal Orders etc. |

**FIGURE 2-9**   The project structure with planned costs

### The Budget

Suggested Transactions: **CJ30**

Even though you have finished planning your costs, you must now decide what your Budget is. Normally, your Plan becomes your Budget, but you can tell PS this—by copying it to the Original Budget. This done, you must then repeat the process in Release Budget (or at least you must release the portion of the budget you want people to use). Budgets can be spread across one year or many years. Once again, it depends on how you configured your Budget Profile. One defining difference between Planning and Budgeting is that Budgets carry with them a record of changes (for example, if you change the Original Budget manually, a record of that change is kept) that can be reported on. Another factor comes into play here—Availability Control. This process determines the levels to which a budget can be expended and how warnings, error messages, or mail to Project Managers are handled (see Figure 2-10). See "Budgeting Profile" in Chapter 5 for more.

---

**TIP**  *Budgeting is by no means mandatory. However, it can only be applied at the WBS level. There is no such thing as budgeting in Networks—they are exclusive to WBSs but can be derived from Networks. There is an audit trail associated with budget changes.*

---

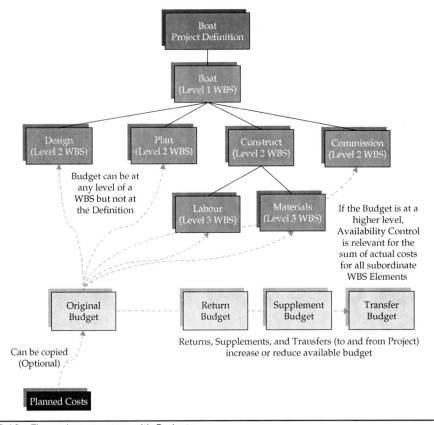

**FIGURE 2-10**    The project structure with Budgets

### The Workforce

Suggested Transactions: **CJ20N, CMP2, CMP3, CMP9**

This process works primarily with Work Centers (which carry the Capacity). Once you have assigned the Work Center/Activity Types you want to use to plan your costs, you take things a step further by assigning people to your Internal Network Activity. Prior to doing this, you must have set up your personnel in the HR minimaster and assigned them to the relevant Work Centers. What this achieves is the ability to select only the people who have been assigned to the Work Center that is featured in the Network Activity. At the same time, you specify the amount of work the individual will contribute. The knock-on effect of this forms the basis of Capacity Planning, which can be performed by Work Center or by Project (see Figure 2-11).

---

*TIP   Capacity Planning not only affects PS—but also Work Centers can be used by other modules such as Production Planning (PP) and Plant Maintenance (PM). These modules could share the Work Centers with PS, hence the needs for Capacity Planning and Leveling Person Assignment are removed when a project is Technically Closed.*

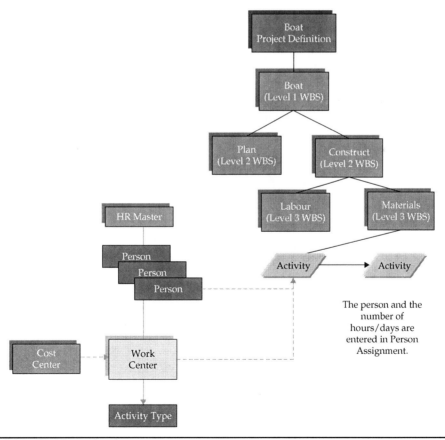

**FIGURE 2-11**   Workforce planning

### The Status

Suggested Transactions: **CJ01, CJ20N, CJ27, CJ2D**

This process will allow you to "Execute" the project and start confirming actual costs. To do this, you must Release. Already, you will notice the Status of your project has changed—it will have a status of CREATED, BUDGETED, COSTS PLANNED, and maybe a few more. But until it is RELEASED, not a lot happens. When you do RELEASE the project, several things will happen, some of which are:

- The Materials will be checked for availability.
- Requisitions will be generated.
- Reservations will be sent.
- Commitments (your Requisitions) will be checked against Availability Control.

Progressively, you may want to control what business transactions can and cannot be permitted, for example, if you change the status of your project (or just one WBS) to TECHNICALLY CLOSED. This status will remove any Reservations and allow commitments to be finalized. You can reverse this status at any time. After final settlement, the project can be CLOSED. If you need to control the status yourself, configure "USER STATUS." See Figure 2-12.

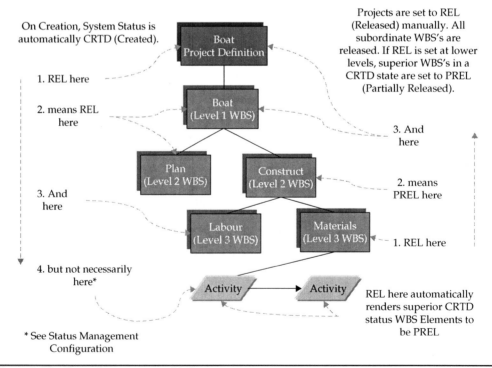

**FIGURE 2-12** The project structure with Status

### The Actuals

Suggested Transactions: **CAT2, CN25, CNMM, CNL1, FB50, KB11N**

There are many ways a project can attract actuals. Some are

- Time-sheet being "confirmed" to an Activity via the Cross Application Time Sheeting System (CATS)
- Activity Allocations (where you simply confirm all the hours without using a Time-sheet)
- Materials ordered via a project being delivered
- FI Journals being posted directly to a Project
- Financial Allocations, Interest, and so on
- Settlement to the Project from other objects such as Maintenance Orders
- Revenue received from Customer

In all cases, the date the event occurred becomes significant because it tells the project when things really happened. This in itself "progresses" the project so you can calculate the "Earned Value" (a facility that compares where you thought you would be, where you are, and where you will be in the future if the trend continues). Remember that every time a cost hits your project, Availability Control checks that you have not broken the budget (see Figure 2-13).

---

**TIP** *Actual Costs and Revenues remain on a Project until settled. You cannot close a Project unless it has been fully settled or been specified as "not for Settlement."*

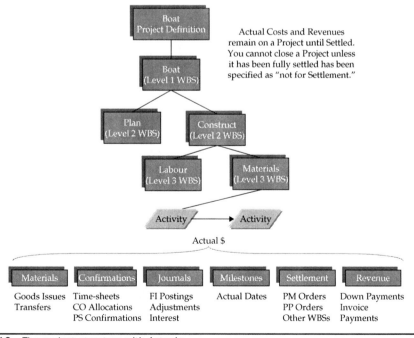

**FIGURE 2-13** The project structure with Actuals

### The Settlement

Suggested Transactions: **CJ88, CJ8G**

Not all projects are subject to Settlement (this is controlled by the Settlement Profile). Settlement transfers actual costs from the Project Object to external objects (such as Assets, Cost Centers, GL Accounts, etc.). Sales-oriented projects could have their costs settled to a Profitability Segment and be subject to RA (Results Analysis), which is performed before settlement. The most common settlement receivers are Cost Centers and Assets Under Construction, which are attributed to Expense and Capital projects respectively. Some Projects have both, where part of the cost is Expense, the balance Capital. Usually, Activity costs settle to the superior WBS. This ensures that all costs are transferred to the WBS structure, which can in turn be settled to an external receiver (see Figure 2-14).

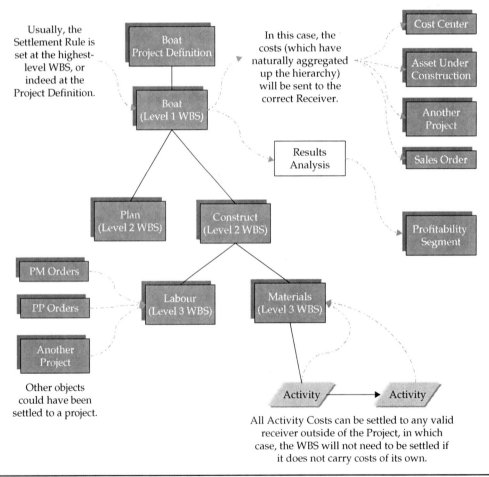

**FIGURE 2-14**   The project structure with Settlement

*TIP* *Unless a Project is deemed "not for settlement," it cannot be Closed until it has been fully settled (balanced to ZERO). One of The best way of analyzing a Project's balance is via transaction CJI3, which among other things provides you with a list of all CO postings.*

## Summary

The preceding scenario is illustrating some of the available permutations—the next chapter will examine the various ways in which PS can be applied, depending on the types of project you want to manage: Asset, Customer, Construction, and so on.

# Methods and Styles

P S can be used to manage projects of many types at the same time, if necessary—typically Asset creation, Customer servicing, Manufacturing, Costing, and so on.

## Ways of Using PS

You will probably have realized by now that the Project and Network Definitions rule the roost and determine the various styles and methods available. So it's perfectly acceptable to mix them in one business (a lot of businesses have Assets they build for Customers, where they may even perform the maintenance). The Business Blueprint will, of course, be the basis upon which you decide how PS will be utilized, but following are the most likely methods.

### Asset Projects

Building an Asset using PS involves the use of IM (Investment Management). Though it is quite possible to achieve a result with the use of PS only, it is not recommended if Capital Funding needs to be monitored. It is the Investment Program that (optionally) distributes the Capital Budget down into the various WBS Elements or Internal Orders. An important ingredient is an object called an Asset Class, and this is what will ultimately trigger creation of the Asset Under Construction (AUC)—that being the term SAP uses to identify the Asset whilst it is being built. The Project can purchase all the materials required (via WBSs in Easy Cost Planning or Networks or both). PS actually creates an AUC at the point a project is released—it is the Investment Profile inside the Budget Profile and the Program Position inside the WBS (called the Measure) that tells PS this is an Investment Project. Settlement Rules for a project like this are automatically created during the first Settlement run. The final Settlement run is called Capitalisation—and this is when the AUC is manually converted into a Fixed

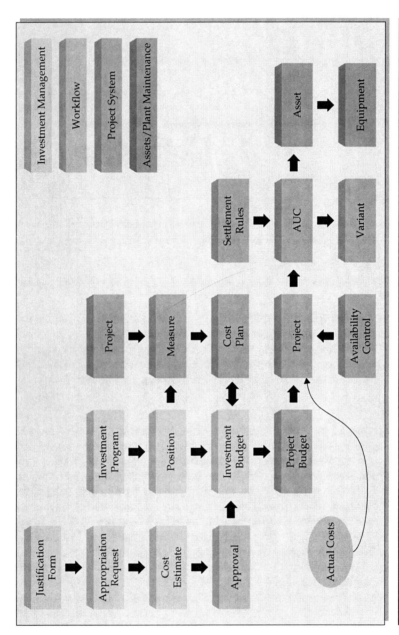

**FIGURE 3-1**   Process relationships for Asset Projects

Asset. See Figure 3-1. This details the logical steps and processes required to bring an asset from "appropriation" through to creation of the fixed asset itself, which may be a piece of equipment.

- **Resource Appropriation Process**   Formal submission of investment plans—approval releases for the sanctioned Capital Investment (CAPEX) spending.
- **IM Planning & Budget Distribution**   The rolling up of submitted investment plans within the investment management hierarchy and the top-down distribution of binding budget.
- **Project setup**   The creation of an appropriate project hierarchy to reflect cost control requirements of complex capital purchases. Bottom-up cost planning at the appropriate level of the project hierarchy is in line with the approved budget.
- **Project execution and reporting**   Actual postings and reporting actuals versus budget and plan.
- **Project Settlement**   The process of periodically reallocating project costs to the appropriate receiver. For CAPEX projects, this is to either a fixed Asset or an AUC. Settlement rules need to be understood to ensure their ongoing relevance and the accurate assignment of costs in the balance sheet.

### Key Terms for Asset Projects

The following terms are used throughout SAP to identify specific processes, objects, or master data elements used in the creation of an Asset.

| Term | Description |
|---|---|
| Applicant | Person who raises a request for capital budget, often a project manager or project accountant. |
| Appropriation Request | Mechanism within investment measure to request investment funds. The appropriation request holds all details of the project/investment proposal and is submitted in the system with the attached project details. Workflow is used to progress the request to the approver. When the appropriation request is approved and released, an Investment Measure is set up. |
| Asset Master | Record set up in Asset Accounting to track the expenditure and depreciation of fixed assets in the asset register. |
| Asset Under Construction (AUC) | Asset Under Construction is a special asset master record to collect expenditure for capital expenditure where the fixed asset is not capitalised and depreciated straightaway. The Asset Under Construction records expenditure in the balance sheet but will not be created as a depreciable fixed asset record until the asset is commissioned. |

| Term | Description |
|---|---|
| Equipment Record | Records maintained in Plant Maintenance (PM) containing all details including location and value of a piece of equipment. There is a one-to-one link between an equipment record and an asset record, and both records reference each other. Workflow can notify PM to create an equipment record when an asset record has been created. |
| Investment Management (IM) | The Investment Management module in SAP R/3. Used to plan investment expenditure, manage the appropriation of funds, control expenditure, and monitor budget vs. actual. IM is highly integrated with the Project System (PS) and the Finance(FI) modules of SAP R/3. |
| Investment Measure | Used to collect actual expenditure against capital projects and installation and service costs for selling equipment. Investment measures are linked to the investment management hierarchy to aid budgetary control. |
| Investment Position | The lowest level of the investment hierarchy—usually at profit or cost center level. Investment measures, that is, projects, are assigned to investment positions. |
| Investment Program | The investment program represents a hierarchy of planned and budgeted costs for capital expenditure. There is usually one IM program per business unit, but this is not a restriction by any means. |
| Service Order | Service orders are used to collect costs associated with selling equipment, for example, the installation and servicing of assets held on customer sites. Service orders are part of the Service Management module of SAP. Service orders are held as investment measures on the investment hierarchy and are raised through the approval of appropriation requests in the same way as other capital projects. |
| Settlement | The periodic process of reallocating costs from a WBS element to an appropriate receiver such as a Fixed Asset or an Asset Under Construction. |
| Variant | Alternative for fulfilling a proposed investment—technical and financial variations. |

Use of all of the preceding terms can be seen as an integrated model in Figure 3-2.

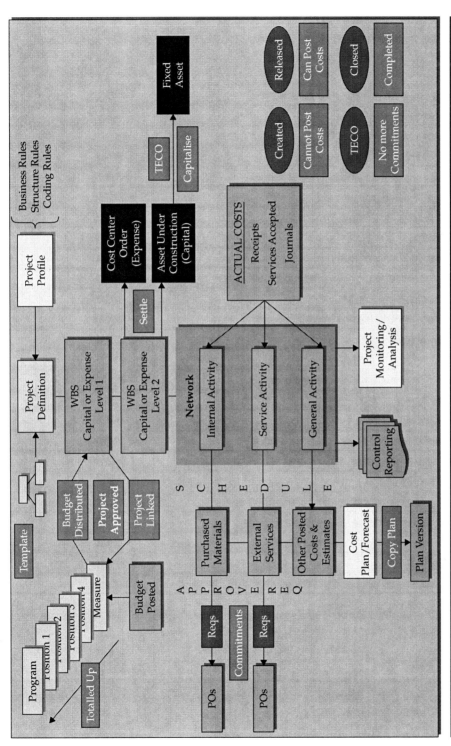

**FIGURE 3-2**  Integrated process flow for Asset Projects

### Detailed Steps for Asset Process

The following transactional steps are the most likely in the process of Asset creation:

| Step | TCode |
|---|---|
| Create appropriation request for capital project | IMA11 |
| Approve appropriation request | IMA11 |
| Plan from appropriation requests | IMAPL |
| Create investment measure | IM12 |
| Replace appropriation request with measure | IM05 |
| Investment management planning | IM35 |
| Determine default plan values from project | IM34 |
| Budget creation | IM32 |
| Convert plan to budget in investment program | IM44 |
| Process budget distribution to investment measures | IM52 |
| Budget updates | IM32 |
| Budget supplement to the investment program | IM30 |
| Budget return in project | CJ34 |
| Budget supplement in project | CJ37 |
| Project builder—maintain project master data | CJ20N |
| Project planning | CJ40 |
| Redistribute project plan | IM34 |
| Redistribute project budget | CJ30 |
| Project builder—release project | CJ20N |
| General ledger posting | FB01L |
| Create asset and enter settlement rule on WBS element | CJ20N |
| Actual project settlement: individual processing | CJ88 |
| Actual project settlement: collective processing | CJ8G |
| Close project | CJ20N |
| Technically close and close project (project builder) | CJ20N |

As an aid to understanding Configuration, Figure 3-3 shows the key object relationships between IM and PS.

## Customer Projects

PS can be used to manage the sale of anything. If you are building something that you will ultimately be selling to a Client after you have built it, you can do it in one of two ways, as described in the next sections.

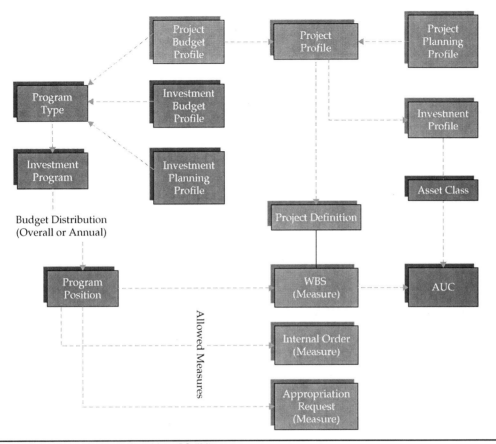

**FIGURE 3-3**    Key object relationships (PS/IM)

## Customer Project with Assembly Processing

You can create a quotation that leads to a Sales Order containing Configurable Material as Line Items. This will automatically generate a Project and in turn automatically trigger the creation of Material Reservations or Purchase Requisitions and Purchase Orders (either from Stock or from a third party). In conjunction with this, you can trigger a request for manufacture of your Configurable items. The project's part in this process is to manage the basic scheduling of the procurement cycle—not the manufacture itself (this is done in Production Planning [PP]). Customer Billing is also performed from the Project based on Milestones, which would have been used to create a Billing Plan in the Sales Order when the project was initially created. Be aware of certain limitations in CN08 - mainly that the material number is the key and you can only have one. It is only possible to have one Standard WBS as well. Figure 3-4 describes the process involved in using Assembly Processing to generate a project.

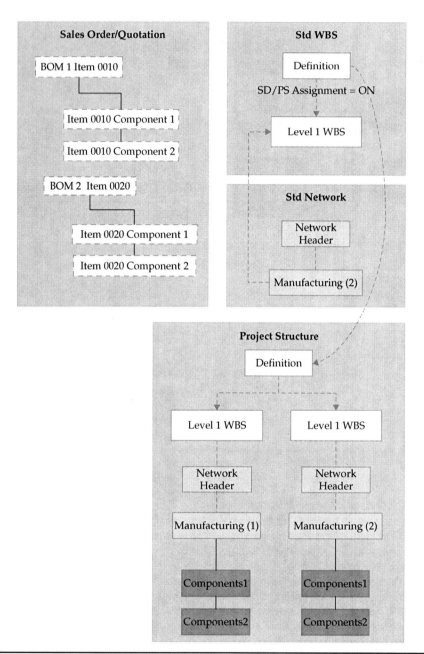

FIGURE 3-4 Assembly processing

---

**TIP** *A Project is automatically generated from a Sales Order when Materials in the Line Item have been "Allocated" in transaction* **CN08**. *This determines which WBS structure is to be used as the basis for project creation, which has also been linked to a Std Network. Because the SD/PS Assignment is* <u>ON</u> *in the Std Project Definition, a WBS leg is created for each Sales Order Line Item, including similar Networks. If the SD/PS Assignment were* <u>OFF</u>, *only one WBS leg with one Network Header would be created, but there would be multiple Activities. To make this process more flexible, you can use the "Class" field in CN08 to identify a characteristic. Then, during Sales Order creation (VA01) you can complete values (for instance, Plant), which can be transferred to the subsequent Network Activity via "Object Dependencies" in the Standard Network.*

Copyright by SAP AG

### Customer Project with Direct Sales

You can create a Project, perform Easy Cost Planning against WBSs, and make PS automatically Execute the procurement/reservation of various items that make up the sale, then create a Sales Document (Quotation or Sales Order). This is achieved using DIP (Dynamic Item Processor) Profiles. Normally, for this scenario, you would use what are called Service Materials on the Sales Order (materials that are not physical, just a description of what you are selling). You might then simply bill the customer based on a marked-up value of your Planned Costs (Order-Related Billing). Alternatively, you could bill the customer based on the resources you have used—this is called RRB (Resource-Related Billing) and again, the DIP Profile is used in a slightly different way to achieve this via transaction DP91. Settlement of Sales-oriented projects usually includes the use of Results Analysis. This is a process that populates Profitability Segments, which are then Settled as normal.

## Service Project

These are projects that exist for the purpose of servicing equipment that may be on a customer site (or even on your own site). In all honesty, you would most probably engage the services of SAP's CS module (Customer Services) in conjunction with PM (Plant Maintenance). But you can easily emulate parts of that facility by creating a project that has a structure representing the various pieces of equipment you are managing. It is a bit like a Sales-oriented project, but you would connect PM Orders to the WBS or Network. The planned costs can be seen by the project and actual costs can be settled to the project. Billing of the customer could utilize RRB, where CATS Timesheets and other actual costs can be transferred to the customer invoice with a mark-up.

# Working with Materials

Materials (as defined in MM—Materials Management) are identified using a Material Number. The various master data values and configuration settings of a material will determine its behaviour within a project.

If **Unit Costing** (UC) is used, Materials are entered against a WBS in the Item View. If General Cost Activities are being used to Plan, you can access Unit Costing from within the Project Builder via the icon shown here.

Copyright by SAP AG

If **Easy Cost Planning** (ECP) is used, Materials are entered against a WBS in the Item View (there is not much difference between UC and ECP). ECP is more user-friendly because of Cost Models but does not distribute costs across time. Also, with ECP, you work exclusively within the Project Builder.

If **Networks** are used, Materials are entered against a Network Activity in the Material Component view.

Further, if **SRM** (Supply Relationship Management) is used, you may enter a material via the Catalogue, which can be accessed using this Icon in the Component Overview screen:

Copyright by SAP AG

*These are the only methods by which you can plan materials directly in a project.*

In all cases, it is possible to control subsequent processes such as creation of a Reservation, Purchase Requisition, and Purchase Order.

The following Material data have an effect on what happens to the material in projects:

- **Item Category** (Most commonly L=Stock Item, N=Non-Stock Item)   This will determine whether a Reservation or Requisition is subsequently created.

- **Procurement Indicator** (Configured in OPS8)   This carries the default Item Category, Priority, and Control settings.

- **Purchasing Info Record**   This carries the source procurement information about a specific material and a specific vendor.

- **Outline Agreement**   Sometimes the purchasing organization has long-term contracts or scheduling agreements with vendors for the supply of materials or services. Specifying them directs MRP to use the contract/agreement.

Consider using ProMan (Transaction CNMM) to make the job of managing the procurement cycle easier.

Active Reservations are removed when a project is Technically Closed (System Status TECO).

### Project Stock

"Project Stock is automatically created to identify in quantity and value all Materials assigned to Planning. It is optional to manage project stock physically from bin location to bin location." (*There is an important synchronization point with PP, MM, FI, and CO because Project Stock can have an impact on the Materials requirements for Production Orders, Inventory Management, and FI postings. The resulting costs on Project Stocks or Projects must be seen in accordance with CO.*)

A Stock Entry credits Project Stock Value and a Stock Issue debits Project Stock Value. A Customer Material Issue decreases the Stock Project Value and posts an Actual Cost on the Project.

### For Purchased Material

- Purchase Requisitions and Purchase Orders will both generate a commitment on a project.

- Goods Receipt and Invoices will valuate Project Stock if the WBS is set to Valuated Project Stock.

- Actual Data will be posted when the Material is delivered to the Customer.

**For Manufactured Material**

- Requirement generates commitment.
- Goods Receipt will valuate Project Stock if the WBS is set to Valuated Project Stock.
- Actual Data will be posted when the Material is delivered to the Customer.

**For Stocked Material**

- Stock Issue will valuate Project Stock if the WBS is set to Valuated Project Stock.
- Actual Data will be posted when the Material is delivered to the Customer.

Generally speaking, the Materials that are needed for a Production Order are managed through MRP. MRP creates a Procurement Proposal that is transformed into a Purchase Requisition.

Sometimes this cannot be done because the Procurement Lead Time for the Material is longer than the MRP Lead Time.

In this case, an Anticipated Procurement (long lead-time) must be created before the Production Order exists. When the Production Order is created, MRP takes into account the Purchase Requisition and does not create a new Procurement Proposal.

When the Material is received, it is entered into the Project Stock. When it is used by the Production Order, the Costs are settled to the Project.

# Working with CRM

CRM (Customer Relationship Management) is an externally managed tool that "replicates" information To and From SAP. It operates in a separate instance of SAP under the mySAP Business Suite. This guide does not cover the implementation of CRM, only one of the main integration points that is useful for PS (Campaigns).

Being a Customer-oriented tool, CRM best works with SD (Sales and Distribution) in the area of Quotations, Sales Orders, and Sales Documents in general. For example, Quotations created in CRM (which contain additional information not found in SAP) can be replicated into SAP in a seamless way.

CRM provides for Marketing Campaigns—which allow for the possibility of having Projects automatically created from a Marketing Campaign structure that has been created in CRM. This process is useful if you want to manage projects whose creation does not depend on tools such as CJ20N or CJ01 and may be under the control of persons who are not necessarily project managers. The created projects may be for simple use, such as collecting costs. CRM is capable of sending Planned Costs and Budgets to the projects.

It goes without saying that all the normal PS configuration must be performed prior to creation of Projects via CRM—usually, you would have to configure:

- Project Profile (note: CRM can only reference one Project Profile)
- Project Type
- Persons Responsible
- Planning Profile
- Budget Profile
- Availability Control tolerances

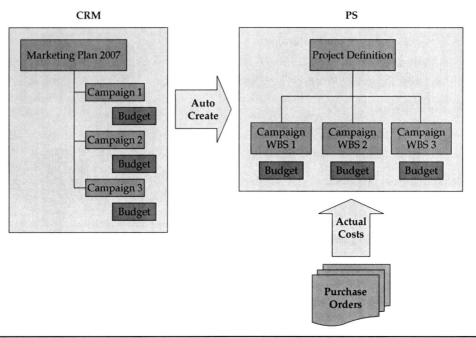

**FIGURE 3-5**  PS/CRM integration

- Coding Mask
- Settlement Rules
- Project Definition and WBS Field Selections
- Network Profiles and Types if you intend to perform scheduling of tasks

One thing you must consider is that CRM will create a new Project Definition and WBS <u>every time</u> you release the Campaign. Further, it does not use the "open number" facility of PS to create the project—it will use the Campaign number assigned (which can be automatic from CRM's point of view, but not PS's). To make the numbering work properly, however, you must create a Project Coding Mask in CRM, which should match the one configured in PS.

Figure 3-5 shows what may be a standard way of integrating Projects to CRM.

Figure 3-5 only serves to illustrate the way CRM would create a project structure. Each node in CRM could potentially create a WBS; however, it will only do this if you tell CRM to by releasing it.

## Summary

Deciding on the style of your projects very much depends on the outcome you're looking for—if you are creating Assets for the business, Billing Customers, Manufacturing something, tracking costs, and so on. All of these outcomes can be combined in one single type of project if you wish—so you would have to be skilled enough to know what Features you may need, which leads us to the next chapter—understanding and choosing the features you could use.

# Features of Project System

PS has many features you can use to develop a Blueprint for a client. They are the building blocks that form the basis of your design. The following pages explain the elements PS offers for managing a project. To assist you in finding where to configure and operate these features, transaction references are provided after each feature description later in this chapter.

PS can be divided into several progressive "working elements." In summary: You need a Structure in order to Plan Costs and Resource, which can be the basis for a Budget. In order to Schedule and Time the work to be done, you need Dates and Resources, which may or may not have a Capacity to perform the work. If you want to get paid for what you manufacture or sell, you need a Revenue Plan. When you're ready with your Planning, you go ahead and Execute the project by changing its Status. Periodically, you monitor your Progress and Settle your Actuals to the correct Financial receiver so the project "sheds" its values.

---

**REMEMBER**  *Projects are a temporary repository for Costs and Revenues—they have a set life and are subject to closure when all work is completed, but cannot be closed if they still have unsettled values.*

---

| Structural Elements |
|---|
| Coding Masks |
| Project Profiles |
| Project Definition |
| WBS Elements |
| Templates |
| Milestones |
| Networks |
| Internal Orders |
| Attachments and PS Text |

| Cost/Resource Planning |
| --- |
| Structure Cost Planning (WBS) <br> Detailed Cost Planning (WBS) <br> Detailed Cost Planning (Network) <br> Easy Cost Planning (WBS) <br> DIP Profiles <br> Plan Versions (CO) <br> Statistical Key Figures <br> Overheads (CO) <br> Value Categories |
| **Budgeting** |
| In Projects <br> In Investment Programs <br> Availability Control |
| **Time and Capacity Planning** |
| Dates in WBS <br> Scheduling in Networks <br> Work Centeres and Activity Types <br> Workforce Planning |
| **Revenue Planning** |
| Structure Revenue Planning <br> Detailed Revenue Planning <br> Sales Orders (SD) |
| **Execution** |
| Status Management <br> Actuals <br> Simulation <br> Versions |
| **Period-End** |
| Settlement <br> Period-End <br> Progress <br> Archiving <br> Billing |

# Structural Elements

A project cannot exist without a structure. At a minimum, you need a Project Definition plus at least one WBS. These two elements are what make up the basis of a project. Extending your project to include Networks makes it more complex and usually means you need scheduling and complex material handling. However, some implementations only use WBSs to plan and capture costs. In all cases, it is wise (though not mandatory) to have a method by which your WBS structure is recognized by its various levels—hence Coding Masks.

Depending on the implementation, a mask that carries intelligence (that is, it contains numbers and letters that mean something to the business) may not be the best approach, as often the coding becomes redundant over time.

## Coding Masks: How Project Numbers Are Coded

Coding Masks are important as follows if you need to have some intelligence in the way your Project Definition and WBS Elements appear to the user:

- There can be many.
- They can reflect the structure of a project.
- They can control project identification.
- They only relate to Project Definitions and WBS Elements.
- They determine what special characters are permitted to separate the structure view.
- They are not connected to Profiles—the "Project ID" used in Operative or Template projects determines the mask.
- Different Masks can be used with one or many Project Profiles.

---

**NOTE** *This information is provided to assist you in finding configuration points and where the functionality may be found in the operation of PS. It is not always clear where either is found because the functionality may be embedded within a transaction, so please use it as a guide only.*

| **Customization:** | OPSK, OPSJ |
|---|---|
| **Operation:** | CJ20N |

## Project Profiles: How a Project Should Behave—What It's Allowed to Do

A Project Profile is mandatory when creating a project:

- There can only be one per project.
- They contain the control parameters used in a project: Business rules, Organizational settings, and so on.
- They influence a project's behaviour by providing default information.

They carry "subprofiles" that further influence a project:

- Version Profile
- Planning Profile
- Budget Profile
- Investment Profile
- Status Profile
- Simulation Profile
- Network Profile

and so on.

| Customization: | OPSA |
|---|---|
| Operation: | CJ20N |

## Project Definition: What a Project's Defaults Are

When a project is created for the first time, all settings from the Project Profile are copied into the Project Definition:

- It cannot Plan Costs or Revenues.
- It cannot have Costs or Revenues posted to it.
- It is the "Header" of the Project.
- There can only be one Project Definition for a project.
- Subsequently created WBS Elements will always inherit key organizational and profile data from the Project Definition (but these can be changed manually).

| Customization: | OPSA |
|---|---|
| Operation: | CJ06, CJ20N |

## WBS (Work Breakdown Structure) Elements: The Hierarchical Structure

A Work Breakdown Structure represents the structural relationship that work elements of a project have with each other:

- It is a model of the work to be performed in a project in a hierarchical structure.
- It forms the basis for organization and coordination in a project.
- It carries the dates associated with a package of work.

Work Breakdown Structures can be represented in a variety of ways:

- Logic-Oriented according to PHASE (Plan, Define, Acquire, and so on).
- Function-Oriented according to FUNCTION (Engineer, Construct, Commission, Support, and so on).
- Object-Oriented according to PHYSICAL objects (Asset, Asset components, and so on).
- WBS Elements can have costs planned and posted to them.
- WBS Elements can have revenues planned and posted to them.
- WBS Elements can have a controlled Budget.

| Customization: | OPSA |
|---|---|
| Operation: | CJ01, CJ11, CJ20N |

## Templates: How a Project Should Look

A template is a neutral structure that can be used to standardize WBS structures, Networks, and Milestones:

- Templates are Master Data.
- You can have many templates to reflect different project scenarios.
- Project and Network Templates contain a Project or Network Profile.
- Templates can contain inherent business rules.
- Templates are not mandatory (unless you are using Assembly Processing), but if you have common, complex structures, they help maintain consistency.
- Operative Projects and their Networks can be used as templates, but are prone to inheriting errors in structure.
- With Assembly Processing, Projects are created in the background from a Sales Order, so you must have Standard WBSs and Standard Networks.
- Milestone Templates (Standard Milestones) can be attached to Standard WBSs and Standard Networks.
- Standard Templates do not carry Settlement Rules.

| Customization: | UPUI, OPUH |
|---|---|
| Operation: | CJ92, CN02 |

## Milestones: Things a Project Must Remember to Do

Milestones carry dates and functions that can be triggered in the future:

- They can be attached to a WBS or a Network (with slightly different functionality).
- In their simplest form, Milestones can just be reminder dates.
- In their most complex form, Milestones can be used for:
  - Automatic triggering of Customer Billing (by Percentage or Amount).
  - Preset Customer Billing Plan (by set amount).
  - Automatic triggering of subsequent events, such as the Releasing of a related Network Activity.
- Milestones can trigger a Workflow message to remind the receiver of an event.
- Milestones form the basis of SAP's "Milestone Trend Analysis" reporting function.
- When Assembly Processing is used to create auto-projects, and Milestones exist in the Standard Networks, the Sales Order Billing Plan is automatically created.
- Billing is sensitive to the Date Categories configured in Milestones:
  - By Percentage
  - By Amount

| Customization: | OPSR, OPT6 |
|---|---|
| Operation: | CN11, CJ20N |

## Networks (Part 1): How to Carry Out Tasks in a Specific Way, Order, and Time Period

Networks are used to provide for scheduling of Activities in a project:

- Unlike WBS Elements (which can only be connected in a linear fashion), Network Activities can be connected to one another using special dependencies called "Start/Finish" rules.
- Networks have a three-tier structure:
  - Network Header
  - Network Activity
  - Activity Element
- Networks are identified by a unique number.
- Network Activities are identified by their owning Network Number plus a sequential number. Activity Elements are identified by a further sequential number.
- Networks are not "effective" until they are Released.

| Customization: | OPUU, OPSC, OPUV, OPSU, OPU6 |
| --- | --- |
| Operation: | CN21, CJ2D, CJ20N |

## Networks (Part 2): What Materials and Resources Are Needed to Carry Out a Task

Network Activities can perform a number of complex tasks:

- Plan/Receive Costs.
- Order/Reserve Materials and Services.
- Book Resources.
- Schedule tasks.
- There are three types of Activity, plus special settings for Service:
  - Internal—for planning Internal resources such as labour
  - External—for planning externally procured Services or Contracts
  - General Cost—for planning by Cost Element
  - Service—for planning Services (for example, Contractors)
- Activity Types are attached to Networks by using Control Keys.
- Subnetworks are other types of Orders (such as Maintenance or CS Orders) that have been manually assigned to a WBS or Network.

| Customization: | OPUU, OPSC, OPUV, OPSU, OPU6 |
| --- | --- |
| Operation: | CN21, CJ2D, CJ20N |

## Networks (Part 3): Internal Activities—Planning Internal Resources

- Internal Activities are defined by Control Keys. Usually, they utilize two objects to make them effective:
  - Work Center—for Capacity Planning
  - Activity Type—for pricing of resources
- Work Centers are independently managed objects. They can be an individual, a group of people, or a piece of equipment. They exist to help manage "Capacities" and to carry all the information required to determine available Capacities and to provide for Capacity levelling.
- Activity Types are independently managed objects. They belong to Cost Centers. They are attached to a "Pricing Schedule," meaning they have a planned cost per unit (which can be a standard Unit of Measure).
- When Work Centers and Activity Types are used in conjunction, they effectively "Plan the Resource" and "Plan the Cost" at the same time.
- Costs associated with a Network Activity aggregate to the WBS to which they are assigned.
- Internal Activities can have attached a set of Components or BOMs (Bills of Materials).

| Customization: | OPUU, OPSC, OPUV, OPSU, OPU6 |
|---|---|
| Operation: | CN21, CJ2D, CJ20N |

## Networks (Part 4): External Activities—Planning External Resources

External Activities are the basis for externally procured resources including Services and Contracts. They are defined by Control Keys.

- External Activities can have attached a set of Components (Materials) or BOMs (Bills of Materials).
- Costs associated with an External Activity aggregate to the WBS to which they are assigned.
- When "Released," External Activities trigger events:
  - A Purchase Requisition if the Material Component is "Non-stock" (becomes a commitment).
  - A Reservation if the Material Component is "Stock" (Assigned Cost).
  - A Reservation is cancelled when a Network Activity is "Technically Closed."
  - A Purchase Requisition/Order remains open when a Network Activity is "Technically Closed."
- Some External Activities are "Services." Services are regarded as being consumed at the time of their performance. They cannot be stored or transported, for example, construction work, cleaning services, legal services.

- They can have a preliminary Total Planned Cost that is reduced as and when Material Components are added.

| Customization: | OPUU, OPSC, OPUV, OPSU, OPU6 |
|---|---|
| Operation: | CN21, CJ2D, CJ20N |

## Networks (Part 5): General Cost Activities—Planning Unspecified Costs

General Cost Activities are the simplest form of Costing in Networks. They are defined by Control Keys:

- They carry an Amount in the currency selected.
- They require a Cost Element to determine what type of cost is being planned.
- They can have attached a set of Components or BOMs (Bills of Materials).
- In themselves, they do not generate any Purchasing Documents. However, if Material Components are attached, they will.

| Customization: | OPUU, OPSC, OPUV, OPSU, OPU6 |
|---|---|
| Operation: | CN21, CJ2D, CJ20N |

## Networks (Part 6): Material Components—Planning Materials

Material Components represent the physical materials you need to plan for within an Activity:

- Components can be added to any Activity.
- There is no restriction on how many Materials you have.
- They form the basis of all your Project Procurement (unless you are using Easy Cost Planning).
- They carry the methods by which MRP will order Materials.
- They can be Stock or Non-stock.
- Each Material Component can trigger a Reservation/Requisition.
- They form the basis of Material Project Cost Planning.
- All Material Components belong to one Activity at a time.

| Customization: | OPUU, OPSC, OPUV, OPSU, OPU6 |
|---|---|
| Operation: | CN21, CJ2D, CJ20N |

## Internal Orders: Objects that Can Be Assigned to a Project Structure

Internal Orders (IOs) are "Project Independent" unless assigned to a WBS or Network Activity. They behave in a similar way to a single WBS Element, except:

- They do not have a structure and are not hierarchical.
- They cannot be scheduled and are not time-oriented.

- There are three types of IO:
  - Type 1—Controlling
  - Type 2—Accrual Calculation
  - Type 3—Model Order
- IOs can have costs planned and posted to them.
- IOs can have revenues planned and posted to them.
- IOs can have a controlled Budget.
- IOs can be Settled.

| Customization: | KOT2_OPA |
|---|---|
| Operation: | KO04 |

### Attachments and PS Text: Attachments to the Project Structure

Attachments can be made to WBS elements and Network Activities. SAP also permits attachment of Standard Text, called PS Text:

- Documents
  - Documents are simple "hyperlinks" or URL references.
  - They can be of any extension type—Word, Excel, Access, and so on.
  - There can be many.
  - You can also create a "Private Note" as a non-hyperlinked attachment.
  - You can "Send" documents and messages to other users.
- PS Text
  - Is predefined with a description.
  - Can be attached to a WBS.
  - Can be assigned to a Template for automatic inclusion in a Project.

| Customization: | OPS3 |
|---|---|
| Operation: | CJ20N |

## Cost and Resource Planning

Any planning you may perform is determined by the amount of detail you need. From a Cost perspective, planning can be as simple as entering a planned value against a WBS. More detail is achieved by specifying where exactly the costs may be incurred (Cost Element) and exactly how many Units you want to plan for (Unit Costing). Even more detail can be applied by planning at a Network level by Material and then integrating it with CO, so the source Cost Centers are informed.

Resource Planning is mainly about the people (or roles) you may want to plan for via Work Centers and Activity Types. This type of planning optionally involves Capacity Planning, where you may share resources from another department.

Further, you may want to plan values where there is no cost involved, only a value that represents volumes or quantities based on Units of Measure. These types of plans can be used to generate Customer Invoices via Statistical Key Figures.

Remember that all planning data totals are kept in Plan Versions against the relevant object (WBS and Network).

### Structure Cost Planning via WBS: Direct Entry of Costs Against a WBS Structure, Without Regard to Cost Elements

These are Costs associated with the WBS as a whole.

- Structure Cost Planning is the simplest form of cost planning.
- It is independent of cost elements.
- Plan values entered hierarchically to estimate the expected costs for a project.
- Usually "Rough-Cut"—meaning that when more detail is known, you will probably be more precise and progress to Detailed Cost Planning.
- Can be entered against any WBS (unless configuration in Plan Profile says otherwise).
- Planning is usually Bottom-up, meaning costs are aggregated from the lowest level WBS upward automatically.
- Can be "integrated" with Controlling.

| Customization: | OPSB |
|---|---|
| Operation: | CJ40 |

### Detailed Cost Planning via WBS: Planning Costs Against a WBS at Cost Element Level

- Costs associated with the WBS, but split by Cost Elements (for example, Labour, Materials, Travel, etc.).
- Cost planning by cost element is used when precise information becomes available.
- It covers planning of primary costs, capacities to be taken, and statistical key figures by cost element.
- WBS cost planning can be applied to any CO Plan Version.

| Customization: | OPSB |
|---|---|
| Operation: | CJ40 |

### Detailed Cost Planning via Network: Planning Costs Against a Network Activity Using Cost Elements, Materials, Services, or Activity Types

- Costs associated with the Network and calculated in one of three ways:
  - General Costs—By Cost Element
  - Internal Costs—By Activity Type (Labour and Machinery)
  - External Costs—By Material and Services

- When performing detailed cost planning at Network Activity level, calculated costs aggregate to the owning WBS Element.
- Network Activity cost planning can only ever be applied to Plan Version 0.

| Customization: | OPUU, OPSC, OPUV, OPSU, OPU6 |
| --- | --- |
| Operation: | CN21, CJ2D, CJ20N |

## Easy Cost Planning via WBS: Planning Costs Against a WBS via Unit Costing, but with the Use of Cost Models to Make Data Entry Simpler

Cost Models need to be designed for Easy Cost Planning (ECP) to work.

- ECP Models have three attributes:
  - Characteristics (the type of data)
  - Derivatives (how the cost is derived)
  - Entry Screen (HTML Code)
- They can be used to calculate costs based on Units × Activity price or Materials.
- They can carry default Cost Elements for manual entry of planned costs.
- They simplify entry of costs against a WBS because the "model" used carries all reference information.
- ECP can only be used in the Project Builder.
- ECP cannot be used for Networks.
- ECP items (the costs) are not distributed over time.
- Execution Services are an extension of ECP for creating subsequent documents such as PRs, POs, and so on.
- Costs Planned in ECP will show under Annual Planning for the start year of the WBS.

| Customization: | SPRO |
| --- | --- |
| Operation: | CKCM |

## Plan Versions: Distinct Repositories for Keeping Your Planned Costs Separate

Plan Versions are designed to keep a history of original and revised versions of your planned costs:

- You can have as many as you want.
- They are created in one of two ways:
  - By directly entering planned costs into them
  - By copying one plan version to another
- They are "Fiscal Year" dependent.
- Plan Version 0 is reserved as the baseline plan and also carries Actual Costs.
- Networks always plan to Plan Version 0.

- Easy Cost Planning can plan against any CO Version.
- Plan Versions can be used to track a project's POC (Percentage of Completion).

| Customization: | OKEQ |
|---|---|
| Operation: | CJ9BS, CJ9CS, CJ9FS, CJ9C, CJ9B, CJ9F |

## Statistical Key Figures: Objects Used for Storing and Planning Invisible Costs or Consumption

- SKFs are designed to carry planned and actual statistical values (usually Quantities).
- Once defined, they can have actual dates and values entered against them that are assigned to a WBSs or Network Activity.
- SKFs are used only for recording purposes and have no accounting impact.
- SKFs can be used as inputs for SD Billing (Resource Related Billing).
- SKFs can be distinguished in three ways:
  - Non-aggregated values
  - Aggregated values
  - Progress level for result determination

| Customization: | KK01 |
|---|---|
| Operation: | CJS2, CJK2, KB31N |

## Overheads (CO): Additional Costs Calculated via Costing Sheets

Planned overhead costs are based on Planned costs plus a mark-up (by percentage or fixed amount):

- Costing Sheets carry the calculation upon which planned overhead costs are based.
- They can be calculated based upon Cost Element, Activity Type, or Material.
- They can be calculated against a WBS or a Network.
- They are calculated "on the fly" when costs are planned.
- They can be seen as separate line-items in the cost plan.
- Costing Sheets are attached to WBSs and Networks.

| Customization: | KZS2 |
|---|---|
| Operation: | CJ20N |

## Value Categories: Giving Meaning to Values

Value Categories are intervals of Cost Centers, Commitment Items, and Statistical Key Figures. They are required for:

- Updating the project information database
- Calculating project interest

- Defining structure reports for costs, revenues, and payments
- Updating quantities in the project info database RPSQT

| Customization: | OPI1 |
|---|---|
| Operation: | Not Applicable |

# Budgeting

A clear understanding of Budgeting is mandatory when used in PS. Though similar to Planning, it is definitely not the same. A budget is used in PS to carry values that are more "definitive" than Planned Costs because they represent an approved value rather than one used to calculate the plan. Usually, the business would perform Planning, then use that Plan as the basis for generating a Budget. Then, any activity that results in a "Commitment to spend" can be monitored and acted upon with Availability Control.

## Budgeting in Projects: When the Budget Is Controlled from Within a Project

Budgeting is the process of transferring the Plan (usually Version 0) to the area reserved in the project for the budget (it is not mandatory to copy from the Plan):

- Whether cost planning was performed at WBS level or not, the budget can be keyed directly.
- Budgets only apply to WBS Elements (or Internal Orders is used).
- The Budget does not have to equal the Cost Plan.
- For Capital Projects, the budget can have originally been distributed from the Investment Program to which it belongs.
- The Budget Profile contains your default settings and it is these settings that will influence PS behaviour.
- A project Budget has the following "columns":
  - Original Budget
  - Supplement Budget (within, or to project)
  - Released Budget
  - Carried-Forward Budget
- Every time a Budget is changed, a record is kept for auditing purposes.
- When a WBS has a budget, its Status is set to BUDG. This can be undone in transaction OPSX, but only if reversal conditions are met.
- Availability Control applies at the lowest level of a WBS—it cannot be applied exclusively at higher WBS levels.

| Customization: | OPS9, CJBN, OPTK |
|---|---|
| Operation: | CJ30, CJ37, CJ38, CJ32, CJ3A, CJBV |

## Budgeting in Investment Programs: When the Budget for All Projects Is Controlled by a Capital Investment Program

Budgeting functionality in Investment Management (IM) programs is almost identical to that of Budgeting in Project Systems:

- An IM Budget is effectively a budget managed and distributed to either WBS Elements or Internal Orders.
- An IM Budget can be derived from a Project Plan as long as:
  - The lowest level IM Position (called the Investment Measure) is linked to a Project or Internal Order.
  - A Cost Plan exists in the Project or Internal Order.
- Even if the budget is distributed to a project from an IM program, the budget can still be managed from within the project (if configured).

| Customization: | OIB1, OIB3 |
| --- | --- |
| Operation: | IM34, IM32, IM44, IM52, IM32, IM30, CJ34, CJ37 |

## Availability Control: When You Need to Control Expenditure

Availability Control (AC) is the process of checking expenditure against allowed limits. It is triggered when you attempt to post costs to a project that has AC activated at the WBS that will get the cost, or at a higher WBS if AC is activated to include subordinate WBSs.

The system uses configured tolerance limits both above and below the actual budget amount to determine what action is taken.

If, when costs are charged to a WBS, the tolerance is detected as having been reached, certain action can be taken. You can configure PS to:

- Display a warning message and allow the transaction to continue.
- Send a mail message to the person responsible for the project detailing what happened (and optionally disallow the transaction).
- If required, have AC activated via a regular batch job (executed in the background) to check which projects have reached a predetermined expenditure level. Any that have, will automatically get AC activated. The advantage of this is more a performance issue (why have a time-consuming calculation occurring before it is really required?).
- Selected Transaction Groups and Cost Elements can be exempted from AC.
- When the budget changes, or tolerance limits change, automatically "reconstruct AC" (that is, all relevant WBS elements will be modified).
- Availability Control in User Status if you want to manage it at individual WBS level.

| Customization: | SPRO |
| --- | --- |
| Operation: | CJBV, CJBW |

# Time and Capacity Planning

These are the methods at your disposal for managing Schedules relating to Dates and Times and the Human Resources within a Project's life cycle. How you manage the dates associated with both WBS and Networks depends on the detail you want: for example, if you only use WBS Elements, you cannot "schedule" your project based on constraints or durations (as you can with Networks). Dates do, however, play a part in Cost Planning, as the duration of the various WBSs determines where in the calendar the planning will show. For Networks, true "Scheduling" can be performed because each Activity can have dependencies on other Activities.

## Dates in WBS: Managing Basic and Forecast Dates

- Dates in WBSs are divided into three categories:
  - Basic—either entered manually or taken from the earliest basic start dates and the latest basic finish date of the activities assigned to the WBS element.
  - Forecast—as for Basic Dates.
  - Actual—can be manually entered or entered via Confirmations and Actuals.
- All dates carry a Duration.
- Dates can be reconciled, extrapolated, and shifted by referencing subordinate WBS Elements.

| Customization: | OPTQ |
|---|---|
| Operation: | CJ21, CJ24, CJ29, CJ20N |

## Scheduling in Networks (Part 1): Managing Start/Finish Rules and Executing Scheduling

Scheduling is only appropriate for projects that use Network Activities. To be effective, it is dependent upon the Start and Finish dates of Activities being associated with one another via "Start/Finish" rules.

The following dates are relevant to scheduling:

- **Scheduled Start**  When you are scheduled to start this work.
- **Scheduled Finish**  When you are scheduled to finish this work.
- **Latest Forecast**  If you will miss the Scheduled Finish, what is your best estimate of a finish date.
- **Actual Dates of events occurred**  When you really did start. This information can be automatically completed by other related triggers (such as a Time Recording, or the completion of a Purchase Order).
- **Latest Start Date**  If you will not make the Scheduled Start, what would be the latest date to start.

- **Latest Finish Dates**   If you will not make the Scheduled Finish, what would be the latest date to finish.

| Customization: | OPU6 |
|---|---|
| Operation: | CJ20N, CN24(N) |

## Scheduling in Networks (Part 2): Managing Start/Finish Rules and Executing Scheduling

- There are two scheduling techniques:
  - Forward—Scheduled activities starting with the basic start date and calculating forwards to determine the earliest start and finish dates.
  - Backward—Scheduled activities where the latest start and finish dates for the activities are calculated backward, starting from the basic finish date.
- Floats are the number of days between the Latest Start Date and the Scheduled Start Date. They can be negative if Backward Scheduling calculates an unrealistic Finish Date:
  - Total Float—Number of days that can be shifted without affecting the Latest dates of the subsequent Network.
  - Free Float—Number of days that can be shifted without affecting the Earliest dates of the subsequent Network.
- A Project can "Start in the Past."
- Activities are connected using Relationship Types: FS—Finish/Start, SS—Start/Start, FF—Finish/Finish, SF—Start/Finish.
- Duration determines the length of time an Activity takes.
- Relationships between Activities determine the sequence of phases in terms of time.

| Customization: | OPU6 |
|---|---|
| Operation: | CJ20N, CN24(N) |

## Work Centers and Activity Types: Planning Capacities and the Cost of Utilizing the Resource

- Work Centers can represent, for instance, a piece of machinery, a role or an individual job. The carry set values that determine the following:
  - Usage—What section of the organization uses it, what Value Key (dimension, time, area) is applied, how it is set up and so on.
  - Defaults—Control Key to determine task lists or Order Types (in the case of PS, the Network Type) and Units of Measure.
  - Capacities—To specify the Formula used when determining the capacity.
  - Scheduling—To calculate how long it takes to perform one unit.

- Costing—Assign a Cost Center and optionally the default (allowed) Activity Type(s) that will be defaulted when the Work Center is used to plan in a project's Activities.

- Technical—Type of machine, Rounding Categories, for instance.

- Activity Types can represent a specific unit of chargeable work, such as a laboratory test or a person's job. They also carry set values that determine the following:

  - Basic Data—Unit of Measure, Cost Center Category, default Cost Element, Pricing Indicator (for instance, based on Plan Price or Manually calculated).

    - They belong to a Cost Center.

    - They have a validity (between dates) and can expire.

  - Activity Types have Planned Prices, which are the basis for Cost Planning in Networks and/or WBS Elements.

| Customization: | OP40, OP45, OP42, OP13 |
|---|---|
| Operation: | CMP2, CNR2, CM01, CM01, CM51 |
|  | KP26, KL01–KL05 |

## Workforce Planning: Planning Who Does What, and When

Workforce Planning involves the HR (Human Resources) module of SAP to provide a Personnel Number for use in determining the actual capacity and cost of providing an individual resource. It is used in relation to a Work Centre, and an Activity Type that have been entered against an Internal Network Activity (if Networks are used) or in Unit Costing (if not).

- When a Personnel Number is added to the Person Assignment tab of a Network Activity, PS will determine the Capacity for the Work Centre to perform the task.

- Entering the Personnel number assists in the process of confirming time in CATS (Cross-Application Time Sheets).

- Data entered in the Network Activity is available for Capacity Planning and Leveling. However, the system will not prevent you from over-utilizing a resource.

| Customization: | CMPC |
|---|---|
| Operation: | CJ20N, CMP9 |

# Revenue Planning

This involves how expected income is planned and managed for Sales-oriented Projects. Revenue can be planned against a project even if there is no connection to a Sales Order. However, the WBS Element must be marked as a Billing Element. The revenue plan can come from a Quotation or a Sales Order, if you configure your Plan Profile to do so (meaning that if you tick the "Automatic Revenue Planning" box, planned revenue will show in project reporting). In essence, the most basic of revenue planning (structural) works in exactly the same way as Structure Cost Planning. At a detailed level (by Cost Element), you use "Revenue Elements," which are just Cost Elements with a special indicator.

Revenue associated with a project always shows up with the Negative (–) symbol in reporting.

### Structure Revenue Planning: Direct Entry of Revenue Against a WBS Structure, Without Regard to Revenue Elements

It is Revenue associated with the WBS as a whole.

- It is the simplest form of revenue planning.
- It is independent of revenue elements.
- Values are entered hierarchically against WBS Elements to estimate the expected revenue for a project.
- It is usually "Rough-Cut"—meaning that when more detail is known, you will probably be more precise and progress to Detailed Revenue Planning.
- Revenue Plan can only be entered against "Billing Elements."
- It bears no relation to Revenue planned in a Sales Order.

| Customization: | OPSB |
|---|---|
| Operation: | CJ42 |

### Detailed Revenue Planning: Planning Revenue Against a WBS by Revenue Element

Revenue associated with the WBS, but split by Revenue Elements (for example, Labour, Materials, Travel, etc.).

- Revenue planning by Revenue Element is used when precise information becomes available (when you know which Revenue Elements to use).
- Revenue Planning cannot take place in a Network.
- If a "Billing Plan" is created from within a WBS, the subsequent Sales Order will recognize it for "Periodic Billing." However, if a Billing Plan is created against a Sales Order that is connected to a WBS, the Project Billing Plan will be deleted.
- WBS revenue planning can be applied to any Plan Version.

| Customization: | OPSB |
|---|---|
| Operation: | CJ42 |

### Sales Orders (SD): Revenue Planning via Sales Order (or Quotation)

It is not mandatory to have a Sales Order (SO) associated with a Project for Revenue Planning if Structure Planning is used.

- Revenue planning to a project via an SO is performed in one of two ways:
  - By entering revenue values against an SO Line Item that is assigned to a WBS.
  - Creating a Billing Plan (must have a Cost Element).

- When performing detailed cost planning at Network Activity level (which can only be done via Sales Orders), revenue plans aggregate to the owning WBS Element.
- WBS revenue planning can be applied to any Plan Version.
- Network Activity revenue planning can only ever be applied to Plan Version 0.

| Customization: | OPSB |
| --- | --- |
| Operation: | CJ20N |

# Execution

Though not specific to PS, "Execution" is a generic term for the point at which a project is ready to be released. It is usually the point at which "Actual" costs, revenues, dates, and so on, will be posted to a project. So, normally, a project that has been Released by System Status would fall into this category. Execution can also be controlled by User Status—meaning that a project can remain in a Created state, but can have Business Transactions opened via a User Status. In any event, it is logical to assume that most projects reach this phase, which would also include the Period-end.

## Status Management: Setting Project Restrictions (Business Processes) by Status

- There are two types of Status:
  - System—Predetermined SAP status.
  - User—Determined by configuration.
- System status CRTD is automatically set by SAP when a project is created.
- The system Status set by user is restricted to:
  - REL—Released.
  - TECO—Technically Closed.
  - CLSD—Closed.
- Other system statuses can be used to LOCK certain information within a project.
- System Status set at higher levels affects all lower levels (not so with User Status—it must be copied down the hierarchy).
- User Status can be configured to prevent certain business transactions.
- A history of Statuses can be kept if you have configured the tick box "Change Documents" in Project Profile Status Management.
- A number of "Hidden" System Statuses inform you of past events, such as Budgeted, Costs Planned, Availability Control, Date not Updated, Activated, and so on.

| Customization: | OK02 |
| --- | --- |
| Operation: | CJ20N |

### Actuals: Posting Actual Costs, Revenues, and Dates to a Project

Actuals are "real" values that hit a project based on actual events.

There are several ways that actuals can hit a project:

- Financial Journals (Cost and Revenue).
- Time-sheets (Confirmations).
- CO Postings (Overheads).
- Material and Service deliveries.
- Activity Allocations.
- Payments.
- Realized Milestones (releases Billing Blocks if connected to a Sales Order).
- Settlement from other objects (for example, Maintenance Orders, Internal Orders).
- Status must be REL to receive Actuals or TECO to receive realized commitments.
- A WBS must have the "Account Assignment" indicator set to On before it can receive costs.
- Actual Dates are automatically updated when costs hit a project.
- Actuals are usually posted to the lowest level of a Project's structure (with the exception of Revenue).

### Simulations: Simulating What You Want to Do Before You Really Do It, Without Committing

Simulations mean what they say—they provide you with a tool to try things out in a project. They carry the following information:

- Structures.
- Dates.
- Costs.
- Material components.
- Milestones.
- Billing plans.
- They are identified by what's termed as a Version Key, which is attached to your "simulated" project.
- They require a Simulation Profile, which tell the simulated project what type of data can be managed.
- In essence, you are using all the functionality of PS structures and Plans, but are not doing any actual postings.
- It's a planning tool and uses the Planning Board to manage structures and planning data.
- Simulations can be created from existing Operative/Standard projects and from other simulated projects.
- Operative projects can be generated from simulated projects.

| Customization: | OPUS, SPRO |
|---|---|
| Operation: | CJV1–CJV6 |

## Project Versions: Snapshots of a Project for Comparison Purposes

- Project Versions should not to be confused with Plan Versions.
- They are exact copies of a project, including all plans, actual costs, and progress information.
- They are subject to a "Profile" that is used to determine the kind of information a version will carry.
- They can be automatically created based on Project Status.
- They cannot be modified.
- They are useful when comparing baseline information with current information.
- They can be seen in most standard reports.

| Customization: | OPTS |
|---|---|
| Operation: | Not Applicable |

# Period-End (and Regular Processes)

This term not only applies to the financial milestone that occurs on a monthly or annual basis, but also to processes within a project that need to be performed on a regular basis, such as Settlement and Billing.

## Settlement: Transferring Actual Values to the "Owner"

Settlement is not mandatory, but if it is not carried out on a project that has received costs, the project cannot be closed. The exception to this is a Settlement Profile that states "Not to be Settled."

- The purpose of Settlement is to balance a project to zero.
- It is necessary because of the temporary nature of a project.
- A project can be settled to almost any other entity:
  - Profitability Segment (for Results Analysis)
  - Asset
  - Another Project
  - A Material
  - A Cost Center
  - A P&L Account
- Settlement "Rules" must be in place—that is, there must be an Origin (by Cost Element) and a Receiver.

- Amounts settled from a WBS or Network can be subdivided by percentage or specific amounts.
- Settlement can be performed "Individually" or "Collectively" using Variants.
- Settlement Rules can be generated automatically (CJB1 and CJB2).
- When a WBS is deemed an Asset Under Construction, Settlement Rules are generated automatically at first settlement.

| Customization: | OKO7, OKEU, OKO6 |
|---|---|
| Operation: | CJB1, CJB2, CJ88, CJ8G, CJIC |

## Period-End: Executing Regular, Cyclical Processes

In Project Systems, Period-end Closing (PEC) is not necessarily based upon a financial period. You perform PEC for the following reasons:

- **Earned Value Analysis**    Each time you run Earned Value (the process of calculating the real progress of a project from a cost/time/percentage of completion viewpoint), EV fields in the project are recalculated and overwritten.
- **Results Analysis**    Each time you run Results Analysis, RA fields in the Project are overwritten. Results can be used as input to Settlement.
- **Settlement**    Depending on the receiver, Project costs are used to transfer costs to Fixed Assets, Profitability Segment, Cost Center, and so on.
- **Project Version**    To take a "snapshot" of the project at a certain time in its life for future comparison purposes.
- **Interest**    Calculate interest to be posted to Projects/Sales Orders and other applicable objects.
- **Periodic transfers**    Postings relevant to cost accounting (such as telephone expenses) are collected in clearing cost centres. The postings collected are then transferred to the receiver cost centers at the Period-end. (Telephone expenses, for example, are transferred to all the cost centers in the business in proportion to telephone units used by the receiver cost centers.)
- **Determining overhead surcharges**    Overheads for provision of machines, buildings, materials, personnel, and so on, are applied to costs using surcharges in Costing Sheets. Both plan and actual values apply for overhead surcharges. All reports should be run at this time to ensure results of PEC are captured.

## Progress (Part 1): Updating and Reviewing a Project's Progress

Progress (Percentage of Completion—POC) is determined by several factors:

- Progress Version.
- Measurement Technique.
  - Start-Finish
  - Milestone

- Estimation
- Time Proportional
- Degree of Processing
- Quantity Proportional
- Secondary Proportional (apportioned effort)
- Cost Proportional
- Actual = Plan
- Individual (user-exit)
- POC can be used as input for Results Analysis.
- A special CO Plan Version must exist for Progress analysis.
- POC is recorded in special Statistical Key Figures (assigned to your Controlling Area).

| Customization: | SPRO |
|---|---|
| Operation: | CNE1, CNE2 |

## Progress (Part 2): Updating and Reviewing a Project's Progress

- Inputs to POC Calculation include:
  - Planned Costs.
  - Actual Costs.
  - Influences for POC calculation are the Measurement Technique used.
  - A Project's POC is updated when you run Progress Analysis.
  - For Milestone Trend Analysis, a Project Version will have been created to record the "before" situation.
- Project Progress can be monitored in a number of ways, including:
  - Planning Board.
  - Standard reporting.

| Customization: | SPRO |
|---|---|
| Operation: | CNE1, CNE2 |

## Archiving: Taking Your Projects out of the Live System

Archiving in Projects requires you to have the Deletion Flag set.

- Archiving is performed in three stages:
  - Set Deletion Flag (CJ20N).
  - Set Deletion Indicator in batch mode (set for all Deleted Projects in CN80).
  - Perform Archive in CN80. (Networks are archived only after residence times 1 and 2 have been met.)

- Some data cannot be archived:
  - Simulation Versions
  - Billing plan for WBS element
  - Invoicing plan for network activity or component
  - Unit costing for network activity or component
  - Additional attributes for project summarization using master data characteristics
  - Classification data for summarization of WBS elements
  - Classification data for order summarization of networks
  - Characteristic value assignments in variant configuration
  - Delivery information for networks/work breakdown structures
  - Delivery addresses for material components in third-party orders
  - Capacity requirements
  - Workforce planning
- Operative Projects will be archived with their respective "Status Dependent" Versions. Time Dependent versions must be archived separately

| Customization: | Not Applicable |
|---|---|
| Operation: | CJ20N, CN80 |

### Billing: Sending the Customer an Invoice

Customer projects can have Actual Costs billed using Resource Related Billing (RRB).

- DIP Profiles are used to gather the relevant actual costs from both WBS Elements and Network Activities.
- Project Milestones can be used to generate a Billing Plan.
- Sales Orders that are linked to projects can have their Billing Plan updated from within a project.
- The project Plan Profile determines how the Revenue Plan is sent to the project.

| Customization: | ODP1 |
|---|---|
| Operation: | DP91 |

## Summary

You should by now be pretty familiar with the main aspects and features of PS. Armed with this knowledge, you can progress to Configuration (or Customization as it is also called). Throughout Chapter 4, there have been references to where the configuration is done—but this does not mean you know it all yet; you still need to know what each configuration transaction contains. In the next chapter, you will be shown how this is done.

# Configuration

The process of configuration is at the heart of any SAP implementation. In itself, the process is relatively straightforward but requires a lot of experience if the implementation is complex. Often, a very small setting in Configuration can make a huge difference to the way a process works. Sometimes, you will tear your hair out trying to work out why something does not function in the way you anticipated. To help solve some of these issues, take a look at the "Inside the Project Builder" section in Chapter 6, where transaction codes for configuration are referenced for your convenience.

*IMPORTANT NOTE  Minor configurations, such as Applicant, Person Responsible, and Priority, are not detailed as they are not complex at all. At the end of this book, you can find the complete Implementation Guide (IMG), where you can have lots of fun trying to find out where you should be! Attempting to include every configuration point would render this book large enough for use in weight training.*

## The IMG and Customization

This icon is used to identify a Configuration point:  Copyright by SAP AG

SAP's Implementation Guide (IMG) is accessed with Transaction Code SPRO. Basic configuration can be achieved with some simple steps:

- Activate Project System in Controlling Area (OKKP).
- Define Special Characters in Project Number (OPSK).
- Create a Coding Mask (OPSJ).
- Create a Project Profile (OPSA).
- Define Plan Versions for Fiscal Year (OKEQ).

Certain other settings must be in place before you can go ahead with the preceding—that is, CO (Controlling) must have set up the basic Organizational values (such as Controlling Area, Company Code, Business Area). These and other integration values (for example, Plant) must be in place before you can attempt any meaningful configuration and therefore create an Operational Project. Be particularly mindful of CO—it has a profound effect on PS in the area of Costing and Settlement.

### How to Proceed

You cannot proceed with PS configuration without discussing the integration points with other module owners. PS is arguably the most integrated module in SAP. To start with, you must take a global view of your requirements by sketching out an integration map.

Ask yourself the following question: What are my primary Organizational elements? (Refer to Figure 1-2, Organization Elements, in Chapter 1.)

| Organizational Element | Comments |
|---|---|
| CO Area | Must be set up, regardless. |
| Company Code | Multiple Company Codes may affect Currency. |
| Business Area | Multiple Business Areas make for complex reporting. |
| Profit Center | Affiliated with Company Code, relevant for PA (Profitability Analysis). |
| Plant | In a manufacturing or procurement-critical environment, it is critical for Materials Management. |
| Responsible Cost Center | Treatment of sales and distribution document items in the event of multiple assignment to WBS element. |
| Sending Cost Center | For plan integration and settlement of Plan/integrated Orders. |
| Investment Program | For Capital Projects and Assets Under Construction. |
| Technical Location | For Plant Maintenance of equipment-type projects. |
| Tax Jurisdiction | For U.S. Tax. |
| Purchasing Organization | An organizational unit in Logistics, subdividing an enterprise according to the requirements of Purchasing. |
| Purchasing Group | Key for a buyer or group of buyers responsible for certain purchasing activities. You need this to generate Purchase Requisitions. |
| Storage Location | Where a Material is stored. |

By analyzing the preceding and deciding what you may need, you are a long way into deciding how far your configuration needs to go.

Following is a table describing the types of projects you may need for each of the Organizational elements. Projects can be divided into the following general categories (you may have others):

| | |
|---|---|
| Costing | Projects that exist only for the purpose of planning costs at WBS level. |
| Assets | Projects that receive Capital funds from Investment Programs. |
| Sales | Projects that are Customer focused. |
| Manufacturing | Projects that are Material/Logistics focused. |
| Statistical | Projects that do not plan or receive costs. |
| Maintenance | Projects that exist for managing Equipment. |

This matrix shows the relationship between Organizational settings and "types" of projects that may use them:

| Organizational Element | Costing | Assets | Sales | Manuf. | Stat. | Maint. |
|---|---|---|---|---|---|---|
| CO Area | ✓ | | | | | |
| Company Code | ✓ | ✓ | ✓ | ✓ | ✓ | ✓ |
| Business Area | ✓ | ✓ | ✓ | ✓ | ✓ | ✓ |
| Profit Center | ✓ | | ✓ | ✓ | | ✓ |
| Plant | | ✓ | ✓ | ✓ | | ✓ |
| Resp. Cost Center | ✓ | ✓ | ✓ | ✓ | | ✓ |
| Sending Cost Center | | ✓ | | | | |
| Investment Program | | ✓ | | | | ✓ |
| Technical Location | | ✓ | | | | ✓ |
| Tax Jurisdiction | ✓ | | ✓ | | | |
| Purchasing Org | | ✓ | ✓ | ✓ | | |
| Purchasing Group | | ✓ | ✓ | ✓ | | ✓ |
| Storage Location | | ✓ | ✓ | ✓ | | ✓ |

Deciding what to configure will depend on your Project type. In summary, think about the following points:

- *If you just want to do costing and do not need to plan your costs using Materials or other Resources:* You don't need Networks, Easy Cost Planning, or Unit Costing. You can use the simple Structure Planning technique of planning costs with or without Cost Elements. All your Actual Costs will be posted via FI Journals or Allocations. Budgeting is optional.

- *If you want to do costing and to plan Materials and other Resources, and you want to trigger the creation of Purchasing Documents, but are not interested in Scheduling:* Use Easy Cost Planning. This option also allows you to create simple Models for data entry of common information. Use Unit Costing if you want, but it amounts to the same thing without a "pretty face." Be aware that Easy Cost Planning does not allow you to distribute your planned costs over a time frame (distribution Rules)— Unit Costing does. Using Easy Cost Planning allows you to do all your planning, including creation of Sales Documents, in the Project Builder. ECP planned values will appear under the year they were planned.

- *If you want to schedule when the activities of your project are to be performed (in relation to one another) and at the same time you want to time your procurement precisely:* You will need Networks. Using Networks can be quite simple for basic Material Component management and General Costing by Cost Element. But it can also be quite complex if you want to plan for Stock/Non-stock Materials, Reservations, PRs, POs, Catalogued Materials, Services, Subcontractors, and Internal Resources. Also, if you want to use Subnetworks (that is, Orders from different modules such as Maintenance, Customer Service), then your config gets a little bit more complex.

- *If your project combines some of the preceding, plus it is managing the creation of Assets Under Construction:* You will need to configure Investment Management. Though in itself this is not too complex, IM is not entirely covered in this book. Asset-based projects are described in a fair amount of detail in Chapter 3.

- *If your project involves a Customer:* You need to consider the method by which you want to process Sales Documents (Quotations, Sales Orders, etc.). This book describes the various methods—Assembly Processing, Sales Simulation, and so on. In some cases, Customer Billing is straightforward (Order Billing); in others, it is not (Resource-Related Billing). For the latter, you need DIP Profiles, which help bill the customer based on resources utilized in a Project.

- *If your projects only exist for the purpose of representing a structure and have no plan at all, but they have costs and those costs may be settled to various other receivers:* You may want to consider the use of Internal Orders.

- *If you are stuck!* Have a look at the section "Inside the Project Builder" in Chapter 6. There you will find config points in relation to the Project Structure. It may help you decide what you need.

The following table shows the highest-level configuration entry points of PS and their basic use:

| IMG Reference | Use |
|---|---|
| Structures | Settings related to managing Project Definition, WBSs, Networks, and Milestones |
| Project Planning Board | Settings for how your Gantt Chart looks |
| Documents | PS Text and Document attachments such as Word, Excel, PowerPoint |
| Collaboration | Settings for Collaborative Engineering & Project Management |
| Claim | Claims Management—recording variances to a project and maybe working with CS (Customer Services) |
| Production Resources and Tools | Integration with Production Planning |
| Costs | Planned costs and Budget management—covers Structure planning, Easy Cost Planning, Network cost planning, Down-payments, and Value categories |
| Revenues and Earnings | Revenue and earnings planning—covers CO Versions, Exchange Rates, Allocations, structure planning, and integration with SD |

| IMG Reference | Use |
|---|---|
| Payments | Project Cash Management with Funding Areas, setting of Cash Management in Company Code |
| Dates | Scheduling in Networks and WBS Date planning methods |
| Resources | Work Centers, Capacities, Formulas, Performance Efficiency Rates (PP), Shift Sequences, and Workforce Planning Profiles |
| Material | Procurement, ProMan, BOM Transfers, Sales-oriented Production |
| Confirmation | PS Confirmation Parameters, Causes for Variance, Field Selection for Confirmations |
| Simulation | Simulation profiles, version keys for simulated Projects |
| Progress | Earned Value, Event Scenarios, Progress Tracking Profiles |
| Workflow | Settings for the standard PS Workflows |
| Information System | Customizing Report Selection/Database Profiles, Views, Technical reports (Dates, Structures), Info Database, Cost and Revenue enhancements, Summarization Interfaces with Excel, MS project, Access |
| Authorization Management | Role Maintenance, Authorization check |
| Project Replication | Profiles for summarizing data for export to external systems |
| Project Versions | Setting up Version Profiles, System and User Status control for version creation |

# Structures

In this section, configuration relating to the Structural elements of your design can be performed. This pertains to all things that affect the Project Definition, WBS, and Network. This includes Coding Masks, Status, Field layout and Master Data settings, Project Types, Milestones, Validations, Substitutions, and so on.

In other words—a lot of the key configuration.

## Coding the WBS

Every project you create (Template and Operative) has Coding Masks Associated with it. Configuration of the mask falls into two areas:

- Special Characters to define formatting rules
- Coding Mask to define the visual representation (the Mask)

### Special Characters

This configuration has dual purpose—to determine the format of your Project Definition and WBS Number Prefixes and to establish the special characters that are permitted within your project numbering.

| Menu Path | Project System->Structures->Operative Structures->Work Breakdown Structure |
|---|---|
| Config Point | Define Special Characters for Projects |
| Transaction | OPSK |

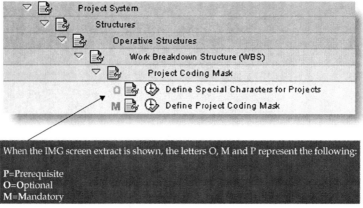

Copyright by SAP AG

---

***TIP*** *Be sure to get your Coding Mask correct from the beginning. Once you have created operative projects, you cannot easily change the mask.*

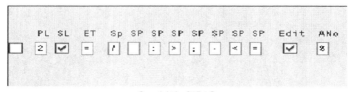

Copyright by SAP AG

- **PL Project Length** Length of the Prefix. This length will determine how long the first part of your project number is (both Project Definition and WBS Elements). Maximum is five characters. It works in conjunction with the SL indicator.

- **SL Structure Length**    If you tick this, all projects must have a prefix equal to the number of characters specified in PL.

- **ET Entry Tool**    Whatever character you enter here can be used to "fast enter" your WBS Elements. For example, if you use the = sign, each time you enter an = (followed by a number) when manually creating a project, the system will determine the new WBS by adding that number to the previous WBS:

  Previous WBS is **XX-00001-01**.
  Enter **=2** in the WBS box.
  You get **XX-00001-02**.

- **Sp Special Character**    Whatever characters are entered in these eight boxes will determine the characters that can be used as separators in your WBS.

- **Edit**    If you tick this, only coded projects will be permitted (that is, based on PL, you will only be able to create projects that have a code associated with them). If you do not tick it, you are free to create projects that are not subject to coding rules.

- **Ano Automatic Number Assignment**    Select a symbol that will be used to automatically assign a Project/WBS Number with the Open Number functionality of PS. The automatic number assignment is active if you enter a character in this field. In this case, the system determines the next free number according to the Search for free number method. The starting value is the extended number by one digit, or in the case of edit masks, by one section, of the higher-level WBS element or project definition. If the system cannot determine a number using this method, it assigns a "help number," which begins with the character entered here. Usually, if SAP cannot assign a number automatically, it is because the mask is at its maximal length.

## Coding Mask

This configuration will determine how your Project Definition and WBS Elements will look. Because it is only a "mask," it is up to you to decide how numbers entered will be represented. Also note that Project numbering in general is only what the user sees—SAP keeps its own numbering (object Number) behind the scenes, so it does not matter what number you enter, it will not make any difference to SAP's internal numbering.

| Menu Path | Project System->Structures->Operative Structures->Work Breakdown Structure(WBS)->Project Coding Mask |
|---|---|
| **Config Point** | Define Project Coding Mask |
| **Transaction** | OPSJ |

| PrjID | Coding mask | Description | Lck | LkS |
|---|---|---|---|---|
| XX | -03000/00-XX.0000 | Sample Masking | ☐ | ☐ |
| | | | ☐ | ☐ |
| | | | ☐ | ☐ |

Copyright by SAP AG

- **PrjID Project Identifier**   Whatever you enter here will be tied in to whatever you enter in the next field (Coding Mask). The way SAP determines a mask is decided right here. So if you enter *XX here, SAP will use that to set out your numbering in all projects.*

  You can have as many different PrjIDs as you want.

- **Coding Mask**   Data entered here determines how the numbers/characters you enter (when creating a project) will look. In the example shown preceding (XX-00000/00-XX.0000), you would get the following result:

  Data entered **PK1/1-GG.1**
  Is Converted to **PK-00001/01-GG.01**
  (This is a complex example and probably not typical.)

  A more usual example would be:
  **XX-00000-00-00-00-00-00**
  In this example, we see the mask representing WBS Levels, with each level represented as a 00.

- **Lck Lock Operative**   Tick this if you want to lock the mask—the effect of this is that no new projects can be created with this mask. This functionality is often used to prevent creation of projects that have special significance.

- **LkS Lock Standard**   As preceding, but for Standard Projects (Templates).

---

**NOTE** *With Coding Masks in general, be aware that once you have created operative projects, it is not so easy to modify your mask (especially in a Sandpit client that already has projects). SAP does not stop you from transporting a new mask into a client, but existing projects may be rendered useless, with short-dumps occurring. For further information on this issue and a solution for converting project numbers, see Note 453280 in SAP's help portal.*

## Status Management

Every time a business transaction is carried out (for example, Create project, Plan project, Release project), SAP automatically changes the Status of a project. The active system status determines which business transactions you can perform with WBS elements. System statuses are passed from the project definition to the WBS elements and passed from the WBS elements to the subordinate WBS elements. The system statuses *Locked* and *Final billing* are exceptions to this. You can cancel certain statuses, for instance, *Technically completed*, *Closed*, and *Deletion Flag*. When you do so, the previous status is set. System statuses are cancelled one by one, until you arrive at a status that cannot be cancelled. You cannot cancel system statuses that are set automatically (in the background by the system); for example, *Partially released* is set by SAP when subordinate WBSs are set and the superior WBS is not Released. If you cancel the statuses *Technically completed* or *Closed*, the system automatically cancels this status in the superior WBS element. However, the system does not cancel the status in subordinate WBS elements.

*System Status* (not configurable). System status is set according to the current status of an element and affects what actions can occur against a WBS element or Network. The main ones (of many) are:

- *Created*   A project has been created but is not yet active and cannot have many business transactions applied.

- *Released*   The project has been released, meaning that it is now active and subject to many business transactions (it can attract costs, generate commitments, etc.). Reservations will be removed.

- *Technically completed*   The project is nearing completion—this status will stop any more commitments from being created, but will allow existing commitments to be fulfilled.

- *Deleted*   The project is flagged for deletion, but not actually deleted. A separate process is required to physically delete (or archive) a project. Additionally, a project must have a "zero balance" to be considered for deletion.

- *Closed*   The project is closed and cannot have any business transactions applied. It can, however, still be maintained. Lockable Elements of a WBS can be locked (Master Data, Dates, Planning, Account Assignment, or all) to prevent update activity.

*User Status* (configurable). User Status can be applied to both WBSs and Networks. They provide user control over what Business Transactions are permitted when the status is set by the user. Complex rules can be configured to set User Status based on what the Status Number of a project is. "Lowest Number" and "Highest Number" are set to determine what can happen. A Project can have several statuses at the same time. However, only one of the statuses has a status number. If another status with a status number is activated, the old status with a status number is deactivated to make way for the new status (provided the new status number does not exceed the "highest number" defined for the old status).

The converse rule applies when using "Lowest Number"—a good example for its use is for determining Phase. If you have, say, two phases for a project—User Status A for Phase 1 and User Status B for Phase 2, you can stop Phase 2 from being initiated if a certain WBS has not been "Settled." This in turn could stop the WBS from being "Released," which would preclude costs from being assigned to it.

## Status Profile

| Menu Path | Project System->Structures->Operative Structures->WBS User Status |
|---|---|
| Config Point | Create Status Profile |
| Transaction | OK02 |

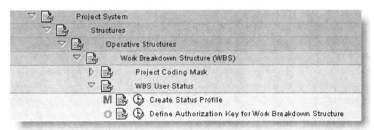

Copyright by SAP AG

Create a New Entry and double-click it.

Copyright by SAP AG

Copyright by SAP AG

- **Stat**   Status Number—unique and tied in to the Status. It is used to identify Lowest/Highest, which follows.

- **Status/Short Text**   Unique Status ID and Description.

- **Init. st**   Tick if the Status is to be set as the initial status when a project using this profile is created.

- **Lowest/Highest**   These numbers are the integer that controls whether the Status can be set after another status with a lower/higher number. A project can have several statuses at the same time. However, only one of the statuses may have a status number. If another status with a status number is activated, the old status with a status number is deactivated. This is only valid under certain conditions. The system makes a note of the status with the highest status number that has been reached up to the present. The "lowest number" of this status number determines which status number a new status must have.

- **Posit / Prior**   There are two types of status display:
  Status line: Up to eight active statuses are displayed in one line (only the four-character status IDs).
  The position specifies at which place in the status line a status should be displayed. If several active statuses have the same position, only the status with the highest priority is displayed. If not all positions of the status line are used, the positions are moved to the left.

- **Auth. code**   A unique code identifying the Authorization Code set in Transaction. This will allow you to be specific about who can do what with the setting of statuses.

Before you can continue to the next step (Business Transactions), you must click the Object Types button and select the Objects allowable (for PS, that is WBS and Network).

Copyright by SAP AG

| Allowed Object Types | |
|---|---|
| X | Obj. Type |
| ✔ | WBS element |

Copyright by SAP AG

*To get to the Business Transactions settings, double-click on a User Status.*

| Status profile | ZZ000001 My User Status Profile |
|---|---|
| Status | zz1 My Status |

Transaction Control

| | Influence | | | | Next action | | |
|---|---|---|---|---|---|---|---|
| Business Transaction | No infl | Allowed | Warning | Forbidd. | No acti | Set | Delete |
| Acct. assignment order/project | ◉ | ○ | ○ | ○ | | | |
| Activate final billing doc. | ◉ | ○ | ○ | ○ | ◉ | ○ | |
| Actual Overhead Assessment | ◉ | ○ | ○ | ○ | | | |
| Actual Overhead Distribution | ◉ | ○ | ○ | ○ | | | |
| Actual Periodic Repostings | ◉ | ○ | ○ | ○ | | | |
| Actual activity allocation | ◉ | ○ | ○ | ○ | | | |
| Actual inverse activity alloc. | ◉ | ○ | ○ | ○ | | | |
| Actual overhead (periodic) | ◉ | ○ | ○ | ○ | | | |
| Actual settlement | ◉ | ○ | ○ | ○ | | | |
| Approval | ◉ | ○ | ○ | ○ | ◉ | ○ | |
| Assign PS texts | ◉ | ○ | ○ | ○ | | | |
| Assignment order/WBS | ◉ | ○ | ○ | ○ | | | |
| Autom. gener. settl. rule | ◉ | ○ | ○ | ○ | | | |
| Autom. gener. settl. rule | ◉ | ○ | ○ | ○ | | | |
| Automat. WIP/results analysis | ◉ | ○ | ○ | ○ | ◉ | ○ | |

Copyright by SAP AG

Extended lists of Business Transactions for WBS and Network follow shortly.
The permissible Business Transactions now can be set by selecting the relevant Radio button:

- **No infl**   Set if the business transaction has no influence on the Status (default setting).

- **Allowed**   Set if this business transaction is allowed when the status is set.

- **Warning**   Set if you want a warning issued when the status is set.

- **Forbidden**   Set if the business transaction is forbidden when the status is set.
- **No Action**   The default setting if the Business Transaction is a System Status.
- **Set**   If the Business Transaction is a System Status, set the User Status when that System Status occurs.

---

**REMINDER**  *User Status CANNOT set System Status.*

The User Status Profile can be inserted into Project Profile and/or Network Type (not in Network Profile). It can be inserted into Standard Projects but not into Standard Networks.

It can be changed within Operative Projects or Networks via the Information button.

Extended list of Business Transactions for **Project Definition** (Highlighted are Statuses):

Copyright by SAP AG

| | |
|---|---|
| Assign PS texts | Change WBS number |
| Change structure | **Complete** |
| **Complete back to tech complete** | **Confirm WBS** |
| Create change document | Delete basic dates |
| Delete element | Expand structure |
| Funds commitment | **Lock** |
| **Lock master data** | **Maintain settlement rule** |
| **Mark for deletion** | **Partially confirm WBS** |
| **Partially release project** | Plan Settlmnt Acc. Assignment |
| **Release** | Remove deletion flag |
| **Revoke status "Closed"** | Revoke technical completion |
| **Schedule basic dates** | Set basic finish |
| Set basic start | **Technically complete** |
| **Unlock** | **Unlock master data** |

Extended list of Business Transactions for **WBS** (Highlighted are Statuses):

| | |
|---|---|
| Acct. assignment order/project | **Activate final billing doc** |
| Actual Overhead Assessment | Actual Overhead Distribution |
| Actual Periodic Repostings | Actual activity allocation |
| Actual inverse activity alloc. | Actual overhead (periodic) |
| Actual settlement | **Approval** |
| Assign PS texts | Assignment order/WBS |
| Autom. gener. settl. rule | Autom. gener. settl. rule |

| | |
|---|---|
| **Automat. WIP/results analysis** | Availability control |
| Budget Release | Budget return |
| **Budget supplement** | **Budget transfer (receiver)** |
| Budget transfer (sender) | Budget transfer (transfer) |
| **Budgeting** | Change WBS number |
| Change structure | **Complete** |
| **Complete back to tech complete** | **Confirm WBS** |
| **Confirm order** | **Copy basic->forecast** |
| FI: Memo postings | FI: Postings |
| FI: Statistical postings | Financial budgeting |
| Funds commitment | Goods Movement |
| Goods issue delivery | **Goods receipt for prodn. order** |
| Goods receipt for purch. order | ISR Account Assignment |
| Incoming invoice | Interest Calculation (Plan) |
| Interest calculation (actual) | Inventory difference |
| **Lock** | **Lock assignment** |
| **Lock budgeting** | **Lock dates** |
| **Lock master data** | **Lock planning** |
| **Maintain settlement rule** | **Manual WIP/results analysis** |
| Manual cost allocation | **Mark for deletion** |
| Material debit/credit | Material purchase order |
| Material purchase requisition | PRC: Activity Backflush |
| **Partially confirm WBS** | **Partially release project** |
| Periodic Reposting: Plan Data | Plan Revenue Types |
| Plan Settlmnt Acc. Assignment | Plan indirect activity alloc. |
| Plan overhead (periodic) | Plan overhead cost assessment |
| Plan overhead cost distrib. | Plan settlement |
| Planning activities | Planning primary costs |
| Planning secondary costs | Planning stat. key figures |
| Post goods issue | **Receiver of carryover** |
| **Release** | **Remove deletion flag** |
| Repost CO line items | Repost costs |
| Repost revenue | **Reset "accepted" flag** |

| | |
|---|---|
| Revenue planning (total) | **Revoke "Fully billed"** |
| **Revoke status "Closed"** | **Revoke technical completion** |
| **Schedule actual dates** | **Schedule basic dates** |
| **Schedule forecast dates** | Schedule order |
| **Sender of carryover** | **Set "accepted" flag** |
| Set basic finish | Set basic start |
| Set forecast finish | Set forecast start |
| Settlement account assignment | Shift basic dates |
| Shift forecast dates | Tech compl revoke created |
| Tech compl revoke part rel'd | Technically complete |
| Total cost planning | Transfer price agreement |
| Transfer price allocation | Unit costing (planning) |
| Unlock | Unlock assignment |
| Unlock budgeting | Unlock dates |
| Unlock master data | Unlock planning |
| Write budget line items | Write plan line items |

Extended list of Business Transactions for Network Header (Highlighted are Statuses):

| | |
|---|---|
| Actual activity allocation | Actual overhead (periodic) |
| Actual settlement | **Automat. WIP/results analysis** |
| **Block assembly order** | Change |
| Change automatically | Check PRT availability |
| Check material availability | **Complete** |
| **Complete back to tech complete** | **Confirm order** |
| Create subnetwork | Debit from actual settlement |
| Determine costs | Earmarked funds |
| Enter statistical key figures | FI: Memo postings |
| FI: Postings | FI: Statistical postings |
| Goods Movement | Goods issue delivery |
| Goods receipt for prodn. order | **Goods receipt for purch. order** |
| ISR Account Assignment | Incoming invoice |
| Interest Calculation (Plan) | Interest calculation (actual) |

| | |
|---|---|
| Inventory difference | **Lock** |
| **Lock assignment** | **Maintain settlement rule** |
| **Manual WIP/results analysis** | Manual cost allocation |
| **Mark for deletion** | Material debit/credit |
| Material purchase order | Material purchase requisition |
| PDC download of order data | **Partially confirm order** |
| Partially release order | Plan Settlmnt Acc. Assignment |
| Plan overhead (periodic) | Planning stat. key figures |
| **Print order** | **Print order (original)** |
| **Release** | **Remove deletion flag** |
| Repost CO line items | Repost costs |
| Reprint order | Reread master data |
| **Revoke status "Closed"** | **Revoke technical completion** |
| Schedule order | **Set deletion indicator** |
| Settlement account assignment | **Technically complete** |
| **Transfer price agreement** | Transfer price allocation |
| **Unblock assembly order** | **Unlock** |
| **Unlock assignment** | **WMS: mat. provisn prodn order** |

Extended list of Business Transactions for **Activity** (Highlighted are Statuses):

| | |
|---|---|
| Actual activity allocation | Actual overhead (periodic) |
| Actual settlement | **Automat. WIP/results analysis** |
| Automatic deletion | **Cancel Scheduling** |
| **Change Activity/Element Number** | Change automatically |
| Check material availability | **Complete** |
| **Complete back to tech complete** | **Confirm order** |
| **Confirm transaction** | Create subnetwork |
| Debit from actual settlement | **Delete operation** |
| **Dispatch** | Earmarked funds |
| Enter statistical key figures | FI: Memo postings |
| FI: Postings | FI: Statistical postings |
| Goods Movement | Goods issue delivery |

| | |
|---|---|
| Goods receipt for purch. order | ISR Account Assignment |
| Incoming invoice | **Individual measure** |
| Interest Calculation (Plan) | Interest calculation (actual) |
| Inventory difference | **Lock** |
| **Lock assignment** | Maintain operation number |
| **Maintain settlement rule** | **Manual WIP/results analysis** |
| Manual cost allocation | **Mark for deletion** |
| Material debit/credit | Material purchase order |
| Material purchase requisition | PDC download of operation data |
| **Partially confirm operation** | Plan Settlmnt Acc. Assignment |
| Plan overhead (periodic) | Planning stat. key figures |
| **Print order** | **Print order (original)** |
| **Release** | **Release operation** |
| **Remove deletion flag** | Repost CO line items |
| Repost costs | Reprint order |
| **Reschedule** | **Revoke status "Closed"** |
| **Revoke technical completion** | Settlement account assignment |
| **Technically complete** | **Transfer price agreement** |
| Transfer price allocation | Unit costing (planning) |
| **Unlock** | **Unlock assignment** |

## Status Selection Profile

Use these if you want to filter the selection of Information Systems records by the System or User Status of a WBS or Network.

Note that in Information Systems, this is the only reliable method you have at your disposal to select information based on Status (the only alternative is to use the Filter in Info Systems). In configuration, you create a unique Selection Profile and optionally attach it to a User Status Profile.

| | |
|---|---|
| **Menu Path** | Project System->Structures->Operative Structures->Milestones |
| **Config Point** | Define Selection Profiles |
| **Transaction** | BS42 |

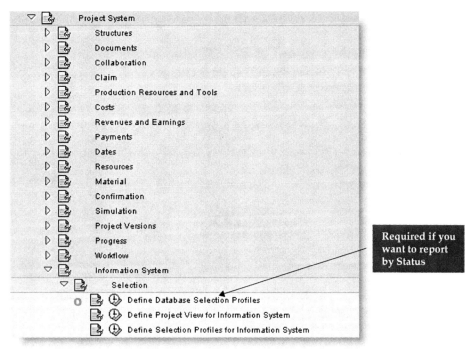

Copyright by SAP AG

Create a new entry and give it a name, then optionally enter the name of the User Status Profile.

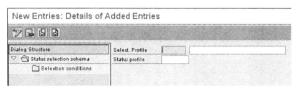

Copyright by SAP AG

Click Selection Conditions.

| | | User | Stat.prof. | Status | | not | State |
|---|---|---|---|---|---|---|---|
| | | ☐ | | | | ☐ | Active |
| | and | ☐ | | | | ☐ | Active |
| | and | ☐ | | | | ☐ | Active |
| | and | ☐ | | | | ☐ | Active |
| | and | ☐ | | | | ☐ | Active |
| | and | ☐ | | | | ☐ | Active |
| | and | ☐ | | | | ☐ | Active |
| | and | ☐ | | | | ☐ | Active |
| | and | ☐ | | | | ☐ | Active |
| | and | ☐ | | | | ☐ | Active |

Copyright by SAP AG

- **User**   Tick this box if the status is a User Status (the system will switch it on or off for you).
- **Stat.prof.**   Optionally, enter a User Status Profile (Matchcode).
- **Status**   Select any status on the pull-down list (if the status is a User Status, an X will indicate this in the pull-down list).
- **Not**   Tick this if you want the selection criteria to <u>exclude</u> your selection in the report.
- **State**   Indicates the selection criteria is Active.

In the left column, you will notice the "and" operator—for multiple lines, you can switch this to "or" by clicking this icon:

Copyright by SAP AG

The symbol you use in Information systems to select your Profile is:

Copyright by SAP AG

Status Selection is specific to the primary elements of a project structure and is tied in to the User Status Profile you have applied to the relevant Project Object. Selection Profiles are not permanently attached to any PS object—they only serve to provide a filter for reporting. If you are not using User Status, you can run the Selection Profile against any of the four project objects and do not need a Status Profile.

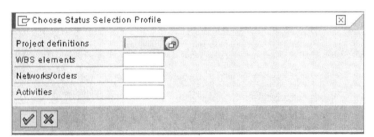

Copyright by SAP AG

## Project Profile

Most of the control parameters for working in the Project System are stored in profiles. These profiles contain default values and control parameters for processing various objects and functions. They influence a project's behaviour. The project profile may have "dependent" profiles (for example, Project Profile contains Planning Profile, which in turn carries Graphics Profile, etc.).The project profile contains default values and parameters for managing your project, for example, key organizational values, settlement profile, factory calendar for scheduling, or settings for graphics. You can change some of these default values when you are working in the work breakdown structure, but not all.

Generally, once a project has been passed into the "execution" phase (released and ready for actual postings), changes made to the Project Profile will have no effect on the project. However, some changes to sub-profiles will have an effect on new WBS elements in that project. For example, If you change the Status Profile, the next time the project is subjected to a User Status change, it will be affected, just as any change to the Planning Profile will affect new WBSs in that Project. Organizational values will remain protected.

To be sure, you should always create a new project when profile configuration has been changed—then you can be certain of a reliable test.

Figure 5-1 is a "roadmap" of the various configuration connections relevant for a Project Profile.

| Menu Path | Project System->Structures->Operative Structures->Work Breakdown Structure (WBS) |
|-----------|----------------------------------------------------------------------------------|
| Config Point | Create Project Profile |
| Transaction | OPSA |

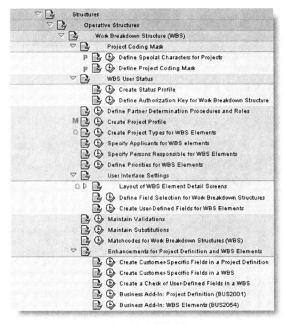

Copyright by SAP AG

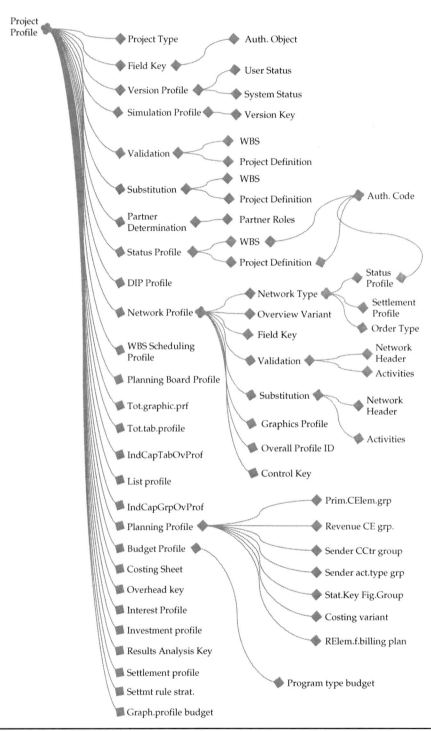

**FIGURE 5-1** Project profile roadmap

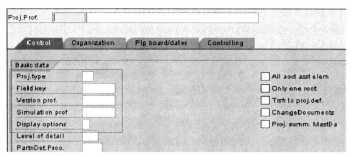

## Proj.Prof./Description

This is the unique ID associated with your project profile and will be used to identify it when a new Standard or Operative Project is created. Be aware that it is good practice to keep Profiles to a minimum and to control such things as organizational differences in Standard Projects that use common Profiles.

## CONTROL TAB: Basic Data

- **Project Type** This is used to "categorize" the project. It is optional, but when used, is selectable in Information Systems via the Dynamic Field Selection.

- **Field Key** If you have utilized the User-Defined-Fields (UDF) facility, this is used to specify which variant. It is important to note that different Profiles can have different Field Keys if desired—therefore giving different projects their own set of UDFs.

- **Version Prof.** Project Versions, when used, can have a profile associated with them that specifies what elements of a project are used to create those versions. This is not to be confused with Plan Versions. Project Versions are physical copies of a project and can be, for example, automatically generated when a project is first released based on the Status.

- **Simulation Prof.** Simulation Profiles can specify what elements of a project are used to create the simulation. A Simulation is very much like an Operative Project, because you can plan costs and perform most functions you could with a real project. The limitation is that the project cannot actually be "executed," meaning it cannot attract real costs or generate commitments of any sort. They can, however, be used to derive a real project by way of copying.

- **Display Options** Determines how your project will be identified when it is first displayed in the Project Builder:

| 1 | Identification using project number |
|---|---|
| 2 | Identification using short description |
| 3 | Identification using text |

- **Level of Detail** Determines how many levels will be displayed when you maintain your project in the Project Builder. This is useful if you have projects with many levels and want to quickly load the project and decide at the time to expand the level of detail.

- **Partn Det. Proc.**   For Projects that will be connected to a Sales Order, the Partner Determination Procedure is used to configure the type of Customer (Sold-to, Ship to, etc.) you want to limit the user to entering. This field is necessary for projects that will utilize the Sales Pricing functionality of the Project Builder (via the icon). See also DIP Profile, as this works in conjunction with the Partner Determination Procedure when performing "Simulated Sales Pricing" (in the Project Builder, use of this field will make the Partner tab visible for completion of Customer details).

- **All Acct Asst Elem**   Tick this if all of the WBSs created via this Profile must have the Account Assignment Element indicator automatically set to ON. Remember, this means that all your WBS Elements can attract costs, so it will be up to the user to tick them OFF in the Operative or Standard Project unless the setting is there for inclusion of Networks or connection to external Orders.

- **Only 1 Root**   Every Operative Project has at least one "root" WBS. This actually means it will have at least one Level 1 WBS. If you tick this, you will not be able to have more than one Level 1 WBS in a project with this setting in the Profile. The benefit of having more than one serves only to make large projects "flatter" and capable of aggregating to logically independent WBSs.

- **Trsfr to Proj Def**   This setting is used when you are creating WBS Elements using the "Single Element" function. A Project Definition is automatically created if you created a single WBS in CJ11. Also, changes made to a single WBS element in CJ12 will be reflected in the Project Definition.

- **Change Documents**   Tick this if you want to keep track of any changes made to a project; for example, if you changed a WBS description from "My WBS 1" to "Your WBS 1," you will be able to see the change history in transaction CN60. Note that this does not include Financial changes; it only applies to WBS content changes.

- **Proj. summ. Mastda**   Tick this if you want to Summarize your project Master Data via Characteristics. SAP have threatened that in the long term, summarization via Classification will no longer be supported, so you might as well tick it unless you have BW (Business Warehouse). If you don't tick it, you can't perform any Summarization reports.

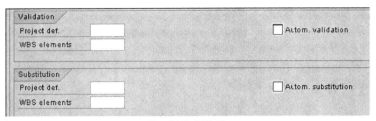

Validation/Substitution at the Project level only applies to the settings shown in the highlight box (this screen extracted from Validation/Substitution Configuration).

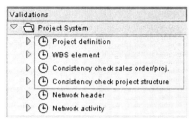

## VALIDATION TAB

Validation and Substitution IDs must be placed in the Project Profile if you want the Standard and/or Operative Projects to execute these tasks automatically in the background when a project is saved. Placing these values in the Standard or Operative WBS (in Settings) does not have the same effect and you will have to manually execute them.

- **Project def.**   If you are using Project Definition Validation, enter the ID. This applies to all Validations relevant for the Project Definition only.

- **WBS elements**   If you are using WBS Validation, enter the ID. This applies to all Validations relevant for the WBS only.

- **Autom. validation**   For both Validations, tick this if you want the system to perform your Validations automatically when the Operative Project is saved. If you do not tick this, you must follow the Edit->Validation/Substitution menu path to activate it when creating/changing an Operative Project.

## SUBSTITUTION TAB

- **Project def.**   If you are using Project Definition Substitution, enter the ID. This applies to all Substitutions relevant for the Project Definition only.

- **WBS elements**   If you are using WBS Substitution, enter the ID. This applies to all Substitutions relevant for the WBS only.

- **Autom. substitution**   For both Substitutions, tick this if you want the system to perform your Substitutions automatically when the Operative Project is saved. If you do not tick this, you must follow the Edit->Validation/Substitution menu path to activate it when creating/changing an Operative Project.

PROJECT STOCK TAB

- **No Stock** No Stock is the default—the Project and all its WBS Elements cannot "own" the materials assigned to the Networks.

- **non-valuated stk** Set this radio button if your project has stock of its own. The project stock is firmly assigned to a WBS element. Components can only be withdrawn for the WBS element.

- **valuated stk** In valuated project stock, the materials are managed on both a quantity basis and a value basis; all goods movements trigger corresponding postings in the stock accounts in Financial Accounting.

- **Automatic reqmnts grouping** For all Materials managed in a project, this indicator is set if you want Grouping for your WBS Elements. The Top-level WBS is considered the Grouping WBS and all Material requirements are grouped thus. Grouping WBS settings can be 1 (Grouping WBS for all WBS Elements) or 2 (Grouping WBS for the selected MRP Groups).

---

**NOTE** *Can only be set if Project Stock or Valuated Stock is set.*

Use value 1 if the grouping WBS element should be valid for all material components that are allocated to a WBS element (which is assigned to this grouping WBS element).

Use value 2 if you want to have different grouping WBS elements for the material components in a WBS element. This could be the case if you plan electrical and mechanical parts separately. Selection of the valid grouping WBS elements is on the basis of the MRP group and the plant for the relevant material.

If you have set the Automatic Requirements Grouping indicator in the project definition, you can only have one WBS element in the project that is the *grouping WBS element for all materials* (value 1).

- **PD sts. Profile/WBS sts. profile** Enter the User Status Profiles applicable to the Status for Project Definitions/WBSs. See "Status Management" in this chapter for details.

- **Change Documents** Tick this if you want to keep a history of changes to all statuses. You can view the history via menu options in all WBS maintenance screens using the Information icon, shown here, in the operative project.

GRAPHIC TAB

This part covers settings by which Graphics are viewed and managed when maintaining a project in Hierarchy Graphics.

Copyright by SAP AG

- **Master data prf. grp** The profile name together with the profile group determines the parameters for displaying the hierarchy graphic.

- **Graph.prfl mstr data** The profile name is used to differentiate among the various graphic profiles within one area according to various applications. The profile name together with the profile group determines the parameters for displaying the hierarchy graphic.

- **Vertical from level** With this value you specify the level in the work breakdown structure where the WBS elements are displayed vertically in the hierarchy graphic. You can specify this value in Customizing for the project profile, but you can change this level in the graphic.

- **SearchTxtIndex1—3** Text index for the text that should be used first for the search. In the graphic, nodes are used that are filled with text. The structure of the nodes is defined in Customizing in the form definitions. These form definitions consist of various fields, each of which is assigned a text index.

## PROJECT SUMMARIZATION TAB

- **All WBS elements** Summarization performed for all WBS Elements, regardless of whether they are Billing or Account Assignment. This setting extends Summarization Reporting to the whole project.

- **Billing elements** Tick this if only WBSs set as Billing Elements are to be considered in Summarization Reporting.

- **Acct asst elements** Tick this if only WBSs set as Account Assignment Elements are to be considered in Summarization Reporting.

## SALES PRICING TAB

This part covers settings used where a project has integration with Sales Documents. The values here are used in conjunction with Partner Determination (the Organizational part).

Copyright by SAP AG

- **Sales Organization, Distribution Channel, and Division** These values will be the Sales & Distribution defaults. Any Sales Documents manually connected to an operative project will have to contain the same values.
- **DIP Profile** DIP is the acronym for <u>Dynamic Item Processor</u>. If you are going to perform "simulated sales pricing" from an operative project, a DIP profile must be entered here. DIP profiles and their use in PS later in configuration.

### ORGANIZATION TAB

Project Profiles can be dedicated to Organizational settings by selection. These values only serve as defaults—they can be changed when the Operational Project is created.

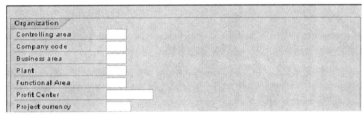

Copyright by SAP AG

- **Controlling area** If an entry is made here, the Controlling Area Currency is defaulted as well.
- **Company code** If a Company Code is entered here, it must belong to the Controlling Area just specified.
- **Business area** If Business Area is entered here, it must belong to the Controlling Area/Company Code.
- **Plant** If Plant is entered here, it must be associated with the Controlling Area/ Company Code. Note that the plant entered here does not influence Networks, only WBS Elements.
- **Functional Area** Used in Cost of Sales Accounting. The functional area is required to create a profit and loss account in Financial Accounting using Cost of Sales Account, for example, Manufacturing, Sales, R&D, and so on.
- **Profit Center** If Profit Center is entered here, it must be associated with the Controlling Area/Company Code.
- **Project currency** Currency is determined by either the Controlling Area, the Object being used (WBS, Network), or the Transaction. If a Company Code was entered in the Project Profile, it will default but you can override it by entering a valid currency here.

### WBS TIME SCHEDULING TAB

The system calculates the scheduled start and finish of the activities in the WBS elements, their capacity requirements, and the float times, when the work breakdown structure (WBS) is scheduled.

The start and finish dates of the WBS elements are the basis for determining the scheduled dates.

```
WBS time scheduling
WBS sched. prof   [            ]
Sched. scenario   [ ]
  [ ] With activities
  Default values
  Factory calend.  [  ]
  Time unit        [  ]
```

Copyright by SAP AG

- **WBS sched. prof**   The Scheduling profile used for WBS Scheduling (see details under "Control Parameters for WBS Scheduling" in this chapter).
- **Sched. scenario**   The method used for WBS Scheduling.
- **With Activities**   If ticked, will display all associated activities when an operative project is maintained in (for example) Project Builder.

| Scheduling scena... | Short text |
|---|---|
| 1 | Bottom-up scenario (pre-defined) |
| 2 | Top-down scenario (pre-defined) |
|  | Free scheduling |

Copyright by SAP AG

## DEFAULT VALUES TAB

- **Factory calend.**   If a Plant is not specified against a WBS, this value will be the default Factory Calendar for all created WBS Elements. It is only a default and can be overridden.
- **Time unit**   For scheduling, the unit that will be the default for new WBS Elements.

| Commerci... | Measurement unit text |
|---|---|
| CH | Hundredth of Hour |
| D | Days |
| DAY | Days |
| DMH | Ten Thousandth of Hour |
| H | Hour |
| HR | Hours |
| MIN | Minute |
| MIS | Microsecond |
| MON | Months |
| MSE | Millisecond |
| NS | Nanosecond |
| PS | Picosecond |
| S | Second |
| WK | Weeks |
| YR | Years |

Copyright by SAP AG

## PLANNING METHOD TAB
Determines how WBS Dates are managed.

| Planning method | |
|---|---|
| Plan.meth/basic | |
| Plan.meth/fcst | |
| Calc. with act. | without taking activity dates into consideration |

Copyright by SAP AG

- **Plan.meth/basic and Plan.meth/fcst**   To plan basic dates, you must specify a planning method. This only applies to work breakdown structure and not to activities:

  1. In Top-down Planning, you plan the dates starting from the top WBS element in the hierarchy. The dates that you maintain in the subordinate WBS elements must lie within the dates periods of the superior WBS elements.

  2. In Bottom-up Planning, you plan the dates starting from the subordinate WBS elements. The dates of the superior WBS elements are only changed if they do not include the dates of the subordinate WBS elements.

  3. In Open Planning, you plan the dates without hierarchical dependencies.

  4. In Strict Bottom-up Planning, you specify that the dates of subordinate WBS elements determine the dates of the superior elements. If you have already entered dates for the superior WBS elements, the system deletes them and calculates new dates based on the dates of the subordinate WBS elements.

| | |
|---|---|
| 1 | Top-down |
| 2 | Bottom-up (taking dates of higher-level WBS into account) |
| 3 | Open planning |
| 4 | Strict bottom-up (without dates of higher-level WBS) |

Copyright by SAP AG

- **Calc. with act**   This indicator specifies how dates from the assigned network activities should be taken into account during WBS scheduling.

| | |
|---|---|
| | without taking activity dates into consideration |
| 1 | taking activity dates into consideration |
| 2 | Consideration of activity dates by user decision |

Copyright by SAP AG

## NETWORK TAB
If you are using Networks, enter its Profile name here. The effect on your project will be to allow the addition of Networks on a WBS—if you do not enter anything here, you will not be permitted to add Networks.

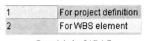

Copyright by SAP AG

- **Network asst**  Stipulates that when you create an activity, the system displays a list of all networks assigned to the WBS element or the project definition.

| 1 | For project definition |
|---|---|
| 2 | For WBS element |

Copyright by SAP AG

- **Display network hdr**  With this indicator, you determine whether the network header will be displayed when you enter dates for a WBS element in time scheduling. (If you are using Network Scheduling, tick this.)

## PROJECT PLANNING BOARD TAB

- **Planning.board prf**  The Project Planning Board is a Gantt Chart that graphically represents a project. It can be customized to suit your needs, though SAP provide one for your use. Generally, it is better to customize the profile to make your projects look better. However, users can modify how their Planning Board looks and save it without needing to customize here.

## CAPACITY REQUIREMENTS TAB

All settings here should be based on Standard SAP settings.

## HIERARCHY GRAPHIC TAB

- **Profile group and Profile**  Key identifying the profile group for the hierarchy graphic in time scheduling. The profile group together with the profile name determines the parameters for displaying the hierarchy graphic.
- **Time schd. Prof**  Key identifying the profile for the settings in the hierarchy graphic in time scheduling.

Copyright by SAP AG

- **Object Class**   The object class categorizes Controlling objects according to their business function and enables you to analyze cost flows within Controlling from different business perspectives.

   The following object classes are available:
   Overhead
   Production
   Investment
   Profitability analysis and sales

   An object class is required to determine or explain certain values in the external accounting components; for example, the balance of all objects in the class "Production" is categorized as "work in process" or WIP.

- **Settlement Profile**   A requirement for creating a settlement rule. You define the following parameters in the settlement profile:

   - Allowed settlement receivers (such as cost center or asset)

   - Default values for the settlement structure and the PA transfer structure

- Allocation bases for defining the settlement shares (using percentages or equivalence numbers—or both)

- Maximum number of distribution rules

- Residence period of the settlement documents

- Document type for settlements relevant to accounting (more specifically, to the balance sheet)

- Definitions for the settlement of actual costs or the cost of sales

- **Settlement Rule Strategy**   Key describing the strategy for generating settlement rules automatically in WBS elements. You use the strategy to determine the following for each settlement parameter:
  Control parameters for the objects to which the strategy applies, such as billing elements.
  Account assignment category, for example:
  –Responsible cost center
  –Treatment of sales and distribution document items in the event of multiple assignment to WBS element

## Networks

Networks are instructions on how to carry out tasks in a specific way, in a specific order, and in a specific time period. They are Order Type 20 and exclusive to PS.

### Network Profile

Conceptually, the Network Profile works in a similar fashion to the Project Profile. However, where the Project Profile controls how WBS Elements behave, Network Profiles determine how Networks behave. For a project to use Networks, the Network Profile would normally be attached to the Project profile (this is not a strict rule, as Standard WBS Elements [templates] can carry it instead).

Configuration of Network Profiles has certain dependencies—the most important being the Network Type.

Following are the configuration connections from Network Type with all PS dependencies. Typical configuration is highlighted in Figure 5-2.

Network Profile carries Network Type, which is connected to Network Parameters and Scheduling Parameters via Plant. Project Profile carries Network Profile.

Though a number of Network Types can be identical, they serve to allow different rules via the Project Profile (for example, Settlement). They also allow for variations in types of Scheduling via Scheduling Parameters.

| Menu Path | Project System->Structures->Operative Structures->Network->Settings for Networks |
|---|---|
| **Config Point** | Maintain Network Profiles |
| **Transaction** | OPUU |

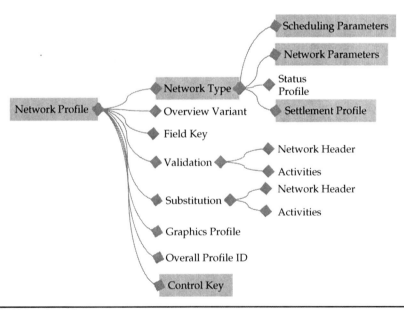

**FIGURE 5-2**   Network roadmap

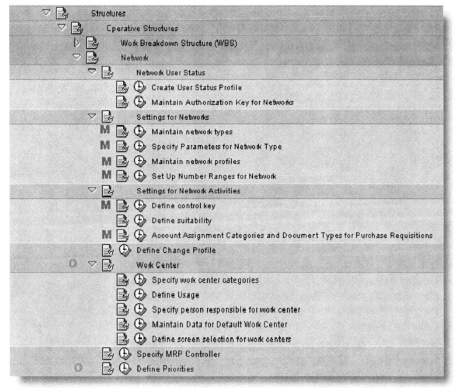

Copyright by SAP AG

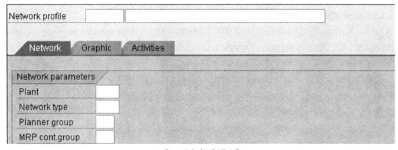

Copyright by SAP AG

### NETWORK TAB: Network Parameters

- **Plant**   The Plant that will be the default for all Activities under the Network header. If it is not specified here, it will have to be entered when a project is created.

- **Network type**   Differentiate the Order Types that may be associated with the Network (Order Types carry number ranges, costing information, etc.). This key is also used in the configuration point "Network Parameters" later in this chapter, which defines what Network Types are valid with what Plants and how they must behave.

- **Planner group**   Which group is responsible for managing the Task List. If it is entered, you will also have to enter an MRP cont.group.

- **MRP cont.group**   The Materials Requirements Planning Group associated with the Planner Group.

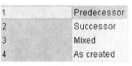

Copyright by SAP AG

- **Rel. view**   The relationship view initially presented when you are defining Start/Finish Rules for linking Networks. The most common is Mixed, as this will show Predecessor and Successor relationships. In CJ20N you can link Activities to each other (and to other projects' activities). As Created will leave them in the order they were created.

| 1 | Predecessor |
|---|---|
| 2 | Successor |
| 3 | Mixed |
| 4 | As created |

Copyright by SAP AG

- **Level of detail**   A number representing the level of detail you want to see when viewing Activity relationships.

- **Comp. increment**   Increment used between Material Components attached to an Activity, for example, 10, 20, 30, and so on.

- **Op.act. incrmnt**   Increment used between each Activity in a Network. Usually 010, which will increment by units of 10. This allows for insertion where necessary. Remember, Network Activities are identified by the Network Number plus the Activity Number.

- **Check WBS act.**   How you want the system to react to WBS Dates that may fall outside the complete range of Activity dates associated with the WBS.

|   | No check |
|---|---|
| E | Exit with error |
| W | Exit with warning |

Copyright by SAP AG

- **Overview var.**   For PP (Production Planning), a list from routings, inspection plans, maintenance task lists, and networks. The variant can be defined with the objects displayed in an object overview and the layout of the object overview lines.

- **Procurement**   Combine various settings for the procurement of components. Which stock the components are to be managed in:
  –The Third-party order indicator
  –The Preliminary order indicator
  –The item category
  The value entered here is the default Procurement Type when a new Material Component is created. When you assign a component to an activity, you have to

enter a procurement indicator in the component overview. After you have confirmed entry, you can no longer change the procurement indicator.

| Rel. view | | | Res./Purc. req. | 3 |
|---|---|---|---|---|
| Level of detail | | | ✓ Cap. reqmts | |
| Comp. increment | | | ☐ Entry tool | |
| Op./act. incrmt | | | ☐ Project sum. | |
| Check. WBS act. | No check | | ☐ Align.Fin. date | |
| Overview var. | | | ☐ Proj. summ. MastDa | |
| Procurement | | | | |
| Field key | | | | |
| Version prof. | | | | |

Copyright by SAP AG

- **Field key**   Determines the Key used for User Defined Fields (UDFs). If you do not use UDFs, you do not need to enter anything here. If you are using UDFs but deliberately leave them out here, you can still manually enter them in an Operative or Standard Project.

- **Version prof.**   Determines the key used if you are using Project Versions. This is also used in the Project Profile, but here you can be specific about what goes into a Network Activity Version via the Status of an Activity rather than the status of a WBS.

- **Res/Purc. req.**   Select a number from 1 to 3 to determine when a Reservation/Purchase Requisition is generated from the Network.

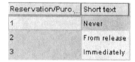

| Reservation/Purc. | Short text |
|---|---|
| 1 | Never |
| 2 | From release |
| 3 | Immediately |

Copyright by SAP AG

- **Cap. Reqmts**   Ticked if you want Capacity requirements calculated when you save the Network.

- **Entry tool**   Tick this if you want the system to automatically go to the data entry screen of the Activity or element (internally, external, general cost).

- **Project sum.**   Tick this to specify that activities in networks with activity account assignment will be taken into account in project summarization. Note, this can only be ticked if the superior WBS Element is also ticked for Summarization.

- **Align. Fin. Date**   Tick this if you want the material components in the Activities staged for the Scheduled Finish Date. You can control the Lead-time days (the number of days before the Finish Date the Materials should be individually staged) in the General Data of the Material Component screen of the Operative Project. To be more precise about the Earliest/Latest Dates, also see configuration for Specify Parameters for Network Scheduling—Trans OPU6.

- **Proj. summ. MastDa**   Tick if you want Summarization via Master Data Characteristics. Note that SAP do not intend to support this in the future.

## VALIDATION TAB

Validation and Substitution IDs must be placed in the Network Profile if you want the Standard and/or Operative Networks to execute these tasks automatically in the background when a project is saved. Placing these values in the Standard or Operative Networks (in Settings) does not have the same effect and you will have to manually execute them. The Validations and Substitutions in the Project Profile work independently from these.

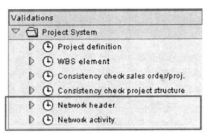

Copyright by SAP AG

**NOTE** *Validation/Substitution at the Network level only applies to the settings shown in the highlight box (this screen extracted from Validation/Substitution Configuration).*

Copyright by SAP AG

- **Network header**  If you are using Project Definition Validation, enter the ID. This applies to all Validations relevant for the Network Header only.
- **Network activities**  If you are using Network Validation, enter the ID. This applies to all Validations relevant for the Network Activities only.

## SUBSTITUTION TAB
Same guidelines as on Validation tab apply.

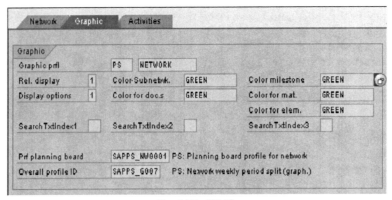

Copyright by SAP AG

## GRAPHICS TAB

Most of the settings in this configuration are standard SAP—it serves no purpose to attempt a full explanation—just use the standard profiles and make adjustments as you see fit.

In summary, these settings affect the way the Network Graphic is shown in the Project Builder, Planning Board, or any other place you see the Network Graphic Symbol, shown here.

Copyright by SAP AG

A Typical Network Graphic using Standard SAP:

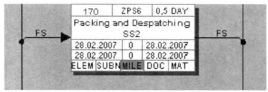

Copyright by SAP AG

---

**NOTE** *The Color settings (for example, Color Milestone), which mean "Milestone Exists," can only be seen in the Expanded Mode of the graphics display as shown next.*

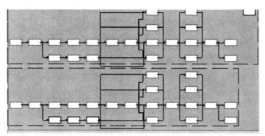

Copyright by SAP AG

## ACTIVITIES TAB

For a network to be functional, it must have Activities (these are the objects that do the work). These Activities are managed via Control Keys, which uniquely identify each type of Activity and what its general settings are. In the Network Profile, you can only have four Control Keys: Internal, External, General, and Service. These four types of activity will be discussed next.

| Internally processed activity | | |
| --- | --- | --- |
| Control key | | Network - internal processing |
| Mat.cost elem. | | |
| Unit for work | | |
| Norm.duratn un. | | |
| Calculation key | | |

Copyright by SAP AG

### Internally Processed Activity

Activities that are managed using internal resources (machines, people, etc.). It can be confusing to tell internal from external, as it is possible to add material components that are purchased externally. However, these types of Activity are the only ones that allow you to use

Work Centers and Activity Types for planning purposes and are the basis for Capacity and internal resource planning.

- **Control key**   The Control Key is configured separately (Trans OPSU). SAP provides standard ones (PS01–PS05) but you can copy/change them to suit your needs (most installations do). Read about Control Keys before you decide which ones to use in your Network Profile.

- **Mat.cost elem.**   Enter a suitable planning Cost Element—Costs planned by Material will appear in reports "by Cost Element."

- **Unit for work**   Unit of Measure—this value appears as the default Unit for all your Internally Processed Activities when planning costs by Work Center/Activity Type. (The Cost Elements associated with this planning are stored in the Cost Center.)

- **Norm.duratn un.**   Unit of Measure—this value appears as the Normal Duration for all your Internally Processed Activities. The value is used in Scheduling for Networks, but can be overridden.

- **Calculation key**   Calculation key for duration, work, or number of required capacities in the activity.
  The basis for the calculation is:
  –Number of capacities with the capacity category
  –Operating (working) time percentage of the entered capacity
  –Duration of the activity
  –Work

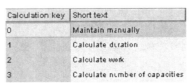

| Calculation key | Short text |
| --- | --- |
| 0 | Maintain manually |
| 1 | Calculate duration |
| 2 | Calculate work |
| 3 | Calculate number of capacities |

Copyright by SAP AG

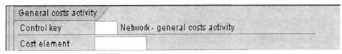

| General costs activity | |
| --- | --- |
| Control key | Network - general costs activity |
| Cost element | |

Copyright by SAP AG

**General Cost Activity**

Costs planned in this way usually relate to things like Travel, Insurance, Royalties, and so on, and do not need to have any materials or Activity Types associated with them—they are a simple form of planning costs at the Activity level.

- **Control key**   The Control Key is configured separately (Trans OPSU). SAP provides standard ones (PS01–PS05), but you can copy/change them to suit your needs (most installations do). Read about Control Keys before you decide which ones to use in your Network Profile.

- **Cost element**   Enter a suitable planning Cost Element—General Costs will appear in reports "by Cost Element."

Following is a screenshot of fields specific for a General Cost Activity in Project Builder:

Copyright by SAP AG

Copyright by SAP AG

### Service Activity

Service Activities are those used to manage external services by way of Outline Agreements and Service Masters. Often, businesses need to plan for subcontractors, and these activities allow you to specify existing contracts and agreements:

- **Control key**   The Control Key is configured separately (Trans OPSU). SAP provides standard ones but you can change them to suit your needs (most installations do). Read about Control Keys before you decide which ones to use in your Network Profile.

- **Cost element**   Enter a suitable planning Cost Element—General Costs will appear in reports "by Cost Element."

- **Material group**   Key that you use to group together several services with the same attributes, and to assign them to a particular material group. Entry of this helps MRP search and find common requirements.

- **Purch. group**   Key for a buyer or a group of buyers responsible for certain purchasing activities. Internally, the purchasing group is responsible for the procurement of a material or a class of materials. Externally, it is the medium through which contacts with the vendor are maintained.

- **Unit of measure**   The Unit used by the purchasing department to order the Service.

Next is a screenshot of fields specific for a Service Activity in Project Builder:

Copyright by SAP AG

Copyright by SAP AG

## Externally Processed Activity

Activities relating to externally purchased goods (and services). These types of activities are used manage the purchase of materials that do not exist in your stock.

- **Control key**   The Control Key is configured separately (Trans OPSU). SAP provides standard ones but you can change them to suit your needs (most installations do). Read about Control Keys in the next section before you decide which ones to use in your Network Profile.

- **Cost element**   Enter a suitable planning Cost Element—General Costs will appear in reports "by Cost Element."

- **Currency**   Default Currency for the Activity (which will be applied to the new Activity).

- **Purchasing Org.**   Default Purchasing Organization (which will be applied to the new Activity).

- **Material group**   Default Material Group (which will be applied to the new Activity).

- **Purch. group**   Default Purchasing Group (which will be applied to the new Activity).

- **Order unit**   Default Unit of Measure (which will be applied to the new Activity).

## Network Type

The function of a Network Type is to categorize the Order Type. Network Orders are Type 20. It is mandatory for a Network to have a Network Type associated with it (via the Network Profile). The Network Type plays a significant role in controlling and managing the network, in particular the Settlement Profile.

| Menu Path | Project System->Structures->Operative Structures->Network->Settings for Networks |
|---|---|
| Config Point | Maintain Network Type |
| Transaction | OPSC |

Order category    20    Network
Order Type

Control indicator
CO partner update        Semi-active
☐ Classification
☐ Planning

Reorganization
Residence Time1    Months
Residence Time2    Months

Costs
Functional Area
Object Class
Settlmt Profile

Status management
Status profile

☐ Release immed.

Number range general

Copyright by SAP AG

- **Order category**    Automatically set to 20 (Network Orders)
- **Order Type**    The ID that is used for this Network Type

## CONTROL INDICATOR TAB

- **CO partner update**    Defined in CO. Settings are:
  - Not active—In allocations between an order and another object, no totals record is produced for the relationship with the order.

- Partly active—In allocations between orders, totals records are produced for each combination. In allocations that are not directly between two orders, such as activity allocations between cost centers and orders, no totals record for the relationships with the order is produced in the other object.
  - Active—In allocations between an order and another object, a totals record is always produced for the combination including the order.
- **Classification**   Tick if Classification of objects is required in reporting.
- **Planning**   Tick if Planning data is to be copied to CO.

## REORGANIZATION TAB

Copyright by SAP AG

When a network is deleted, it is archived according to time frames (Residence) set here (1 and 2). There are three steps involved in deleting a Network:

1. Setting the delete flag (can be reset).

2. Setting the final deletion indicator (cannot be reset).

3. Reorganizing (writing the object to a sequential dataset and physically deleting it from the system).

- **Residence Time1**   Residence time 1 determines the time interval (in calendar months) that must elapse between setting the delete flag (step 1) and setting the deletion indicator (step 2).

- **Residence Time2**   Residence time 1 determines the time interval (in calendar months) that must elapse between setting the delete flag (step 2) and setting the deletion indicator (step 3).

## COSTS TAB

- **Functional Area**   Used for external accounting. The functional area is required to create a profit and loss account in Financial Accounting using Cost of Sales Accounting (a type of profit and loss statement that matches the sales revenues to the costs or expenses involved in making the revenue). Often used in government applications.

- **Object Class**   Can be Overhead, Production, Investment, or Profitability Analysis/ Sales. While certain object types automatically belong to a particular class (for example, cost centers belong to the "Overhead" class), others need to be explicitly assigned to an object class in their master record (this is the case with internal orders and work breakdown structure elements).

- **Settlmt Profile**   The profile configured in Settlement Config (OKO7). This will become the default for Activities.

## STATUS MANAGEMENT TAB

Any User Status configured can be set as default for all Networks created.

| Order category | 20 | Network |
|---|---|---|
| Order Type | | |

Control indicator
CO partner update    Semi-active
☐ Classification
☐ Planning

Reorganization
Residence Time1 ___ Months
Residence Time2 ___ Months

Costs
Functional Area ___
Object Class ___
Settlmt Profile ___

Status management
Status profile ___

☐ Release immed.

Number range general

Copyright by SAP AG

- **Status profile**   The profile configured in User Status Config (OKO2). This will become the default for Activities.

- **Release immed.**   If ticked, all activities will be released the moment they are created.

**NOTE** *You can only use the indicator for orders that use general SAP status management. Maintenance Orders and Service Orders are released automatically only if they are created from maintenance calls, from a background notification, or from a sales order. Service orders are also released immediately if they are created from a sales document item.*

- **Number range general**   Takes you into transaction OPSC (Maintain Number Ranges for Orders). Here you can set the number ranges required for your Network Header based on your Network Types.

## Network Parameters

It would not be possible to use Networks and process Purchase Orders, Reservations, Maintenance Orders, and other Orders unless you have set up the Parameters by which the Orders are processed, especially if the orders are attached to different Plants. Parameters are the "binding" of the Plant to the Network Type (attached to the Network Profile), which is achieved here. If you have multiple Plants in your Organization, you will need one Parameter entry for each Plant (assuming the Plant is suitable for Networks).

| Menu Path | Project System->Structures->Operative Structures->Network->Settings for Networks |
|---|---|
| Config Point | Specify Parameters for Network Type |
| Transaction | OPUV |

Copyright by SAP AG

- **Plant**   The Plant that will use the Network Type. Not all Plants would use a Network—for example, if you have a Service Plant where you do not want Service Orders to appear in Project Planning.
- **Network type**   The Network Type (as configured in OPSC) associated with the Plant.

## NETWORK TYPE PARAMETERS TAB

- **Strategy**   How the Settlement Rule is determined in the Network Activity.
- **Default Rule**   In a CO settlement rule, the distribution rules are, in certain cases, generated automatically. The default rule determines how this kind of distribution rule is structured. The default rules are predefined by SAP and cannot be changed.

| 01 | as WBS element/project definition |
| 02 | to WBS element |
| 03 | Default rule |
| 04 | Manual settlement rule |
| 05 | No settlement rule |

Copyright by SAP AG

Plant ☑
Network type ☑

**Network type parameters**
Strategy
Default Rule
Red. strategy
CstgVariantPlan
CstgVariantActl
Plan Cost Calc.   Determine plan costs

☐ Wrkflw PO chg.
☐ ActvtyAcctAsgn.
☐ Net Order Price
☐ CollctveRequstn

**Status change documents**
☐ Change document

**Documents**
☐ OrdStatChangeDc
☐ OpStatChangeDoc
☐ MatStatChngeDoc
☐ PRTStatChangeDc

**BOM Usage**
BOM application

**Change Management**
Change profile

☐ PDC active

Copyright by SAP AG

- **Red. strategy**   Key that specifies the strategy for reducing the lead-time of an Activity.

- **CstgVariantPlan**   Key that specifies which Costing Variant is used to determine the planned costs. The Costing Variant refers to a Valuation Variant, which combines all the parameters for evaluating materials, internal activities, and external activities in Preliminary Costing. It also determines which calculation schema is proposed for determining the overheads for production and Process Orders.

- **CstgVariantActl**   Key that specifies the Costing Variant that is used to determine the actual costs. The Costing Variant refers to a Valuation Variant, which determines which activity prices are used from cost center accounting to evaluate the confirmed internal activities in Simultaneous Costing (a process that assigns to a cost object the actual costs incurred to date for that cost object). It also determines which Costing Sheet is proposed for calculating the Overheads in the order (Production Cost Collector or Production Order).

- **Plan Cost Calc.**   When you want your Planned Costs updated.

| Plant | ☑ | | |
|---|---|---|---|
| Network type | ☑ | | |

**Network type parameters**

| Strategy | | Wrkflw PO chg. |
|---|---|---|
| Default Rule | | ActvtyAcctAsgn. |
| Red. strategy | | Net Order Price |
| CstgVariantPlan | | CollctveRequstn |
| CstgVariantActl | | |
| Plan Cost Calc. | Determine plan costs | |

**Status change documents**

| ☐ Change document | |
|---|---|

**Documents**

- ☐ OrdStatChangeDc
- ☐ OpStatChangeDoc
- ☐ MatStatChngeDoc
- ☐ PRTStatChangeDc

**BOM Usage**

| BOM application | |
|---|---|

**Change Management**

| Change profile | |
|---|---|

☐ PDC active

- **Wrkflw PO chg.**   Tick this if you want changes to quantities or dates of non-stock components, external activities to create a workflow (and whether a purchase order already exists).

- **ActvtyAcctAsgn.**   Tick this if you want Account Assignment (postings) at the Activity level. If you do not tick this, Account Assignment will be at the Network Header level.
- **Net Order Price**   Tick this if the net price cannot be changed when copied over from the purchase requisition into the purchase order.
- **CollctveRequstn**   Tick this if you want all external operations (Orders) to be associated with a Collective Purchase Requisition. If you do not tick the box, separate PRs will be created for each external Operation.

## STATUS CHANGE DOCUMENTS TAB

Tick this if you want changes to Networks to be recorded (before/after and who made the change).

- **OrdStatChangeDc**   Tick this to record Status changes at the Network Header level.
- **OpStatChangeDoc**   Tick this to record Status changes to an Operation.
- **MatStatChngeDoc**   Tick this to record Status changes to a Material Component.
- **PRTStatChangeDc**   Tick this to record Status changes to a Production Resource Tool.

## BOM USAGE TAB

Represents a process for automatic determination of alternatives (Production Planning) in the different organizational areas within a company.

Copyright by SAP AG

## BOM Application

To select the right alternative for a specific application area, the following criteria are defined for each application:

- Priority for BOM Usage
- Priority of a specific alternative for a particular material BOM
- Production version from the material master
- Checking of certain status indicators

## CHANGE MANAGEMENT TAB

- **Change profile**   This profile determines the change process in PP for production orders and how automatically executed changes to orders or networks are dealt with in PS and PP.
- **PDC active**   Tick this if Plant Data Collection is active (Cross Application).

## Order Value Updating

In this configuration, you make settings that determine how the various Order Types (Networks, PP Orders, Maintenance Orders, etc.) update the Project Cost Plan. The costs can be either Apportioned or Appended.

- **Apportioned** (Appended not set)   The plan value of an order is added to the committed value of the corresponding WBS element.
- **Appended**   The plan value of an order is added to the plan value of the corresponding WBS element.

The most useful purpose of this configuration (outside of Networks) is to ensure that other Orders (such as Maintenance Orders that are assigned to a Project), will have their planned costs showing in a Project.

*Also, see Transaction OPTP (Parameters for Subnetworks).*

| Menu Path | Project System->Costs->Planned Costs->Automatic costing in Networks/ Activities |
|---|---|
| Config Point | Define Order Value Updating for Orders for Projects |
| Transaction | OPSV |

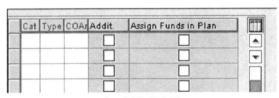

Copyright by SAP AG

- **Cat**   Enter an Order Category (for example, 20, 30, 50).

- **Type**   If you want all Order Types of the Category to be considered for Cost Planning, enter ++++. Or enter an Order Type (for example, there may be several Types of Maintenance Order, so you can be specific about which ones have which settings).

- **COAr**   Enter a CO Area or ++++ for all CO Areas.

- **Addit.**   Tick if Costs from the Orders are Additive (that is, Appended). If you do not tick this, Costs are Apportioned (see preceding notes).

- **Assign Funds in Plan**   Tick this if the plan values for an order with status "Opened" are entered in the assigned values for the PSP element as the order requests. If your Order Type is a Network and your Network Type has a setting in the Control Indicator and you attempt to be specific about which Order Types are affected, then you will get an information message stating that Assign Funds to Plan has been controlled by the Network Type.

Copyright by SAP AG

### Parameters for Subnetworks

Subnetworks are Orders (other than Networks) that may be assigned to a Project for planning purposes. In this configuration, you are making settings that point one Network Type to another. If, for example, you want Service Orders to be Subnetworks of a Project, you first specify the Network Type from PS that a Subnetwork will be part of, then you specify the Network Type that it will be replaced by when an Order is assigned to a project, then you specify the Control Key that must be used to define how the Subnetwork is managed (see OPSU Control Key). Finally, you specify which Dates are copied from the Network to the Subnetwork.

*Also, see Transaction OPSV (Order Value Updating).*

| Menu Path | Project System->Structures->Operative Structures->Network |
|---|---|
| **Config Point** | Define Parameters for Subnetworks |
| **Transaction** | OPTP |

Copyright by SAP AG

- **Network type subntwk**  Specify the Network Type from PS that a Subnetwork will be part of.
- **NtwkTy replaced act.**  Specify the Network Type that the Subnetwork will be replaced by when an Order is assigned to a project.

## CONTROL PARAMETER TAB

- **Control key**  Specify the Control key that must be used to define how the Subnetwork is managed.
- **Copy dates**  Specify which Dates are copied from the Network to the Subnetwork—Earliest, Latest or Earliest Start, and Latest Finish.

A reminder of how the Control key looks in Transaction OPSU:

Copyright by SAP AG

### Control Key

Determines which Business Transactions are carried out when a Network Activity is processed. The most important thing is that its function is to uniquely identify whether a Network Activity is one of the following:

- Internally Processed (for internal resources by Work Center/Activity Type)
- Externally Processed (for externally sourced Materials)
- General Cost (for nonspecific planning by Cost Center)
- Service (for externally sourced Services [contracts])

SAP provides a set of typical settings, but you can subtly change their behaviour here by including special settings. For Subnetworks, there may be a specific Control Key—see Transaction OPTP.

| Menu Path | Project System->Structures->Operative Structures->Network->Settings for Networks->Settings for Network Activities |
|---|---|
| **Config Point** | Define Control Key |
| **Transaction** | OPSU |

Copyright by SAP AG

- **Control key**   A unique identifier and a Description

## INDICATORS TAB

- **Scheduling**   Tick this if you want your Activities and Activity Elements scheduled according to the Scheduling Parameters.

- **Det. Cap. Req.**   Tick this if you want your Activities and Activity Elements to have your Capacity requirements determined. This should only be ticked if you have also ticked Scheduling, as the scheduling results determine Capacity.

- **Gen. costs act.**   Tick this if you want your General Cost Activities to use this Control Key.

- **Cost**   Tick this if you want the costs associated with your Activities and Activity Elements to be included in Costing.

Copyright by SAP AG

- **Print time tic.**   Tick this if you want to print time tickets. You must also set the *Print* indicator in the Control key. Set a number greater than "0" of time tickets to be printed in the order (see *General Data* for the respective operation, sub-operation, or phase).

A Time Ticket is a document on which an employee's actual times and quantities produced are recorded. This document is used for confirmation of work order completion and remuneration for work performed. Time tickets are created for all operations printed on job tickets if certain conditions are fulfilled, for example, operation released, not completed, not deleted, or not confirmed.

The time ticket is a means of recording working times and allocating labor costs to cost centers or cost objects. When used to record piecework, it comprises data that describe a work unit in its entirety.

The fields used on time tickets are account assignment fields, such as order number; operation or cost center; actual data fields, such as time required, number of units completed, or setup time; and reference data fields, such as standard time for each unit, quantity to be completed, and target time based on the number of units and the standard time for each unit.

- **Confirmation**    Select an appropriate setting if you want to allow Confirmations.

| Confirmatio... | Short text |
|---|---|
| 1 | Milestone confirmation (not PS/PM) |
| 2 | Confirmation required |
| 3 | Confirmation not possible |
| | Confirmation possible but not necessary |

Copyright by SAP AG

- **Ext. processing**    If you want this Control Key to be used for External Processing, specify how.

| Extern... | Short text |
|---|---|
| | Internally processed operation |
| + | Externally processed operation |
| X | Internally processed operation/external processing possible |

Copyright by SAP AG

- **Service**    Tick this if you want this Control Key to be used for Services.

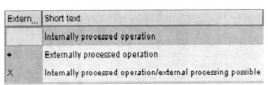

Copyright by SAP AG

- **Print confirm.**   Tick this if you want to print confirmations. You must also set the *Print* indicator in the Control Key. Set a number greater than "0" of time tickets to be printed in the order (see *General Data* for the respective operation, sub-operation, or phase).

    This setting is only taken into account if, in Customizing for print control (section *List control for transaction*).

- **Print**   Tick if you have set either Print Time Ticket or Print Confirmation.

- **Sched.ext.op.**   This indicator determines that Network Activities can be scheduled using their standard values if they are externally processed. If the indicator is not set, then these objects are scheduled using the planned delivery time when they are externally processed.

    This setting is only taken into account if the object is marked as externally processed in the Control Key (field *external processing*).

## Account Assignment Categories

This configuration applies to settings against Purchase Requisitions/Purchase Orders that have been created as a result of Networks. Purchase requisitions/orders can be assigned to:

- The network. (Planned costs are updated in the network.)
- The WBS element. (If the network is assigned to a WBS element, planned costs are updated in the WBS element.)
- The sales order. (If the network is assigned to a sales order, the planned costs are updated in the sales order.)

| Menu Path | Project System->Structures->Operative Structures->Network->Settings for Networks->Settings for Network Activities |
|---|---|
| **Config Point** | Account Assignment Categories and Document Types for Purchase Requisitions |
| **Transaction** | OPTT |

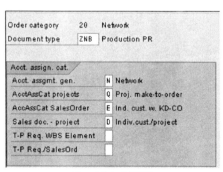

Copyright by SAP AG          Copyright by SAP AG

- **Order category**   Always 20 for Networks.
- **Document type**   Specify the document Type. These are created in Purchasing configuration (the standard PR/PO Document Type is NB, but you can have your own).

### ACCT. ASSIGN. CAT. TAB
Account Assignment Category is a "statement" for CO Settlement receivers:

- **Acct. assgmt. gen.**   Category for consumption
- **AcctAssCat projects**   Category for Project Stock
- **AccAssCat SalesOrder**   Category for Sales Order Stock
- **Sales doc.-project**   Category for Sales Order Settlement
- **T-P Req. WBS Element**   Category for 3rd Party request for WBS
- **T-P Req./SalesOrd**   Category for 3rd Party request for Sales Order

## Milestones

### Overview

Milestones carry dates that represent planned events. They can be used to simply identify important events, or they can have functions attached to them. Example: You are planning the construction of a glass elevator using a network. A milestone is attached to the activity "approval." After the activity "approval" is released, the network will be automatically updated to include a standard network "procurement" containing all activities related to purchasing.

Milestones can also trigger a Workflow (for example, an internal mail reminding someone that an event has occurred when it was planned to).

Milestones are events in the life of a project. They are date-controlled and can influence the behaviour of a project when certain dates are confirmed as having arrived. Milestones can be attached to both WBS and Network Activities.

### Milestone Functions

Based on the value of System and User status (which changes as a project progresses), you perform special tasks that can release subsequent activities or create new networks. This is useful when you require "behind the scenes" activity to be triggered when milestones are reached.

---

**NOTE** *"Release Stop Indicator" exists to control release of subsequent activities.*

### Sales Document Date

If the network is linked to a Sales Order, the scheduled date for the Milestone can be replicated in the Sales Document (based upon the Date Key, which determines which specific date in the Sales Document is overwritten).

### Offsets

If you want a Milestone date to be calculated for you, you can do one of the following:

- tick the Latest Date indicator, which will transfer the latest date of the WBS into the Milestone Schedule Date

or

- tick the Offset to Finish indicator, which will transfer the Finish date of the WBS into the Milestone Schedule Date

Subsequently, you can (optionally) complete the dependencies (for example, after 20 hours of the Activity has elapsed). Or you can specify a Percentage representing the Percentage of Completion an Activity has reached (as specified in the Percentage of Completion of the Milestone.

### Billing Plan

A Billing Plan is a list of dates when customers are scheduled to receive their accounts. It is possible to trigger the sending of those accounts via Milestones. This is done in two stages:

1. Create the Milestones in PS.
2. Attach Milestones to the Billing Plan in SD (Sales & Distribution).

Figure 5-3 details the object relationship in Milestones (both Network and WBS).

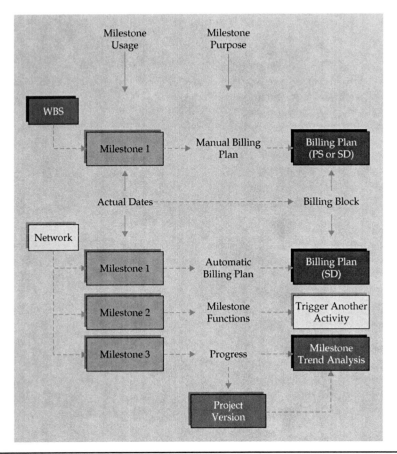

**FIGURE 5-3** Milestone object relationship

**NOTE** *When Milestones are used with Networks to form the basis of a Customer Billing Plan, only the initial % entered into the Milestone is transferred to the Billing Plan. Subsequent updates must be managed manually in the Sales Order.*

### Milestone Trend Analysis (MTA)

MTA is a simple method for analyzing the dates in a project and comparing them with planned data. You use it to quickly recognize trends and deviations from the planned schedule. The scheduled dates of the milestones, which are relevant for the course of the project, are compared at various points in time. Deviations from the planned schedule are made apparent. In the graphical form, an MTA chart is used whose triangular sides are the time axes. As shown in Figure 5-4 (extract from SAP documentation), milestone dates are plotted against the report dates.

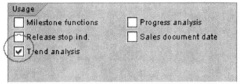

FIGURE 5-4 Milestone trend analysis

To make a Milestone relevant for MTA, you must set the indicator in the Milestone to ON.

In conjunction with this, you must have configured a Project Version Profile with MTA-Relevant set to ON (see "Create Profiles for Project Version OPTS" in this chapter). This will form the basis upon which MTA can compare your operative project to the original baseline.

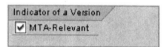

Copyright by SAP AG

Create a Project Version via the following path in Project Information System:

*Structure->Structure Overview (or in the Project Execution menu) Period-End closing->Project Versions*

Then select Evaluation->Save project version.

MTA can be run via the Planning Board or by accessing this path:

*Logistics or Accounting->Project System->Information System->Progress->Milestone Trend Analysis*

The SAP Library contains excellent information on this subject.

### Milestone Usage

You need do no more configuration than create a Usage and a Description if you are using Milestones in their most basic form (that is, you only want them as dates on a Gantt Chart and do not use Billing).

If you want to set up Standard Milestones, you will need a Usage.

---

**NOTE** *Configuration of Usage is the same for both Standard and Operative projects.*

---

| Menu Path | Project System->Structures->Operative Structures->Milestones<br>Project System->Structures->Templates->Standard Milestones |
|---|---|
| Config Point | Define Milestone Usage |
| Transaction | OPSR |

IMG for Milestone Usage:

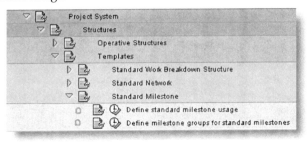

IMG for Milestone Billing:

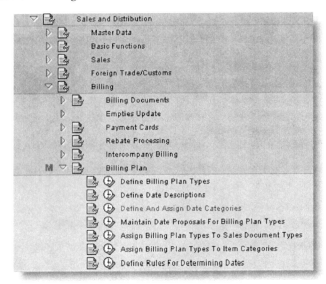

| Usage | Description | BillPlanTy | Date catg | S/F | No dialog | |
|-------|-------------|------------|-----------|-----|-----------|---|
| | | | | | ☐ | |
| | | | | | ☐ | |
| | | | | | ☐ | |
| | | | | | ☐ | |

- **Usage**   A unique identifier for the use of this Milestone.

- **Description**   A description. (If you are using Milestones for Order Billing purposes, this is the description that appears on your SD Billing Plan. Take note that even though the description is 40 characters long here, you will only be able to see 13 characters on the SD Billing Plan.)

- **BillPlanTy**   If you are using Milestones for Billing purposes, you will have to enter a Billing Plant Type here. This controls which fields are offered for processing (see "Maintain Billing Types for Milestone Billing OVBO.")

- **Date catg**   Date Category—Again, if you are using Milestone Billing, this controls Billing Rules, Billing Types, Billing Blocks, and other date-related information (see "Define and Assign Date Categories OVBJ.")

| Start/Fini... | Short text |
|---|---|
| 1 | Milestone at the start of an activity |
| 2 | Milestone at the finish of an activity |

Copyright by SAP AG

- **S/F**   Start/Finish—specify whether you want the Milestone date to be at the start or the end of an activity.

- **No dialog**   Specifies that when a milestone function or trigger point function is triggered, you are not informed about the execution of this function. This presumes that you have maintained the usage for the milestone or trigger point.

Once you have performed this configuration, you can attach Milestones to a Project Definition, a WBS, and a Network.

## Field Selections

This configuration is about the Project fields you see when working with Project Definitions, WBSs, and Networks. In this book, configuration is only shown for Project Definitions—however, conceptually it is the same for WBS Elements and the same rules apply to Standard Projects. In summary, if you apply an influence to a project, the Master Data you influence will control what you see in data entry screens such as CJ20N, CJ01, and so on. If you do not use Influencing, nearly all fields will be allowed for input.

### Project Definition, WBS, Network

Selected fields can be one of the following:

- **Input**   The field can be input.
- **Required**   The field is input and mandatory.
- **Display**   The field is displayed only (greyed out).
- **Hidden**   The field is not visible.
- **Highlighted**   The field is input and highlighted but not mandatory.

There are two ways of managing which fields are shown in a project:

- **Without Influencing**   You select the fields you want and the settings will apply to all projects, regardless.
- **With Influencing**   You select the fields you want but apply an "influence." This means that the fields are available based on the value of certain Master Data in your project.

In the case of **Project Definition**, you can influence the following key data:

- Business Area
- Company Code
- Controlling Area
- Plant
- Profit Center
- Project Profile

In the case of **WBS**, you can influence the following key data:

- Acct asst elem
- Billing element
- Business area
- Company Code
- Controlling area
- Field key

- Level
- Planning element
- Plant
- Priority
- Profit Center
- Proj.type
- Project Profile
- Statistical

In the case of **Network Header**, you can influence the following key data:

- Business Area
- Company Code
- Controlling Area
- MRP controller
- Network profile
- Order Type
- Profit Center

In the case of **Network Overview**, you can influence the following key data:

- Business Area
- Company Code
- Control Key
- Controlling Area
- Field key
- MRP controller
- Network profile
- Order Type
- Priority
- Profit Center
- Work center

In the case of **Network Details**, you can influence the following key data:

- Business Area
- Company Code
- Control Key

- Controlling Area
- Field key
- MRP controller
- Network profile
- Order Type
- Priority
- Profit Center
- Work center

| Menu Path | Project System->Structures->Operative Structures->Work Breakdown Structure->User Interface Settings |
|-----------|------------------------------------------------------------------------------------------------------|
| Config Point | Define Field Selections for Work Breakdown Structure |
| Transaction | OPUJ |

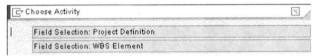

Copyright by SAP AG

To proceed, double-click either Project Definition or WBS Element.

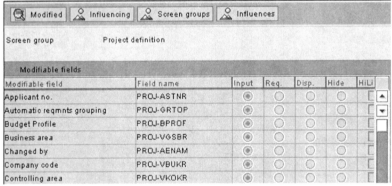

Copyright by SAP AG

If you do not want Influencing, simply click the relevant radio buttons. If you do want influencing, click the Influencing button:

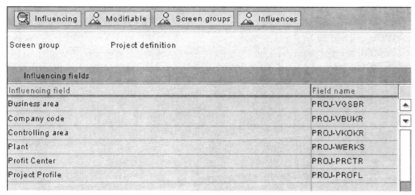

Then double-click on the Master Data field for which you want influence to apply (Project Profile in this case). Then enter a value. Now all you have to do is click the radio buttons you want.

## Validation/Substitution

These two procedures are dealt with together because they work in a very similar fashion—they are initiated at the time a Project is saved or when you manually trigger the procedure. The difference is Validations only report on a situation as it happens, whereas Substitutions make changes to master data in a project.

Validations are the process of checking data that has been entered into a project and issuing a message to inform the user of the validation error (Warning, Error, or Information).

In simple terms, SAP provides for a method of comparing values in fields against other fields and constant values. This can be done against a project Definition, a WBS, a Network Header, and a Network Activity. You <u>cannot</u> validate data in any other project object (for example, Milestones, Components, and some other areas such as Settlement Rules). If you accept that you can only validate data in the primary PS tables, then validation may work for you.

As an additional "bonus," SAP do permit you to validate data between the Project Definition and its subordinate WBSs and between WBSs and their subordinates.

The same <u>does not apply</u> between Network Header and subordinate Network Activities—you cannot validate between these two objects.

| Menu Path | Project System->Structure->Operative Structures->Work Breakdown Structure |
|---|---|
| Config Point | Maintain Validations |
| Transaction | OPSI |

Validations are constructed in two phases:

- **Validation**   This identifies the Validation.
- **Step**   This identifies the first (and maybe only) step and carries the Prerequisite, the Check you want to make, and the Message you want to issue if the validation fails.
- **Rule** (optional)   Boolean Rules can be created and used in both Validation and Substitution.

To best describe the many ways this function can be used, we will use an example. In this case, we will validate the Project Definition to make sure it has XX in the first two characters.

Use the three "Create" buttons, shown here, to create a new validation.

Step 1 is to click the Create Validation:

Copyright by SAP AG

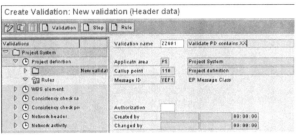

Copyright by SAP AG

Step 2 is to click the Create Step:

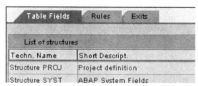

Copyright by SAP AG

Step 2 Prerequisite tells the validation rule the first thing it must check before it performs the actual validation. As we want all entries checked, we don't need to enter a prerequisite, so we will go straight to the Check:

| Table Fields | Rules | Exits |
| --- | --- | --- |
| **List of structures** | | |
| Techn. Name | Short Descript. | |
| Structure PROJ | Project definition | |
| Structure SYST | ABAP System Fields | |

Copyright by SAP AG

As we are validating the Project Definition, double-click the table name to display the available fields and use the page-down till you find field PROJ-PSPID and it will appear in the dialogue box.

| Table Fields | Rules | Exits |
| --- | --- | --- |
| **Project definition** | | |
| Techn. Name | Short Descript. | |
| PROJ-ABGSL | RA Key | |
| PROJ-AEDAT | Changed on | |
| PROJ-AEDTE | Last basic schd | |
| PROJ-AEDTP | Last fcst sched | |
| PROJ-AENAM | Changed by | |
| PROJ-ASTNA | Applicant | |
| PROJ-ASTNR | Applicant no. | |

Copyright by SAP AG

Double-click the field PROJ-PSPID and see the field name appear in the dialogue box:

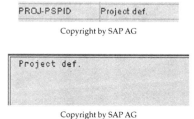

| PROJ-PSPID | Project def. |
| --- | --- |

Copyright by SAP AG

Project def.

Copyright by SAP AG

Click FldComp. Then enter From 1 to 2.

 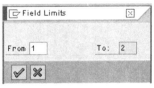

Copyright by SAP AG          Copyright by SAP AG

Now click the equal sign:

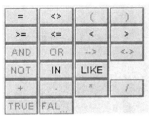

Copyright by SAP AG

And specify Constant so we can enter a value:

Copyright by SAP AG

Enter **XX** and press ENTER.

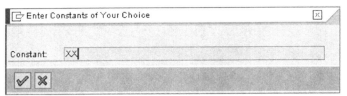

Copyright by SAP AG

Your dialogue box will now look like this:

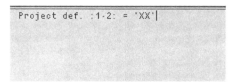

Copyright by SAP AG

Step 3 is to select the message you want displayed when the validation fails. This step requires you to have Developer access if the message class has not been created. If your message needs to include values, use the Message Variables, which allow you to enter a field and a symbol that represents it. This functionality is useful when (for example) you want to say something like "Value *XX* is not permitted" instead of "Value is not permitted."

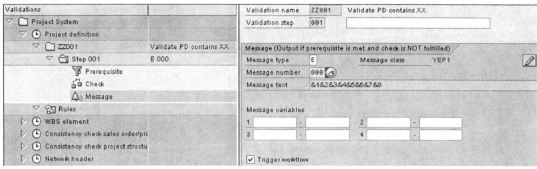

Copyright by SAP AG

# Documents

Document Management is only required if you are attaching external documents to a Project. Simple configuration can be performed by specifying the types of documents you wish to attach to a Project (Word, Excel, PowerPoint, etc.). This approach is not true "document management" because it does not manage the filing and management of the versions. This is normally configured under Cross-Application in Document Management and is not covered in this book.

Do not confuse DM with PS Text.

## PS Text

PS Text has very basic configuration. In the Project Builder (or any other tool for maintaining a Project), you attach the text based on this configuration. Once you have done the attachment, the description and long text are available for use in other projects.

| Menu Path | Project System->Documents |
|---|---|
| Config Point | Define Text Types for PS Texts |
| Transaction | OPS3 |

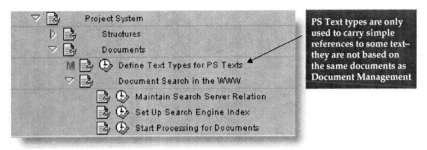

Copyright by SAP AG

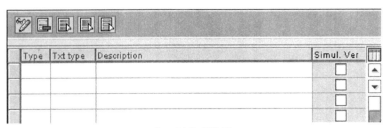

Copyright by SAP AG

- **Type**  Enter a two-character Identifier.
- **Txt type**  Enter a unique type, for example—Serial#, Webname, Problem—anything you want to sufficiently describe the type of text.

- **Description**   A more detailed description of the Type.
- **Simul. Ver**   With this indicator, you stipulate that the PS Text should only serve to describe changes in simulation versions. PS texts for simulation versions are **not** transferred to the operative project.

In the Project Builder, you use this icon to maintain PS Text:

| S | Text typ | Description | Created | Changed by | Change |
|---|----------|-------------|---------|------------|--------|
| ☑ |          | ☑           |         |            |        |
| ☑ |          | ☑           |         |            |        |
| ☑ |          | ☑           |         |            |        |
| ☑ |          | ☑           |         |            |        |

*PS texts*

Long Text is maintained via this icon:

## Costs

In this section, configuration relating to the Cost in your design can be performed. This pertains to the various methods by which costs are planned, how they integrate with other modules, and how actual costs affect the project.

## Planned Costs

Planned Costs can be related to both WBS Elements and Networks.

### Easy Cost Planning (ECP) and Execution Services (ES)

Easy Cost Planning differs from the following types of Cost Planning because it allows you to trigger procurement events in a similar fashion to Networks. However, ECP does not support scheduling:

- *Structure Planning* is keyed directly into a WBS with reference to a Plan Version.
- *Detailed Planning* is keyed directly against a WBS with reference to a Plan Version and Cost Element.
- *Unit Costing* is similar to ECP but is managed via Planning Forms. It is different from Structure and Detail Planning because you can plan by number of Units.
- *Network Planning* is Costs planned within Network Activities and not directly against a WBS (though costs aggregate to the WBS). Network Costs are always planned against Plan Version 0.

ECP has two disadvantages—planning items do not have Scheduling capabilities, and the planned costs cannot be distributed across time (as in Unit Costing). So the decision to use ECP should be made with the restrictions described next in mind.

Costs can optionally be planned with "Cost Models," meaning that a costing template is used to facilitate calculations and defaults not available in any other type of cost planning (except Standard Networks, which can do so but are not as easy to use). If Cost Models are not used, the costs can be planned manually, directly in what is termed the "Item View."

Costs in ECP can be planned against any predefined CO Plan Version.

Material planning can be extended to Execution Services, which allow you to generate Purchase Requisitions, Purchase Orders, and Reservations (including Services).

Planned Labour costs based on Cost Center/Activity Types can trigger Activity Allocations in Execution Services.

A major advantage of ECP is its unique ability to integrate planned costs with Sales Pricing in the Project Builder.

This facility allows you to simulate and generate Sales Documents (Orders, Quotes, etc.) via DIP Profiles (with the source as ECP). Network Costs cannot be used in this way.

Creation of Costing Models (Transaction CKCM) is Master Data, not configuration. You will use Characteristics in Cost Models (Transaction CT04). However, note that you can also create Characteristics within CKCM, but it uses Transaction CT05, which does not give you access to the Additional Fields functionality, which is useful for creating F4 type searches in SAP Tables within your finished Cost Model (this is explained in "Cost Models") in this chapter.

Easy Cost Planning is performed exclusively against WBS Structures. It differs from Unit Costing by virtue of the fact that you can create "templates," which are models of common, repeatable costing. Please note: ECP does <u>not</u> work with Integrated Planning.

ECP and ES is structured as detailed in Figure 5-5.

| Menu Path | Project System->Costs->Planned Costs->Easy Cost Planning and Execution Services->Easy Cost Planning |
|---|---|
| Config Point | Define CO Versions for Easy Cost Planning<br>Create Costing Variant<br>Assign Plan Profile to Costing Variant<br>Assign Plan Profile to Project Profile<br>Define Cost Component Structure<br>Define Alternative CO Versions<br>Activate Multiple CO Versions |
| Transaction | SPRO |

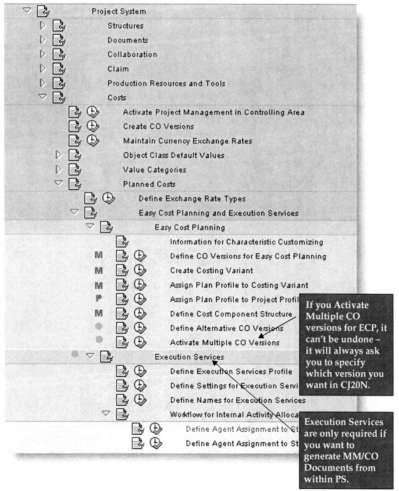

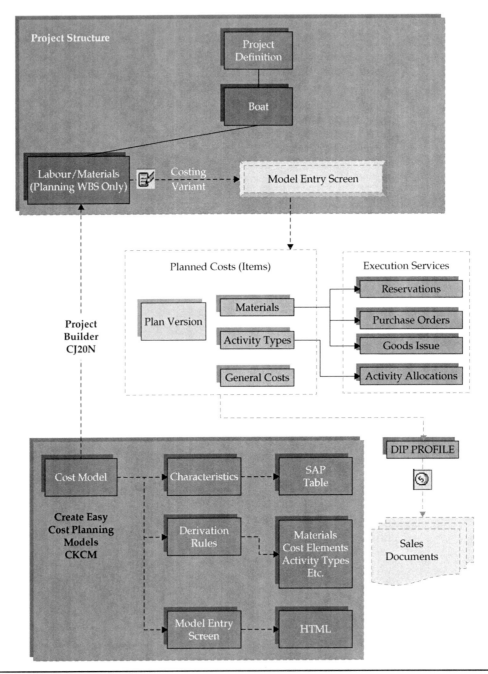

**FIGURE 5-5**   Easy cost planning

Most of the work specific to ECP is performed in Cost Models and Characteristic definition, which is Master Data. Following is a summary of the Configuration points affecting ECP:

- **CO Versions**   ECP defaults to Plan Version 0. Here you stipulate which versions may be used by CO Area and whether Planned Revenue from the Project Billing Plan is to be kept in the version.

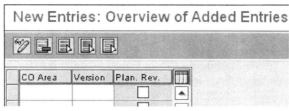

Copyright by SAP AG

- **Create Costing Variant**   For ECP to be effective, you must create a costing Variant. It is wise to create a special one for ECP. See config for Costing Variants under "Detailed Cost Planning."
- **Assign Plan Profile to Costing Variant**   This can also be done in the Plan Profile.
- **Assign Plan Profile to Project Profile**   This can also be done on the Project Profile.
- **Define Cost Component Structure (extract from SAP Help)**   In the cost estimate, the Cost Component Groups are displayed, and you can analyze the costs there. The cost component split, however, is not saved and consequently is not available in the information system. The information in this section applies in principle to Easy Cost Planning, with the following exceptions: It is not possible to transfer the costing results to *Profitability Analysis* because the cost component split is not saved. You cannot view the costs in the auxiliary cost component split.

  You can only see the differences between the transfer prices (delta profit) if your operational valuation view is group valuation. You create the operational valuation view in the operational version (000) in Customizing for *General Controlling* under *Organization->Maintain versions.*

- **Define Alternative CO Versions**   Here, you define the CO Versions available for ECP—you are able to choose them in CJ20N.
- **Activate Multiple CO Versions**   This procedure activates the ability to make selections of specific CO Versions in CJ20N. Once activated, it cannot be undone, so be careful because if you decide to revert to only one CO Version, you will always be given the choice, which is annoying.

### Execution Services for ECP

Execution Services are an extension of Easy Cost Planning—meaning they are the means by which you can trigger certain subsequent events, such as Purchase Requisitions, Purchase Orders, Activity Allocations, and so on.

Any planning performed in ECP has the potential for Execution, as long as an Execution Profile exists. Execution Services are managed in the Project Builder (CJ20N).

### Execution Services Configuration Part 1

| Menu Path | Project System->Costs->Planned Costs->Easy Cost Planning and Execution Services->Execution Services |
|---|---|
| **Config Point** | Define Execution Services Profile |
| **Transaction** | SPRO |

### Execution Services Profile

You need one of these if you intend to perform functions such as "Create PO, Create PR, and so on." You have to tell the system which of the Execution Services will be available when you run ECP in the Project Builder.

ECP defaults to Plan Version 0. Here you stipulate which versions may be used by CO Area and whether Planned Revenue from the Project Billing Plan is to be kept in the version.

Copyright by SAP AG

After creating the profile, click Execution Services, New Entries, and enter the Services you want.

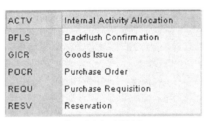

Copyright by SAP AG

Decide which Execution Services Profile you want as the default in your Project Profile(s).

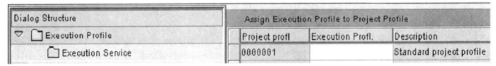

Copyright by SAP AG

Now all you have to do is create some Cost Models. In ECP, Cost Models are optional, as you can if you like use the Item View to enter values. Cost Models just make data entry easier.

**Execution Services Configuration Part 2**

| Menu Path | Project System->Costs->Planned Costs->Easy Cost Planning and Execution Services->Execution Services |
|---|---|
| Config Point | Define Settings for Execution Services<br>Define Names for Execution Services<br>Workflow for Internal Activity Allocation |
| Transaction | SPRO |

- **Define Settings for Execution Services**   This config applies to the Document Types that are used in Purchase Requisitions, Purchase Orders, and Reservations/ Goods Issues. You would not normally change these standard settings unless you had your own special document types for Orders. For PS, you would normally only be interested in WBS Element.

| Dialog Structure | Purchase Requisition | | | | |
|---|---|---|---|---|---|
| 📁 Purchase Requisition | ObjectType | Doc. Type | Name | Acct Ass. Cat. | |
| 📁 Purchase Order | KS Cost center | NB | Non Applicable | K | |
| 📁 Reservation/Goods Issu | OR Internal order | NB | Non Applicable | F | |
| | PR WBS element | NB | Non Applicable | P | |

Copyright by SAP AG

- **Define Names for Execution Services**   Though you cannot create your own "Execution Service" names, you can change the descriptions if you like.

| Name of Execution Services | |
|---|---|
| Service | Name |
| ACTV | Internal Activity Allocation |
| BFLS | Backflush Confirmation |
| GICR | Goods Issue |
| POCR | Purchase Order |
| REQU | Purchase Requisition |
| RESV | Reservation |

Copyright by SAP AG

- **Workflow for Internal Activity Allocation**   Because Internal Activity Allocations are directly posted, you may find it desirable to send a Workflow to the Cost Controller so they can perform a posting as well.

## Cost Models

In ECP, Cost Models are optional, as you can if you like use the Item View to enter values. Cost Models just make data entry easier.

Transaction CKCM is used to create the Model. See Figure 5-5 to understand how all the components of ECP work together. Here we will show an example of creating one cost model for the purpose of entering a Material against a Plant and one Cost Model for entry of an Activity Type.

---

**NOTE**   *If you do not want to create a project to perform an Easy Cost Planning estimate, you can create an ad hoc cost model in the menu path:*
*Accounting->Controlling->Product Cost Controlling->Product Cost Planning->Easy Cost Planning & Execution Services->Edit Ad Hoc Cost Estimate*

When using this facility, you <u>cannot</u> use existing WBS Cost Models; you must create new ones that use "All Objects" as their Reference Objects.

Here is what Cost Objects for WBS Elements will look like in the Project Builder:

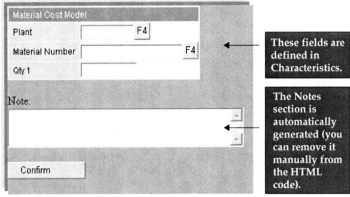

Copyright by SAP AG

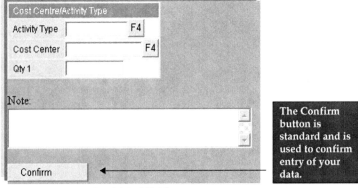

Copyright by SAP AG

Transaction CKCM looks like this for both Cost Models:

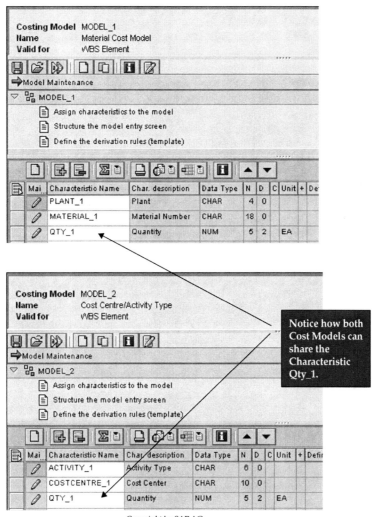

Copyright by SAP AG

   Maintaining the Characteristics in CT04 will allow you to specify a Table for the Cost Model to "look up," that is, to work like a Matchcode. You have to create characteristics that perform table look-ups in CT04 because transaction CKCM calls CT05, which is a cut-down version of CT04.

Plant 1 will look like this in CT04:

## Change Characteristic

| | |
|---|---|
| Characteristic | PLANT_1 |
| Change Number | |
| Valid From | 08.02.2007 — Validity |

**Basic data** | Descriptions | Values | Addnl data | Restrictions

### Basic data
| | |
|---|---|
| Description | Plant |
| Chars Group | PPPI_04 Special Applications |
| Status | 1 Released |
| AuthGrp | |

### Format
| | |
|---|---|
| Data Type | CHAR Character Format |
| Number of Chars | 4 |
| ☐ Case Sensitive | |
| Template | |

### Value Assignment
- ◉ Single Value
- ○ Multiple Values

☐ Restrictable

☐ Entry Required

Copyright by SAP AG

With Additional Data completed as shown next (Table CKF_RES_TPL Field WERKS):

| | |
|---|---|
| Characteristic | PLANT_1 |
| Change Number | |
| Valid From | 08.02.2007 — Validity |

Basic data | Descriptions | Values | **Addnl data** | Restrictions

### Reference to Table Field
| Table Name | CKF_RES_TPI | Field name | WERKS |
|---|---|---|---|

Copyright by SAP AG

### Creating a Cost Model
Load transaction CKCM and create the Cost Model using the Create icon:

Copyright by SAP AG

| Maintain char. | Characteristic Name | Char. description | Data Type |
|---|---|---|---|
| | | | |

Copyright by SAP AG

### Assign Characteristics to the Model

Enter the name of your characteristic—you will then be taken to CT05 to create it (unless the characteristic already exists, having been created in CT04).

Define the Derivation Rule. Here you need to specify what you want "derived" from the characteristic. For example, you may have a predefined Plant, Cost Element, or simply a default value. To achieve this, you must create at least one Item line. Depending on the type of Item you create, you do different things. To create a Material line (which will subsequently be the basis for creating Planned Costs by Material in CJ20N), you select Material from the list. The following screens show the views you have.

In Change Mode, you can add new items:

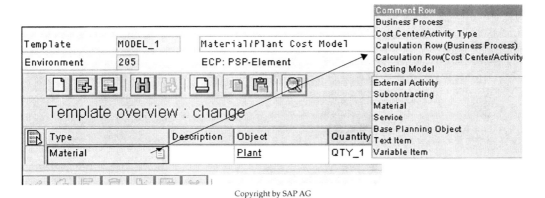

Copyright by SAP AG

Pressing ENTER puts you in Display Mode but able to enter the "Rule":

Copyright by SAP AG

By default, you get a blank set of values—waiting for you to enter the Plant and the Material. The trick is to kind of fool the system into performing a look-up by using the IN function, as shown next:

Copyright by SAP AG

What this means is, "Plant must become whatever the user entered in Characteristic PLANT_1 and the Material must be whatever the user entered in MATERIAL_1." It just so happens that what the user entered was taken from a Matchcode look-up. By double-clicking on the QTY_1 field, you can now enter the value you want to be considered as the Material Quantity—in this case, whatever the user entered:

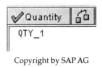

Copyright by SAP AG

Here is the same kind of thing for Cost Center/Activity Type items:

### Structuring the Model Entry Screen

Here you can customize how your Model Entry screen looks in CJ20N. Basically, SAP writes HTML code. If you select WEB STYLE, you get a much bigger looking (uglier) screen in CJ20N.

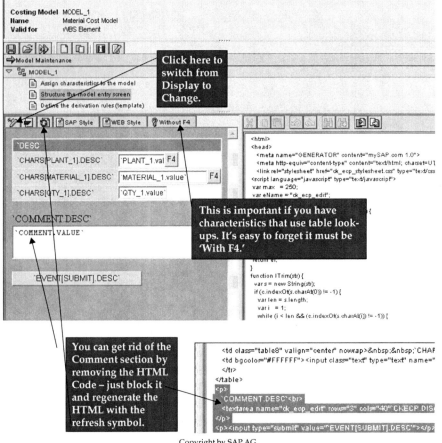

**Activating ECP in CJ20N**

Requires certain prerequisites:

- The WBS must be a Planning Element.
- You must have specified a Costing Variant in Configuration.
- You must have specified a CO Version.

ECP is activated in CJ20N via the Planning icon:

Copyright by SAP AG

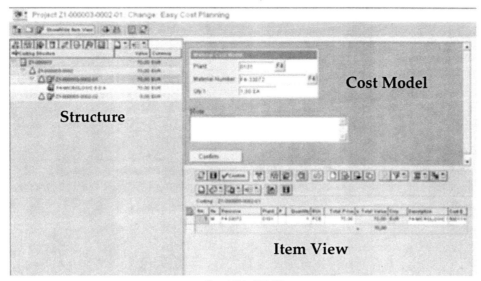

Copyright by SAP AG

When you first place the cursor against a WBS that has no Planning, you will see this tab—simply click it and select the form you want:

Choose Planning Form

Copyright by SAP AG

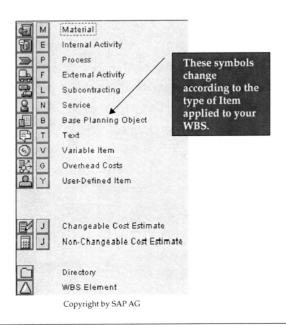

Copyright by SAP AG

***TIP*** *Before you go into ECP via the Planning icon, you may want to change the way your WBS is displayed—if you right-click on the Structure section, you can switch from WBS Number to Description.*

Copyright by SAP AG

### Costing Variants

***NOTE*** *Costing Variants are CO configuration—so here we only cover the key points.*

Use costing variants to combine all the controlling parameters for costing. The costing variant represents the link between the application and customizing because all costings must reference a costing variant as they are made and stored. The costing variant controls how costing is to be carried out. With it, you control:

- Whether the costing results are to be regarded as plan costs or actual costs
- Which prices are used to value the materials, internal activities, and external activities
- How overhead surcharges are calculated

The following are part of a costing variant:

- Costing type 08 for the project unit costing
- Valuation variant

| Menu Path | Project System->Costs->Planned Costs->Manual Cost Planning in WBS->Unit Costing |
|---|---|
| Config Point | Create Costing Variant |
| Transaction | OKKT |

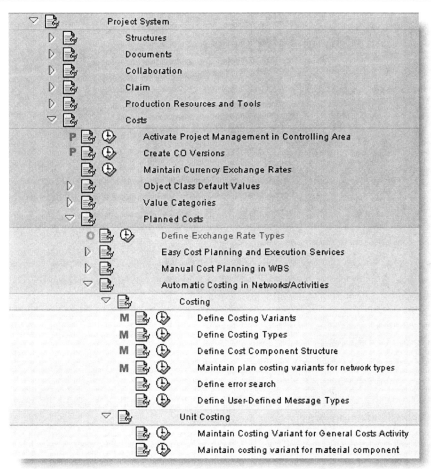

Copyright by SAP AG

### Standard Settings
SAP standard contains a number of predefined costing variants.

### SAP Recommendation

For Easy Cost Planning, they recommend you use costing variant PS06, which they deliver as standard.

Assign a different valuation variant to each of the costing variants you want to use to store costings. If you do this, you will subsequently be able to change the valuation strategies as and when you want.

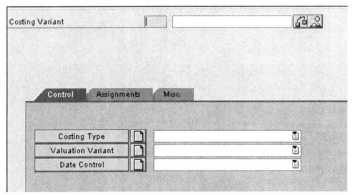

Copyright by SAP AG

**Step 1.** Enter an alphanumeric key and an appropriate short text for the costing variant.
**Step 2.** In the detail screen, assign a costing type and a valuation variant to the costing variant.
**Step 3.** If you want to use your own parameters, you must carry out the steps Define costing types and Define valuation variants.

If you are using the costing variant for a model costing, you stipulate whether cost elements have to be assigned to the costing items. The costs for other reference objects in the unit costing must be totaled using cost elements.

You need the costing variant for your costing (plan costs) and cost determination (actual costs) for networks and network activities.

Create two costing variants, one for plan costs and one for actual costs:

- As default values for the application in the Project System implementation guide in the network parameters for the network type

- In the application, in the extras for the network header (if you did not define a costing variant in the network parameters)

In the network header data, choose Go to->Network header->Supplement.
In unit costing for projects or WBS elements, you define the costing variant:

- As a default value for the application in the cost planning profile

- In the application, when you access the unit costing from structure-oriented cost planning

## Planning Profile

If you are planning Costs and/or Revenues at the WBS level, you need a Plan Profile. This profile is linked to the Project Profile. If it is not linked to the Project Profile, it is possible to attach it to WBS Templates.

The Plan Profile defines the method by which all your Costs/Revenues are planned at the WBS level—it has <u>no influence</u> on Network Activities whatsoever.

| Menu Path | Project System->Costs->Planned Costs->Manual Cost Planning in WBS->Hierarchical Cost Planning |
|---|---|
| Config Point | Create/Change Planning Profile |
| Transaction | OPSB |

IMG for Structure Cost Planning:

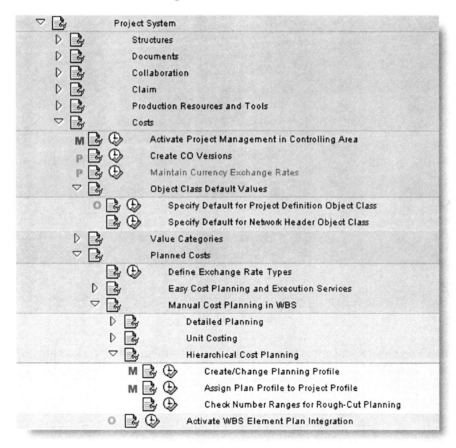

IMG for Detailed Cost Planning:

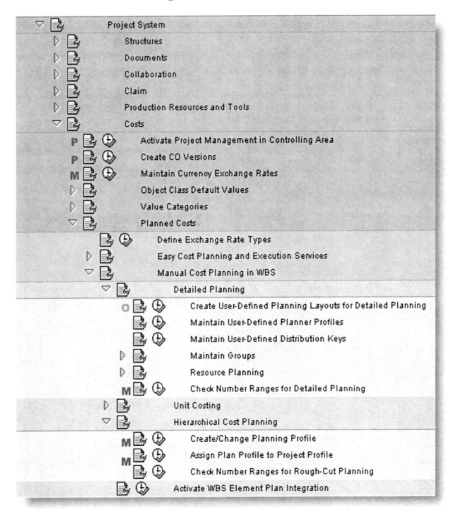

Use a Plan Profile if you are performing Structure Planning, Detailed Planning by Cost Element, or Unit Costing.

The Plan Profile is primarily used in Transactions CJ40 and CJ42.

Copyright by SAP AG

- **Profile/Description**   Enter a unique identifier and a Description.
- **Bottom-up planning**   Tick this if you want the Structure Planning process (CJ40/CJ42) to automatically "Total Up" to the top working level when you save.
- **Planning elements**   Tick this if you want to be specific about which WBS elements are allowed to have Cost Planning performed on them (by ticking Planning Element in a WBS). If you do not tick this box, you can plan against any WBS.

### TIME FRAME TAB

- **Past**   Enter the number of years in the past you permit planning to take place (relative to the current year).
- **Future**   Enter the number of years in the future you permit planning to take place (relative to the current year).
- **Start**   Value which determines the start year for planning. The reference value is the current fiscal year.
- **Total values**   Tick this if you allow planning to take place for the whole WBS, regardless of year.
- **Annual values**   Tick this if you also allow planning by the year. This will allow you to be specific about each year's planning values.

## DETAILED PLANNING AND UNIT COSTING TAB

- **Prim.CElem.grp**   For Detailed Cost Planning, specify the Cost Element Group you want your planning to be limited to.

- **Revenue CE grp.**   For Detailed Revenue Planning, specify the Cost Element Group you want your planning to be limited to.

- **Sender CCtr group**   Organizational unit for saving a group of cost centers in the SAP System for which activity types were planned. Each cost center in this group can also function as a sender in activity input planning. One example of this group is a cost center area of the original hierarchy or other alternative hierarchies (such as the group "Energy"). You can also define any number of your own cost center groups in order to make working in your application easier, using the relevant maintenance transactions to do so.

- **Sender act.type grp**   Organizational unit for storing a group of Activity Types in the SAP System for which activity type planning has been completed. Each activity type in this group can appear as a sender activity type in activity input planning.

- **Stat.Key Fig.Group**   For Activity Input Planning, specify the SKF Group you want your planning limited to.

- **Costing variant**   Key that determines how a cost estimate is performed and valuated in Unit Costing. To calculate the costs of producing a material, you create a product cost estimate with or without a quantity structure. In a cost estimate with a quantity structure, the costing variant determines which dates are valid for the cost estimate itself and for exploding and valuating the quantity structure.

## REPRESENTATION TAB

- **Decimal places**   The number of decimal places your costs will be planned to.

- **Scaling factor**   The scaling factor will determine the constant units—for example, Factor of 3 with a value of 1234 will be represented as 1,234,000.

## CURRENCY TRANSLATION, OVERALL PLAN VALUE TAB

- **Exchange Rate Type**   When planning costs and revenues, the currency used is determined by the Planning Currency (Controlling, Object, Transaction). PS can only work with two currencies, so it is necessary to specify the exchange rate you want to use in planning. It is possible to use a special one for project planning, to keep your planned values static and not subject to daily fluctuations. It is a Finance decision.

- **Value Date**   The value date in planning determines which daily exchange rates apply for currency translation. If you enter a date, the R/3 System uses the exchange rate for that day in all periods. If you do not enter a value date, the system translates currency by period. The R/3 System determines an exchange rate based on the starting dates from each period, which includes potential exchange rate fluctuations in a fiscal year. This does not apply to accrual calculations or overheads in the plan. You enter the value date in the transaction manually, by choosing Extras->Value date.

- **Remainder translat.** Tick this if you want the system to translate only the remainder, not the full overall value. This remainder is calculated as: Remainder = overall value – sum of annual values. In other words, this is that part of the overall value that was not distributed to the years. This value is translated in accordance with the plan profile. To then have the full translation of the overall value, the translated remainder value is added to the total of the translated annual values.

## PLANNING CURRENCY TAB

- **Controlling Area/Object/Transaction**   Select the default planning currency.
- **Default Object Currency**   This indicator is only relevant if planning is permitted in a user-defined transaction currency in the budget profile. It determines the default per WBS element for the transaction currency in which the planning takes place if a transaction currency is not explicitly specified. If the indicator is set, the relevant object is planned by default in the object currency. If the indicator is not set, the relevant object is planned by default in the controlling area currency.

## AUTOMATIC REVENUE PLANNING TAB

This relates to "integrated planning." Sales Quotations and Sales Orders are effectively Planned Revenues if they are Account Assigned to a Billing Element WBS. To make this integration work, it is required to set the Integrated Planning indicator in transaction OPO8. See further SAP notes following:

- **From quotation**   Tick this if you want planned revenues of an associated Quotation to be copied into the project.
- **From Sales Order**   Tick this if you want planned revenues of an associated Sales Order to be copied into the project and available in Information Systems.

These two settings can also be applied in transaction OLPE.

### Integrated Planning Notes

Setting the indicator in OPO8 specifies whether an order/project participates in integrated planning. This is defined per project profile for projects. For orders, you can store a default value in the order type, which you can change in the order master data when required.

Activity inputs planned in a plan-integrated order/project are updated directly on the sending cost center if "Integrated planning with Cost Center Accounting" is activated in the version. You can then also settle plan-integrated orders/projects to cost centers. Plan data is passed on to the profit center and the extended general ledger if both "Integrated planning with Cost Center Accounting" and the "Integrated planning" indicator are activated in the version.

### Changing the "Integrated Planning" Indicator

You can change the "Integrated planning" indicator at a later date under the following conditions:

- Unit costing was never performed on the job affected. That is, no unit costing was carried out, even if it was later undone.
- Planning data was never entered on the job.

or

• If planning data was entered, then all plan values and quantities from internal allocations must be zero. Data from primary cost planning is possible. The "Integrated planning" indicator may not be set in the fiscal year–dependent data from the plan version.

No plan line items may exist.

### Budgeting Profile

If you want to maintain a controlled budget at the WBS level, you need a Budget Profile. This profile is linked to the Project Profile. If it is not linked to the Project Profile, it is possible to attach it to WBS Templates.

The Budget Profile defines the method by which all your Costs are budgeted by WBS— it has <u>no influence</u> on Network Activities whatsoever—budgeting is only ever maintained at the WBS level of a project (or Internal Order). However, costs posted at the Activity level are recognized and checked at the aggregate WBS (assuming Availability Control is active).

Capital Budgets for Projects can optionally be managed via an Investment Program.

The Budget is maintained in Transactions CJ30 (Original Budget), CJ32 (Release), CJ34 (Transfer), CJ37 (Supplement), and CJ35/CJ38 (Return).

Documents in relation to Budgeting are maintained in CJ3A.

| Menu Path | Project System->Costs->Budget |
|---|---|
| Config Point | Maintain Budget Profile |
| Transaction | OPS9 |

IMG for Budgeting:

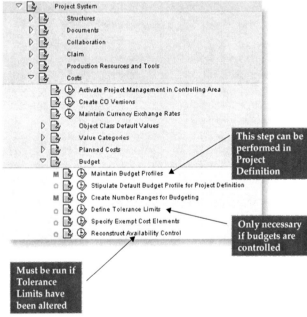

| | |
|---|---|
| Profile | ☑ |
| Text | |

**Time frame**
Past
Future
Start
☐ Total values
☐ Annual values

**Investment management**
Program type budget

**Representation**
Decimal places
Scaling factor

**Availability control**
Activation Type ☑ Usage
☐ Overall ☐ Object Currency
☐ Releases

**Currency translation**
Exchange Rate Type ☑
Value Date
☐ Remainder translat.

**Budgeting Currency**
◉ Controlling area currency
○ Object currency
○ Transaction curr.
☐ Default Object Currency

Copyright by SAP AG

- **Profile/Text**   Enter a unique identifier and a description.

### TIME FRAME TAB

- **Past**   Enter the number of years in the past you permit budgeting to take place (relative to the current year).

- **Future**   Enter the number of years in the future you permit budgeting to take place (relative to the current year).

- **Start**   Value that determines the start year for budgeting. The reference value is the current fiscal year.

- **Total values**   Tick this if you allow budgeting to take place for the whole WBS, regardless of year.

- **Annual values**   Tick this if you also allow budgeting by the year. This will allow you to be specific about each year's budget values.

### INVESTMENT MANAGEMENT TAB

- **Program type budget**   Enter the Program Type if you want your Budget maintained by an Investment Program. This is a critical integration point for IM (Investment Management). An Investment Program can control distribution of the Project's overall budget (see screen extract here from IM Program Position).

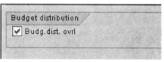

Budget distribution
☑ Budg.dist. ovrl

Copyright by SAP AG

## REPRESENTATION TAB

- **Decimal places** The number of decimal places your budget will be planned to.
- **Scaling factor** The scaling factor will determine the constant units—for example, Factor of 3 with a value of 1234 will be represented as 1,234,000.

## AVAILABILITY CONTROL TAB

- **Activation Type** Specify the method by which you want Availability Control activated (0 will negate any settings you make next).

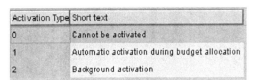

| Activation Type | Short text |
|---|---|
| 0 | Cannot be activated |
| 1 | Automatic activation during budget allocation |
| 2 | Background activation |

Copyright by SAP AG

- **Usage** The "credit limit used" expresses the ratio of assigned funds to the budget as a percentage. This value is used only in combination with activation type 2—if the background activator determines that this value has already been exceeded by too high assigned funds, availability control is activated for the WBS.

---

**NOTE** *The advantage of Background Activation is mainly response times—it means that AC will not be checked as the transaction is posted, it will be checked only once the limit has reached the percentage specified in Tolerances. Use Transaction CJBV to do this.*

- **Overall** Tick this if you want Availability Control to be activated based on Overall Values. If you do not tick this, it will be checked against Annual Values (the year in which the transaction is posted).
- **Object Currency** Tick this if Availability Control is to be carried out in the Object currency.
- **Releases** Tick this if Availability Control must be activated at the point at which a budget is Released (Transaction CJ32).

## CURRENCY TRANSLATION TAB

- **Exchange Rate Type** When budgeting, the currency used is determined by the Planning Currency (Controlling, Object, Transaction). PS can only work with two currencies, so it is necessary to specify the exchange rate you want to use in budgeting. It is possible to use a special one for project budgeting to keep your budget values static and not subject to daily fluctuations. It is a Finance decision.
- **Value Date** The value date in budgeting determines which daily exchange rates apply for currency translation. If you enter a date, the R/3 System uses the exchange rate for that day in all periods. If you do not enter a value date, the system translates currency by period. The R/3 System determines an exchange rate based

on the starting dates from each period, which includes potential exchange rate fluctuations in a fiscal year. This does not apply to accrual calculations or overheads in the plan. You enter the value date in the transaction manually, by choosing Extras->Value date.

- **Remainder translat.**   Tick this if you want the system to translate only the remainder, not the full overall value. This remainder is calculated as: Remainder = overall value – sum of annual values. In other words, this is that part of the overall value that was not distributed over the years. This value is translated in accordance with the budget profile. To then have the full translation of the overall value, the translated remainder value is added to the total of the translated annual values.

## BUDGETING CURRENCY TAB

- **Controlling/Object/Transaction currency**   Select the default planning currency.
- **Default Object Currency**   This indicator is only relevant if budgeting is permitted in a user-defined transaction currency in the budget profile. It determines the default per WBS element for the transaction currency in which the budgeting takes place if a transaction currency is not explicitly specified. If the indicator is set, the relevant object is budgeted by default in the object currency. If the indicator is not set, the relevant object is budgeted by default in the controlling area currency.

## Availability Control

- **Tolerance Limits**   Used with Budgeting to warn/prevent the user from spending beyond the "tolerance" allowed. In the Budget Profile, you decide on the "Activation Type." Whatever your settings there, the configuration here is called to effect the tolerance; that is, whether you are performing "inline" or "background" activation, these tolerances are the ones used. You can have more than one entry per CO area in this configuration to cater for the Warning plus Error situation. Example: A warning will be issued whenever the value of a commitment or direct posting plus total of previous expenditure is made that is calculated as >= to the WARNING tolerance limit. This does not prevent the transaction from completing as long as the next tolerance limit for the error message is not reached. For example, Tolerance limit = 80%, Budget = 1000, Expenditure in total = 810, Warning is issued. An error will be issued whenever the value of a commitment or direct posting plus total of previous expenditure is made that is calculated as >= to the ERROR tolerance limit. This does prevent the transaction from completing. For example, Tolerance limit = 110%, Budget = 1000, Expenditure in total = 1100, Error is issued.

| Menu Path | Project System->Costs->Budget |
|---|---|
| **Config Point** | Define Tolerance Limits |
| **Transaction** | SPRO |

IMG for Tolerance Limits:

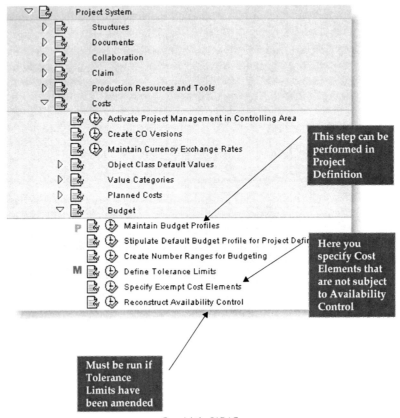

Copyright by SAP AG

Copyright by SAP AG

- **COAr** Specify the Controlling Area.
- **Prof.** Specify the Budget Profile to which these tolerances apply.
- **Text** Display of Budget Profile Description.
- **Tr.Grp** Select the Group of transactions that the tolerance applies. Selecting anything but ++ will limit the checking of budget overspending to those groups of transactions.

| Activity group | Short text |
|---|---|
| ++ | All activity groups |
| 00 | Purchase requisition |
| 01 | Purchase order |
| 02 | Orders for project |
| 03 | Goods issue |
| 04 | Financial accounting document |
| 05 | CO document |
| 06 | Budgeting |
| 07 | Funds reservation |
| 08 | Fixed prices in project |
| 09 | Payroll |

Copyright by SAP AG

- **Act.** Availability Control Activation—indicator that controls what action is triggered if the defined tolerance limit is exceeded.

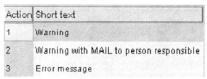

- **Usage**  The percentage of the expended budget that must have been reached to trigger the Activation. **Note** that if ever this value is modified from its original value (and Availability Control had been activated), you will need to "Reconstruct Availability Control" using transaction CJBN. This will allow you to perform a mass change of all the project's current expenditure so the new Usage can be effected.

- **Abs.variance**  Maximum permissible absolute variance—if the difference between the assigned funds and the budget exceeds the absolute variance, availability control triggers the Activation (this option should be used instead of Usage, not as well as).

### Plan Versions (CO)

Plan Versions are usually managed by Controlling—however, as they have such a profound effect on PS, there must be extensive liaison between the two modules to make them work for both.

Though in a simple environment, CO Versions are not complex at all (they only serve to provide a repository for Planned Costs), basic settings are needed (in particular for definition of Fiscal Year).

Some of the controls with a CO Version have relevance in Integrated Planning, Work In Progress (WIP), and Progress Versions. Plan Versions that are relevant for Progress Analysis have to be created and configured so that EV (Earned Value) can be determined.

| Menu Path | Project System->Costs |
| --- | --- |
| Config Point | Create CO Versions |
| Transaction | SPRO |

IMG for CO Versions:

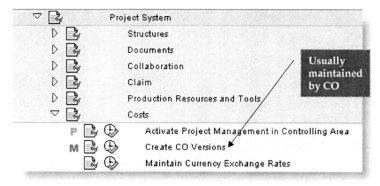

The first step is to Create the individual Plan Versions and to specify whether they contain Planning, Actual WIP/Results Analysis, and Variance data.

**General Version Definition**

| Dialog Structure | General Version Overview | | | | | | |
|---|---|---|---|---|---|---|---|
| ▽ 🗀 General Version Definition | Version | Name | Plan | Actual | WIP/RA | Variance | Exclusive Use |
|   🗀 Settings in Operating Concern | ☑ | | ☐ | ☐ | ☐ | ☐ | 0 |
|   🗀 Settings for Profit Center Accounting | ☑ | | ☐ | ☐ | ☐ | ☐ | 0 |

Copyright by SAP AG

A plan version can also be assigned for Exclusive use:

Budget Control System (BCS): Frozen Version
Cost Estimate in Maintenance Order
Cost Forecast
Material Ledger: Actual Version Cumulated in Parallel
Progress Analysis
Transfer Price for Jobs

Copyright by SAP AG

You must define the Operating Concern (not to be confused with CO Area) under which this Plan Version belongs. It is the representation of a part of an organization for which the sales market is structured in a uniform manner.

| Dialog Structure | Operating concern | 1000 Core Model Operating Concern |
|---|---|---|
| ▽ 🗀 General Version Definition | Version | |
|   🗀 Settings in Operating Concern | | |
|   🗀 Settings for Profit Center Accounting | **Attributes** | |
|   ▽ 🗀 Controlling Area Settings | ☑ Version Locked | |
|     🗀 Settings for Each Fiscal Year | | |
|     🗀 Delta Version: Bus. Transactions from Ref. Version | Currency type | |
|   🗀 Settings for Progress Analysis (Project System) | Exch. Rate Type ☑ | |
| | ☐ Check derivation | |
| | Derivation date ☑ | |
| | **Transfer to SOP** | |
| | Characteristic group | |

Copyright by SAP AG

Each Fiscal Year assigned to a Plan version controls validity, integration (whether WBS element planning in a version is integrated with cost center or business process planning), and Pricing.

| Dialog Structure | | CO Area | 1000 EURO CONTROLLING AREA | | | |
|---|---|---|---|---|---|---|
| ▽ 🗀 General Version Definition | | Version | 0 | Current forecast/ActualVersion | | |
| 🗀 Settings in Operating Concern | | | | | | |
| 🗀 Settings for Profit Center Accounting | | **EC-PCA: Fiscal-year dependent version parameters** | | | | |
| ▽ 🗀 Controlling Area Settings | | Year | Online transfer | Version Locked | Line items | ExRateT |
| 🗀 Settings for Each Fiscal Year | | 2005 | ☐ | ☐ | ☑ | M |
| 🗀 Delta Version: Bus. Transactions from Ref. Version | | 2006 | ☐ | ☐ | ☑ | M |
| 🗀 Settings for Progress Analysis (Project System) | | 2007 | ☐ | ☐ | ☑ | M |
| | | 2008 | ☐ | ☐ | ☑ | M |
| | | 2009 | ☐ | ☐ | ☑ | M |

Copyright by SAP AG

Plan Versions can be used for Progress Analysis as long as they have been set exclusively for this purpose.

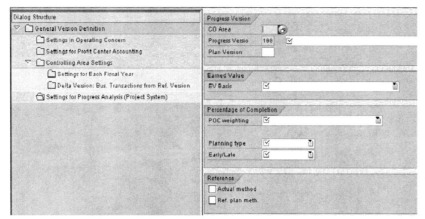

Copyright by SAP AG

| Progress Version | | |
|---|---|---|
| CO Area | ☑ | |
| Progress Versio | 100 | ☑ |
| Plan Version | | |
| **Earned Value** | | |
| EV Basis | ☑ | 🗒 |
| **Percentage of Completion** | | |
| POC weighting | ☑ | 🗒 |
| Planning type | ☑ | 🗒 |
| Early/Late | ☑ | 🗒 |
| **Reference** | | |
| ☐ Actual method | | |
| ☐ Ref. plan meth. | | |

Copyright by SAP AG

### Statistical Key Figures (SKFs)

SKFs are primarily CO Objects and need minimal configuration—you can simply create them using existing Units of Measure and then start entering statistics. However, apart from creating the SKFs themselves, it makes sense to create a Group hierarchy of some kind so that you can differentiate your SKFs from other parts of the business for reporting purposes. Assigning your SKFs to Value Categories can also be useful to make sure they are valuated properly in CO. SKFs are always keyed into the system against a Unit of Measure.

| Menu Path | Controlling->Activity based costing->Master data->Statistical Key Figures |
|---|---|
| Config Point | Maintain Statistical Key Figures |
| Transaction | KK01 |

IMG for SKFs:

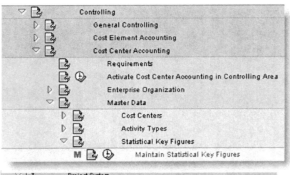

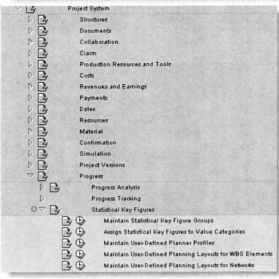

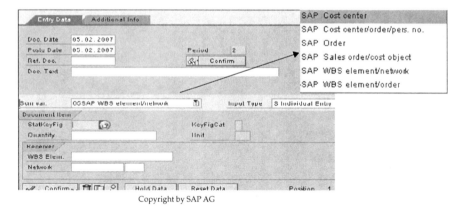

Copyright by SAP AG

- **Stat. key fig. UnM.**   The standard unit of measure assigned to this SKF.
- **Key fig. cat.**   Select whether the SKF is a Fixed Value (it is distributed across the whole year) or Total Value (it is one amount for the period you are entering).

Entry of SKFs into the system can be performed via Planner Profiles and works much the same as entry of any other planning data, including the use of Distribution Rules.

For WBS Element and Network entry, you should just use the standard SAP entry screens, or copy one to suit your specific requirements.

All that is required to make an SKF stick to a project object is the use of a simple data entry screen, such as KB31N (see below), where you can choose the object type to which you want the SKF to be assigned.

Copyright by SAP AG

Data entered here can be used as input data in DIP (Dynamic Item Processor) Profiles for Customer Billing. Basically, values input here are used as "Quantity" inputs for calculation of values for billing purposes.

### Dynamic Item Processor (DIP)

DIPs have a dual purpose—for Cost Planning in Easy Cost Planning and for Billing in Revenues and Earnings. In short, DIP Profiles calculate and summarize information for use in both Planning and Billing. Both methods will be covered in this section.

Dip Profiles are the basis upon which Sales Pricing determines two things:

- What Easy Cost Planning sources are used for Simulated Sales Pricing
- What Actual Values are used to prepare Customer Billing

DIP Profiles are capable of providing the basis upon which both of the preceding are detailed.

They carry the following information:

- **Usage**   How the DIP Profile is to be used:
  - Billing & Results Analysis
  - Quotation Creation and Sales Pricing
- **Characteristics**   The type of data that is used as Input for analysis. If you make a characteristic *relevant,* it is *dynamic* and will be created for you as the billing line.
  - Activity Type
  - Cost Element
  - Personnel Number
  - WBS Element
  - Work Center
    and so on.
- **Source**   The origin of your characteristics data
  - Actual costs—Line items
  - Actual costs—Totals records
  - Easy Cost Planning
  - Funds—Line items
  - Funds—Totals records
  - Inter-company—Line Items
  - Plan Statistical Indicator—Totals records
  - Planned costs—Totals records
  - Statistical Indicator—Totals records
  - Statistical Indicator—Line items
- **Selection Criteria**   The filters that apply when selecting data
  - Period
  - Currency
  - Unit of Measure

- **Material Determination**   The Material against which all inputs will be attached
- **Criteria**   The criteria that define the Material Determination

The schematic in Figure 5-6 shows the various elements you can configure in DIPs.

| Menu Path | Project System->Costs->Revenues and Earnings->Integration with SD Documents->Creating Quotations and Project Billing |
|---|---|
| **Config Point** | Maintain Profiles for Quotation and Billing |
| **Transaction** | ODP1 |

To proceed, Create a New Entry and give your Profile a Name/Description:

Copyright by SAP AG

- **Usage**   Decide how you want your DIP to be used. There are only two options here:

Copyright by SAP AG

- **Sales Document Type**   Will determine the Output that will be generated. In the case of Quotation creation and sales pricing, that would normally be a Quotation but could be a Sales Order or some other Sales Document. In the case of Billing and Results Analysis, it is likely to be a Debit Memo.

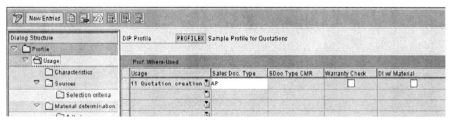

Copyright by SAP AG

- **Characteristics**   Select the types of data you want to be considered as input to your Quotation/Billing run.

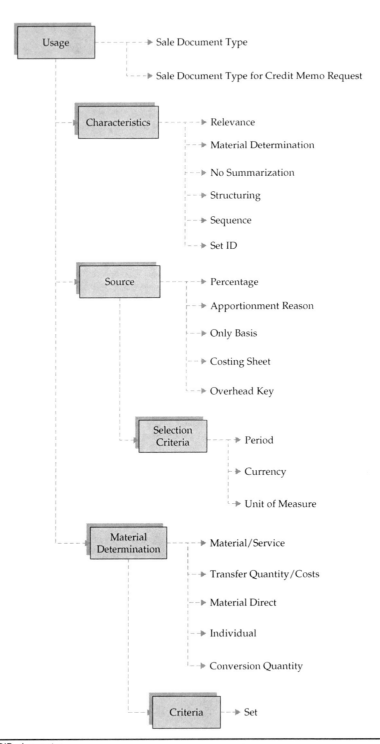

If you further select the tick box **Mat. determination**, it means whatever information is selected as input will be pointed to a Material later in the process.

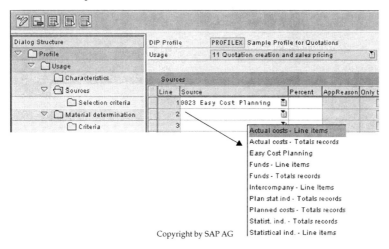

| Char. | CharactRelevant | Mat. determination | NoSummarization | Structuring |
|---|---|---|---|---|
| Accounting Indicator | ☐ | ☐ | ☐ | ☐ |
| Activity Type | ☑ | ☑ | ☐ | ☐ |
| Activity number | ☐ | ☐ | ☐ | ☐ |
| Billing form | ☐ | ☐ | ☐ | ☐ |
| Business Process | ☐ | ☐ | ☐ | ☐ |
| Commitment item | ☐ | ☐ | ☐ | ☐ |
| Cost Center | ☐ | ☐ | ☐ | ☐ |
| Cost Element | ☑ | ☑ | ☐ | ☐ |
| Document Number | ☐ | ☐ | ☐ | ☐ |
| Functional Area | ☐ | ☐ | ☐ | ☐ |
| Fund | ☐ | ☐ | ☐ | ☐ |
| Funds Center | ☐ | ☐ | ☐ | ☐ |
| GM Value Type | ☐ | ☐ | ☐ | ☐ |
| Grant | ☐ | ☐ | ☐ | ☐ |
| Material | ☑ | ☑ | ☐ | ☐ |

Copyright by SAP AG

- **Sources**   You have several choices here and you can select as many as you wish. In the case of Usage for Quotations (that is, Simulated Sales Pricing in CJ20N), Easy Cost Planning is the obvious choice. For normal Resource-Related Billing, you can select any form of input. All other fields are optional: **Percent** defaults to 100%. If you select a percentage, also enter an **Apportionment Reason** for Results Analysis. The system transfers the apportionment reason together with the costs of sales from the results analysis. **Costing Sheet** can be entered for Overhead calculation. **Only Basis** controls whether the data determined by the system from the selected source is used directly in the construction of dynamic items or whether only surcharges for the source data are used as the basis for dynamic items. **Overhead key** is used to determine order-specific or material-related overhead rates.

Copyright by SAP AG

- **Selection criteria**   Depending on the Characteristics you selected, you have the opportunity of limiting what is selected via **Set ID** (which can be, for example, Cost Element Groups that have already been set up or new ones you generate now). Here you enter a range of, for example, Activity Types, Cost Elements, etc.). If you do not enter a Set ID, all data will be considered for input.

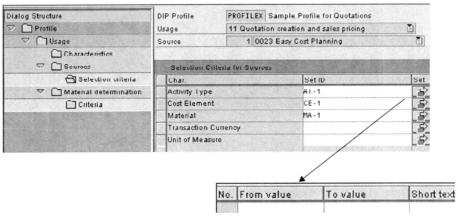

Copyright by SAP AG

- **Material determination**   Here you can enter the names of the Materials that will be used to apply the values. For example, if the system found five records with a Cost Element that fitted the Selection Criteria, they would all be applied to the Material (as long as they <u>also</u> fit into the Criteria set out in **Criteria**). The main purpose of these settings is to direct all the source data into the Materials you want them to belong to in any Sales Item.

- In **Transfer Quantity/Costs**, you decide if you only want Costs, Quantities, or both transferred for each material. This becomes important if you don't want Quantities on Sales Documents, for example. **Material direct** controls whether the Actual Material found is transferred, rather than the values posted into the Dynamic Material. This is useful if you want the Customer to see details of the physical material. **Individual** means that you want one dynamic material per entry found in the source—if not ticked, they will be summarized into one Dynamic Material. **Conversion Quantity** is ticked if you want the source material's Unit of Measure to be converted into the Sales Item's Unit of Measure.

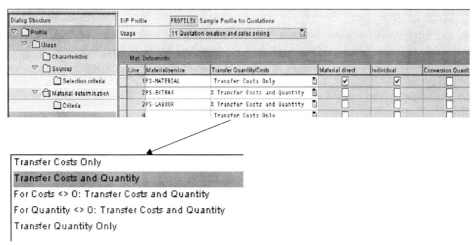

Copyright by SAP AG

- **Criteria** For each of the Dynamic Materials, you can be specific about the source data that fits into them. This is useful when you have a large range of input data (controlled by Selection Criteria under Sources) that you then want to direct into specific Materials in your Sales Item. You can use Sets or individual values.

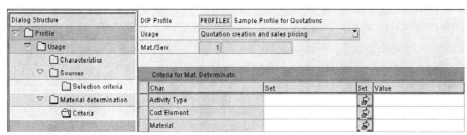

Copyright by SAP AG

# Dates

Dates in relation to WBSs and Networks have a different purpose.

- **In WBS Elements** They have limited function—apart from inheriting dates from subordinate WBS Elements and/or Networks if they are used. WBS Dates form the basis of Gantt charting in the Project Planning Board. Within the WBS, it is possible to "extrapolate" and copy dates manually from subordinate WBS Elements. WBS Dates can also be used in Project Progress. Rudimentary scheduling can be performed in WBS Elements. See Dates in WBS for more in Chapter 4 under "Time and Capacity Planning."

- **In Networks** Dates in Networks are used for Scheduling.

## WBS Scheduling

For Scheduling to take place at the WBS level, a profile must be created. This profile has a relationship with the Network Activities that are attached to the WBS.

| Menu Path | Project System->Dates->Date planning in WBS |
|---|---|
| Config Point | Define Parameters for WBS Scheduling |
| Transaction | OPTQ |

IMG for WBS Scheduling:

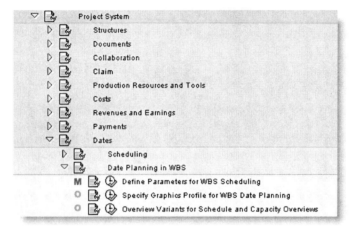

Copyright by SAP AG

Copyright by SAP AG

## SCHEDULING TAB

- **Scheduling type**   This setting determines the method by which Scheduling is to be performed (Backwards, Forwards, etc.). This subject is covered in more detail in "Network Scheduling."

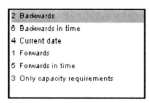

Copyright by SAP AG

- **Start in past**   Number of days that scheduling allows the start date to be in the past. If this number of days is exceeded, the system automatically overrides the set scheduling type and uses "today" scheduling.

Copyright by SAP AG

- **Schedul. method**

  <u>WBS determines dates</u>   In the case of Forwards scheduling, the earliest start date of the activities (or in the case of Backwards scheduling, the latest finish date) is determined by the basic dates of the WBS elements to which the activities are assigned.

  <u>Network determines dates</u>   In the case of Forwards scheduling, the earliest start date of the activities (or for Backwards scheduling, the latest finish date) is determined by the basic dates of the network header.

- **Adjust bsc date**   Tick this to schedule your WBS dates based on subsequent Network Activity dates (which will have been determined during scheduling). This fits in with SAP's Bottom-up scenario. Basic Dates in the WBS will be overwritten.

- **Automatic log**   Tick this to automatically create a log of messages that may have occurred during scheduling (accessed via Extras on menu).

- **Shift order**   Tick this if you <u>do not</u> want a partially confirmed activity's actual dates taken into account during a rescheduling run.

- **Autom.schedul.**   Tick this indicator if you want scheduling to be always carried out when you save the network or the order. If you do not tick it (and make a change relevant to scheduling in the network), the system gives the network the status "Dates are not updated" (NTUP) when you save.

  If you do not maintain the indicator, the system will still update the capacity requirements if you make changes in the order or network. You can override the indicator in the order or network.

- **Latest staging**   Tick this to apply Latest Activity Dates in the requirements date of a component related to the dates of an activity.

<u>For components with a positive requirements quantity</u>:

If the indicator is set, the requirements date is the latest start date of the operation/ activity.
If the indicator is not set, the requirements date is the earliest start date of the operation/activity.

<u>For components with a negative requirements quantity</u>:

If the indicator is set, the requirements date is the latest finish date of the operation/ activity.
If the indicator is not set, the requirements date is the earliest finish date of the operation/activity.
A negative requirements quantity means that the material is produced in the operation/activity.

- **Max. redn. level**   Specifies the maximum level to be used to reduce the lead time for scheduling bottlenecks. Reduction is only relevant for detailed scheduling.

- **Reduction type**   Defines which operations are taken into account for the reduction of the lead time of the following objects: Routings, Production orders, Planned orders, Collective orders, Networks.

You can choose between the following reduction types:

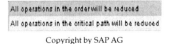

Copyright by SAP AG

### Reduction of All Operations
The reduction measures are carried out step-for-step for all operations until the whole lead time has been sufficiently reduced. After reduction all the operations have the same reduction level.

### Reduction of Operations on the Critical Path
You can only use this type of reduction for:

- Collective orders

- Routings, planned orders, and production orders that contain parallel sequences

- Networks

In each reduction step, reduction measures are only applied to those operations for which a reduction of the lead time results in a reduction of the whole lead time. In collective orders and orders with parallel sequences, the sum of these operations is known as the critical path. Since there can be different critical paths for each reduction step, operations can have different reduction levels before a sufficient reduction of the whole lead time is achieved.

In both types of reduction the order floats are reduced according to their settings.

For Routings, planned orders, and production orders that are not part of a collective order (and do not contain parallel sequences), there is no critical path. Consequently, the second type of reduction has no effect, resulting in a reduction of all operations.

---

**CAUTION** *Reduction of operations on the critical path makes greater demands on the system than standard reduction and can cause a reduction in performance.*

## Network Scheduling

### Scheduling—General

Both types of scheduling are possible in PS: backward and forward. The critical path is always highlighted. Latest and soonest dates are calculated. Constraints can be set on starting or finishing dates of activities.

For Assembly Processing, Backward Scheduling should be the default. That means you can enter (manually or from sales order) the ending date to which you want to have finished activities; the system can calculate automatically the starting date to which you must begin activities to respect this latest date according to specific constraints dates.

This can be turned to forward scheduling if required (enter starting date and automatic calculation ending date). There is no automatic postponing of the planned Project dates due to events coming either from delivery or from other events. In standard SAP, some dates can be managed both on WBS and on activity Networks. SAP allows three types of link between the various objects:

- **Descending** (Top-down), elements at the highest level are a constraint toward elements at the lowest levels (from highest WBS element to activities through all the structure)
- **Bottom-up**, lowest level is a constraint on higher-level scheduling
- **Open Planning**, dates do not interact between each level

Different sets of dates are available:

- **Basic date**   Used to communicate with other modules, they are the reference. These dates are linked to material requirement and capacities requirement.
- **Forecast dates**   Used to manage other aspects of the Project. They can be initialized by a copy of basic date sets. It's just a forecast vision without links with other requirements (material, capacities, etc.).
- **Constraints dates**   Used to determine if there is a scheduling constraint for the start and the end of an activity. They can be available for basic or forecast dates set.
- **Actual dates**   Filled when a task is realized or confirmed.

Difference between "Forecast dates" and "Project Version": Project Version will be used to keep a history of the Project at the Project Event (first scheduling). Forecast dates set can be used to store other visions of scheduling (pessimistic or optimistic visions).

The planning board allows the displaying of a Gantt view of the dates. Basic dates and/or forecast dates can be displayed in this planning board. In the PS Information system, a comparison between forecast and basic date is available.

If an individual is assigned to an activity and if this activity is postponed, the task must be assigned again to align the workload on a new date (no automatic rescheduling of day-to-day work to be done for an individual resource regarding Project schedule changes, etc., just to avoid uncontrolled modification permanently). Following is a schematic explanation of how Backward and Forward Scheduling works.

Delivery <u>can</u> be met (see Figure 5-7).

Delivery <u>cannot</u> be met (see Figure 5-8).

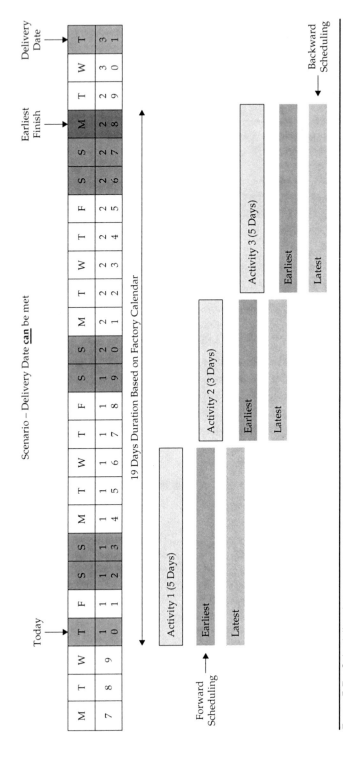

**FIGURE 5-7** Scheduling 1

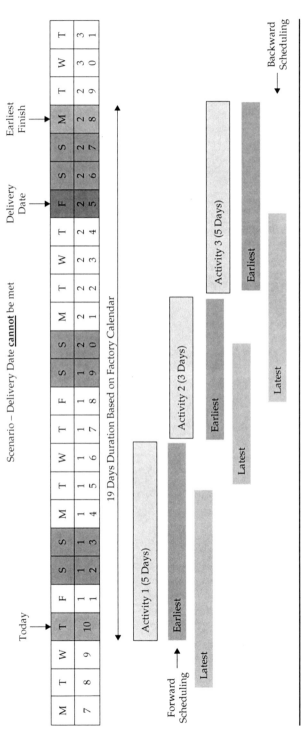

**FIGURE 5-8** Scheduling 2

## Parameters for Network Scheduling

**IMPORTANT NOTE** *Configuration point Define Control Key (OPSU) contains a tick box to enable "Scheduling."*

Parameters for Network Scheduling are tied into both Plant and Order Type (meaning Network Type in the case of PS). If you don't have an entry here, scheduling will not take place and you will get errors in your project.

| Menu Path | Project System->Dates->Scheduling |
| --- | --- |
| Config Point | Specify Parameters for Network Scheduling |
| Transaction | OPU6 |

IMG for Scheduling in Networks:

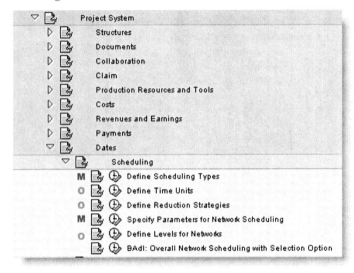

Copyright by SAP AG

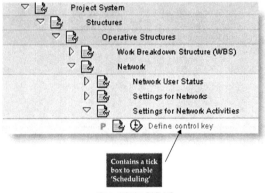

Copyright by SAP AG

| | |
|---|---|
| Plant | |
| Order type | |
| ProdScheduler | |

**Adjust scheduling**

| | |
|---|---|
| Adjust Dates | Adjust basic dates, adjust dep. reqmts to operation date |

**Scheduling control for detailed scheduling**

| | |
|---|---|
| Scheduling Type | ☑ | ☐ Automatic Scheduling |
| Start in the Past | | ☐ Automatic log |
| | | ☐ Scheduling with breaks |
| | | ☐ Shift Order |
| | | ☐ Latest dates f. material |

**Reduction**

| | |
|---|---|
| Reduction type | All operations in the order will be reduced |
| Maximum reduction level | 0 Do not reduce |

**Workforce Planning**

| | |
|---|---|
| Rescheduling | Distribute distributed work according to old distribution |

- **Plant**   The Plant for which Network Scheduling applies.
- **Order type**   The Network Type for which Network scheduling applies.
- **ProdScheduler**   Scheduler responsible for a material in production activity control. The production scheduler determines how capacity requirements are calculated for a material during a scheduling run.

## ADJUST SCHEDULING TAB

**Adjust Dates** determines if and how the basic dates or the dependent requirements dates are adjusted during lead-time scheduling, and after scheduling, how the new basic dates differ from the old basic dates. In backward scheduling, the system adjusts the basic start date if necessary (if there is a negative float); in the case of forward scheduling, it adjusts the basic finish date. The basic finish date is not adjusted in planned orders (that is, the Sales Order is not changed automatically).

## SCHEDULING CONTROL FOR DETAILED SCHEDULING TAB

- **Scheduling Type**   Determines the Scheduling type to be used for all Detailed Planning Operations (Usually Backwards for Production).

"In Time" means by 24-hour clock.

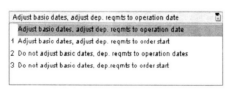

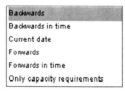

- **Start in the Past** Number of days that scheduling allows the start date to be in the past. If this number of days is exceeded, the system automatically overrides the set scheduling type and uses "Today" scheduling.
- **Automatic log** Tick this if you want the scheduling log to be displayed automatically after each scheduling run. The scheduling log is displayed for information purposes or when errors occurred during the scheduling run.
- **Scheduling with breaks** Tick this if you want to determine that the exact time of a break should be taken into account. If you set this indicator, it is no longer possible that a calculated time occurs during a break time.
- **Shift Order** Defines that for partially confirmed operations the actual dates already existing are not taken into account during a new scheduling run. You can use this indicator if, for example, the basic dates change during the execution of the order/network and operations have already been partially confirmed. The actual dates are then no longer taken into account in the next scheduling run.
- **Latest dates f. material** Tick this if you want the "Latest Date" scheduled for the Activity to be used to order the Material Component (as opposed to the Start Date). Also see Align Finish Date in your Network Profile for more information.

### REDUCTION TAB

- **Reduction type** Reduction Types represent a decrease in the lead time of your network in scheduling. If the basic dates specified cannot be respected, the system takes reduction measures. Reduction measures are performed in steps:
  1. Which times are reduced
  2. Steps in which reduction takes place

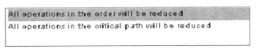

All operations in the order will be reduced
All operations in the critical path will be reduced

- **Maximum reduction level** Specifies the maximum level to be used to reduce the lead time for scheduling bottlenecks.

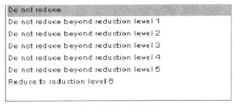

Do not reduce
Do not reduce beyond reduction level 1
Do not reduce beyond reduction level 2
Do not reduce beyond reduction level 3
Do not reduce beyond reduction level 4
Do not reduce beyond reduction level 5
Reduce to reduction level 6

**NOTE** *Reduction is only relevant for Detailed Scheduling.*

### WORKFORCE PLANNING TAB

- **Rescheduling**   Specifies how the system handles work that has already been distributed if the activity dates change.

    The following options are available for work that has been distributed but is now outside the new dates:

    - Distribute it according to the new distribution.
    - Delete it.
    - Distribute it to the start or finish of the new activity period.

In this case, the system distributes the work to the start if the previous dates were before the new dates, and to the finish if the dates have been moved forward in time.

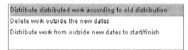

Copyright by SAP AG

## Material

Configuration of all matters pertaining to the procurement of Materials in Networks is controlled by Procurement Indicators, Account Assignment Categories, Movement Types, and MRP Groups.

## Procurement

The process of managing Purchase Requisitions and Purchase Orders, that is, Materials bought from external sources.

### Procurement Indicator

This setting applies the default values for Material Components entered in Networks. Its use can help determine such settings as "Long Lead-Time" or "3rd Party Orders sent directly to Customer."

| Menu Path | Project System->Material->Procurement> |
|-----------|----------------------------------------|
| Config Point | Define Procurement Indicators for Material Components |
| Transaction | OPS8 |

IMG for Material Procurement in Projects:

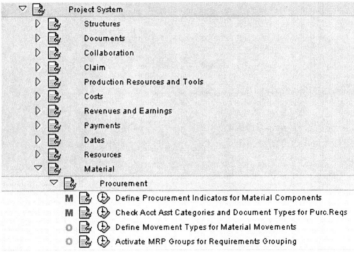

Copyright by SAP AG

Copyright by SAP AG

- **Procurement**   A unique key and a description. This value will be specified when you enter the Material Component against a Network Activity/Element.

## PRIORITIES TAB

By entering priorities for the various stock types, you control in which stock type a component is kept. For example, if you are using Valuated Project Stock, you might set Project to 1, Plant to 2, and Sales to 3.

- Priorities plant   Set 1–9.
- Priorities project   Set 1–9.
- Priorities sales ord   Set 1–9.

## CONTROL DATA TAB

- **PReq network**   Tick this to specify that a requirements-replenishing purchase requisition should be generated for a component in a network as well as an MRP-relevant reservation. This is only possible for components that are managed in individual stock. Generating a PR from a Network has the effect of immediately creating a commitment. PRs generated outside of a Network (and assigned to the Network) <u>do not</u> generate a commitment on their own—they must first become a Purchase Order to effect a commitment.

- **3ʳᵈ party**   Tick this if externally procured material should be delivered directly to the customer (or another location). You will need to enter a Delivery Address at the time the Material Component is entered.

- **Prelim.reqmnts**   Tick this if you want to register requirements (planned independent requirements or preliminary purchase requisitions) in advance via a network (long lead-time items). These can later be offset against real requirements.

## DEFAULT ITEM CATEGORY TAB

- **Item Cat MRP**   Whatever you enter here will be the default Item Category for the Material Component using this Procurement Indicator. This is usually *N* for Non-Stock or *L* for Stock.

### ProMan (Project-oriented Procurement) Define Exceptions

The use of ProMan as a tool is described in Chapter 6. As there are many ways ProMan can be configured, an extract of SAP's Best Practice is described here.

| Menu Path | Project System->Material->Project-oriented Procurement (ProMan) |
|---|---|
| **Config Point** | Define Exceptions |
| **Transaction** | SPRO |

Exceptions can be attached to Profiles but if not attached, they can be selected when you run the ProMan transaction CNMM. Exceptions are the "Traffic Light" Rules you want to apply to a particular set of conditions.

If you want Exceptions, you must specify an Exception Profile. This will later be linked to the actual Exception Rule (Red or Yellow traffic lights).

In the example following, we will be creating a Red Rule that will check if a Reservation has yet led to a Purchase Order. Once this has been done, the Exception will be attached to the Profile.

Select New Entries and key in an Exception Profile ID and Description:

New Entries

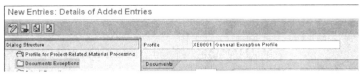

Now place the cursor on Document Exceptions and double-click.

Select New Entries and key in a Document Exception ID and
Description. In this example, we are going to set up a Red Rule if there is
no Purchase Order.

New Entries

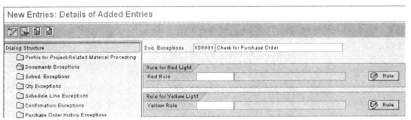

Click the RED Rule icon (you must not enter anything in the Red Rule box yet).
You will be presented with this screen:

Click the Create Rule icon.

| □ Rule |

Enter a suitable Rule Name and press ENTER.

**Create Rule: XDR001**

| Rule name | XDR001 | Check if PO Exists |

| Rules | |
| --- | --- |
| ▽ □ | |
| ▽ ⏰ Orders/Documents | |
| ▽ ⊘ XDR001 | Check if PO Exists |
| 📄 Rule definition | |
| ▷ ⏰ Dates | |
| ▷ ⏰ Quantities | |
| ▷ ⏰ Schedule Lines | |
| ▷ ⏰ Confirmations | |
| ▷ ⏰ Purchase order history | |

Applicatn area  PM
Callup point  1  Orders/Documents

Content of rule

Click Rule definition and you will be able to select the type of data you want to check. Then double-click Structure CNMMD0—the structure for Documents:

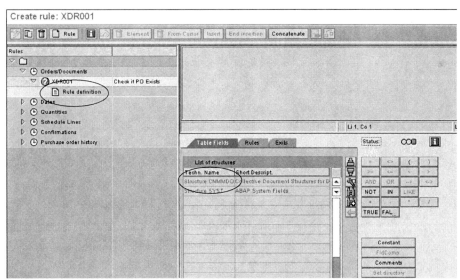

**Create rule: XDR001**

Double-click field Purchase Order:

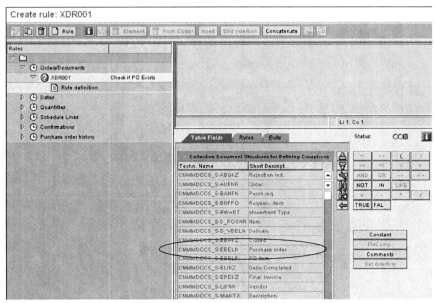

Copyright by SAP AG

Purchase Order will appear in the dialogue box.
Click the = operand.
Click the Constant button.
Do not enter anything in Purchase Order.
Click the green tick.

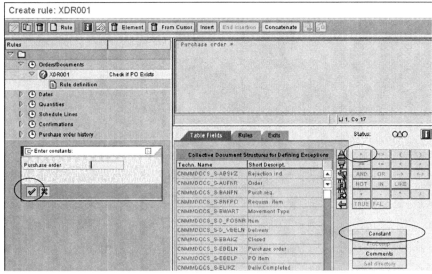

Copyright by SAP AG

Status should be Green, meaning your syntax is okay.

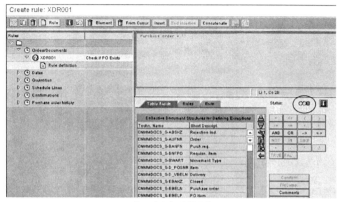

Copyright by SAP AG

Status should be Green, meaning your syntax is okay.
Go back one level:

Copyright by SAP AG

Save the Rule:

Copyright by SAP AG

Go back four levels by clicking the Back icon four times:

Copyright by SAP AG

Enter the name of your Exception for Document in the field Red Rule:

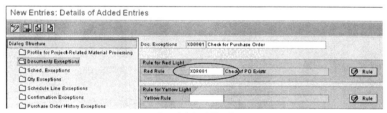

Copyright by SAP AG

Save the Exception:

Copyright by SAP AG

Go back three levels by clicking the Back icon three times:

You can now apply more Exception Rules as you see fit.
Below is the rule just created working in CNMM…before the Exception is applied:

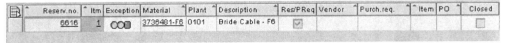

| | Reserv.no. | Itm | Exception | Material | Plant | Description | Res/PReq | Vendor | Purch.req. | Item | PO | Closed |
|---|---|---|---|---|---|---|---|---|---|---|---|---|
| | 6616 | 1 | OO■ | 3736481-F6 | 0101 | Bride Cable - F6 | ☑ | | | | | ☐ |

And after the Exception is applied:

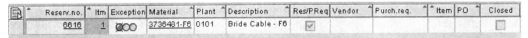

| | Reserv.no. | Itm | Exception | Material | Plant | Description | Res/PReq | Vendor | Purch.req. | Item | PO | Closed |
|---|---|---|---|---|---|---|---|---|---|---|---|---|
| | 6616 | 1 | ■OO | 3736481-F6 | 0101 | Bride Cable - F6 | ☑ | | | | | ☐ |

### ProMan (Project-oriented Procurement) DefineProfile

| | |
|---|---|
| **Menu Path** | Project System->Material->Project-oriented Procurement (ProMan) |
| **Config Point** | Define Profile |
| **Transaction** | SPRO |

Here you create the Profile, connect the Exception Profile to it, and tick the relevant Documents and Views for use in the operation of ProMan.

The Profile determines the type of data that is available. There can be many profiles. They serve to filter what you will see in the ProMan transaction CNMM. Profile can have Exception Profiles attached to them.

Simply Create a Profile, specify the Description, and tick the relevant boxes.

New Entries: Details of Added Entries

ProMan Profile  XX0001
Description  General ProMan Profile

Settings
Except. Profile

Orders/Documents
☑ Purchase Req.
☑ Inquiry
☑ Purchase Order
☑ Delivery
☑ Material Docum.
☑ Planned Order
☑ Production Ord.
☑ Maint.order
☑ Res. for WBS

Views
☑ Components
☑ Activ./Elements
☑ Quantities
☑ Dates
☑ Deliveries
☑ Stock
☑ Orders/Docs

Below is a list of field names used in ProMan Exceptions for each category of information. These fields can be used when defining Exceptions.

| DOCUMENTS | SCHEDULE (1) | SCHEDULE (2) | QUANTITIES (1) | QUANTITIES (2) |
|---|---|---|---|---|
| Rejection ind. | Rejection ind. | CW Mat. Staging | Rejection ind. | RFQ |
| Order | Changed On | CW Fin. Plnd Or | Order | RFQ Item |
| Purch.req. | Order | CW Start PlnOrd | Purch.req. | Record type |
| Requisn. item | Requisn. date | Delivery DatePO | Req.Qty ProdOrd | Reservation |
| Movement Type | Purch.req. | Del.PS Delivery | Reserv. Req.Qty | Item no. |
| Item | Reqmts date | Description | Requisn. item | Debit/Credit |
| Delivery | Requisn. item | Material | Order quantity | RFQ status |
| Closed | PostDateMatDoc | Mat.avail.date | Item | Sales document |
| Purchase order | Movement Type | Material Doc. | Delivery | Qty.f.avail.chk |
| PO Item | Item | Mat. Doc. Year | Closed | Activity |
| Deliv.Completed | Closed | Network | Purchase order | Plant |
| Final invoice | Purchase order | Order finish | PO Item | PO History |
| Vendor | PO Item | Planned order | Deliv.Completed | Confirmations |
| Description | PO Delivery | Item | Withdrawal Qty | Schedule Lines |
| Material | Deliv.Completed | WBS Element | Final invoice | Mat. Doc. Item |
| Material Doc. | Created on | Order start | Order quantity | |
| Mat. Doc. Year | Final invoice | RFQ | Delivery qty | |
| Network | Release date | RFQ Item | Description | |
| Planned order | Basic fin. date | Record type | Material | |
| Item | Sched. finish | Reservation | Material Doc. | |
| WBS Element | Bas. start date | Item no. | Base Unit | |
| RFQ | Sched. start | Debit/Credit | Order unit | |
| RFQ Item | CW Change Date | RFQ status | UoM Product.Ord | |
| Record type | CW Request Date | Sales document | Base Unit | |
| Reservation | CW Req. Date | Delivery | UoM Mat. Doc. | |
| Item no. | CW Post. MatDoc | Activity | UoM Planned Ord | |
| Debit/Credit | CW DeliveryDate | Plant | Base UoM Reserv | |
| RFQ status | CW Creat.Delltm | PO History | PReq Quantity | |
| Sales document | CW Release PReq | Confirmations | Order quantity | |
| Activity | CW Fin. ProdOrd | Schedule Lines | Qty in Mat. Doc | |
| Plant | CW SchFin ProdO | Mat. Doc. Item | Mat. Doc. Year | |
| PO History | CW Start Pr.Ord | | Network | |
| Confirmations | CW SchedStrt PO | | Planned order | |
| Schedule Lines | CW Deliv. Date | | Item | |
| Mat. Doc. Item | CW DeliveryDate | | WBS Element | |

| SCHEDULING AGREEMENT | ORDER CONFIRMATIONS | PO HISTORY |
|---|---|---|
| Reserv. Req.Qty | Reserv. Req.Qty | Reserv. Req.Qty |
| Reqmts date | Reqmts date | Reqmts date |
| PurchOrderDate | Purchase order | Qty. in OPUn |
| Committed date | Item | Order prce unit |
| Purchase order | Confirm. cat. | GR blocked stck |
| Item | Delivery date | PostDateMatDoc |
| Delivery date | Created on | Item |
| CW Req. Date | CW Req. Date | Purchase order |
| CW OrderDateScL | CW Del.Confirm. | Item |
| CW Confirmed | CW Create Conf. | Mat. Doc. Year |
| CW DeliveryDate | CW Deliv. Date | CW Req. Date |
| CW Deliv. Date | Delivery date | CW Post. MatDoc |
| Delivery date | Description | CW Deliv. Date |
| Description | Material | Delivery date |
| Material | Base Unit | Description |
| Base Unit | Unit Meas.Ordlt | Material |
| Unit Meas.Ordlt | Base UoM Reserv | Base Unit |
| Base UoM Reserv | Quantity | Base UoM Reserv |
| Quantity | Quantity | Quantity |
| Scheduled qty. | Network | Qty in Mat. Doc |
| Network | Item | Network |
| Item | WBS Element | Item |
| WBS Element | Record type | WBS Element |
| RFQ | Reservation | Record type |
| Item | Item no. | Reservation |
| Record type | Sales document | Item no. |
| Reservation | Activity | Debit/Credit |
| Item no. | PO History | 15 |
| RFQ status | Confirmations | Activity |
| Sales document | Schedule Lines | GR bl.st.in OUn |
| Activity | | PO History |
| Received | | Confirmations |
| PO History | | Schedule Lines |
| Confirmations | | |
| Schedule Lines | | |

## Summary

You have now seen most of the important configuration points available in PS. This should easily get you started—now you can get online and get further assistance from SAP's help.

# 6

# CHAPTER

# Tools

T his chapter looks at the available tools for working with Projects—the Project Builder, Planning Board, ProMan, and Reporting.

## The Project Builder

The Project Builder is SAP's primary tool for creating and maintaining most elements of a Project. There are some things you cannot manage here, such as Budgets, Claims, and Subnetworks. However, you can do just about anything else.

### Project Builder Structure

The Project Builder is divided into three main sections:

- Structure
- Worklist and Templates
- Identification and View Section

#### Structure

Here the structural elements of a project are shown in a Hierarchical format. As you move down the Hierarchy, the object content is shown in the Identification and View Section.

- **Worklists and Templates**   In here you will see the last projects worked on, so you can return to them quickly. Also, by selecting Templates, you will see the various templates available.
- **Identification and View**   For the Worklists and the Templates that appear in this section of the screen, you can double-click or drag-and-drop objects  to convert them into operative objects in the Structure. In here the currently highlighted object will be shown for you to change contents and perform other actions.

Figure 6-1 shows how the screen is structured.

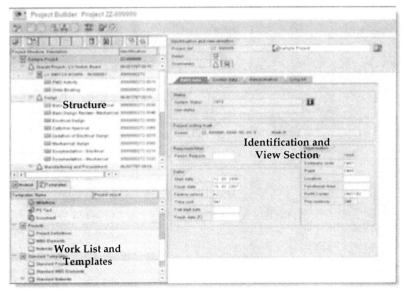

Copyright by SAP AG

**FIGURE 6-1** Project Builder

## Project Builder Icons

The following table describes all the available icons inside the Project Builder:

| Icon | Description |
|------|-------------|
| Copyright by SAP AG | Switch from Edit to Display mode. Be aware that when you switch, the object you have highlighted will go to the top of the screen and you will only be able to edit the relevant tree. |
| Copyright by SAP AG | Open a Project. |
| Copyright by SAP AG | Move the object a level UP in the hierarchy. Subordinate WBSs are also affected. |
| Copyright by SAP AG | Move the object a level DOWN in the hierarchy. Subordinate WBSs are also affected. |
| Copyright by SAP AG | Cut the highlighted object (ready for Paste). |
| Copyright by SAP AG | Copy an object. |
| Copyright by SAP AG | Paste a cut or copied object. |

| | Description |
|---|---|
| Copyright by SAP AG | Services for Object (allows you to send a Workflow to other office users or external recipients). The pull-down gives a list; the call-out provides icons. |
| Copyright by SAP AG | Launch the Planning Board (Gantt Chart) for all objects from where your cursor is currently highlighted. |
| Copyright by SAP AG | Switch to Graphics mode (for WBS only). |
| Copyright by SAP AG | Switch to Graphics mode (for Network only). |
| Copyright by SAP AG | Perform Mass Changes (search and replace common information) against the current project. |
| Copyright by SAP AG | Launch Easy Cost Planning (only applies to Planning WBS Elements). |
| Copyright by SAP AG | Launch Simulated Sales Pricing (requires a DIP Profile and Partner determination information). |
| Copyright by SAP AG | Delete (physically remove) the highlighted object and any subordinate objects. |
| Copyright by SAP AG | Expand project hierarchy from highlighted object. |
| Copyright by SAP AG | Compress project hierarchy from highlighted object. |
| Copyright by SAP AG | Undo last Cut/Paste. |
| Copyright by SAP AG | Switch to Relationship Overview (for linking Network Activities with Start/Finish Rules, Durations, Intervals, etc.). |
| Copyright by SAP AG | Search the Project hierarchy. |
| Copyright by SAP AG | Overview WBS Elements or Network Activities. This lets you maintain the objects in a tabular view. |
| Copyright by SAP AG | Maintain Long Text for WBS Elements, Network Activities, and Milestones. |
| Copyright by SAP AG | Generic symbol representing a WBS. |
| Copyright by SAP AG | Generic symbol representing a Project Definition. |

| | |
|---|---|
| <br>Copyright by SAP AG | Generic symbol representing a Network Header (different in Planning Board). |
| <br>Copyright by SAP AG | Generic symbol representing a Network Activity. |
| <br>Copyright by SAP AG | Generic symbol representing a Network Activity Element. |
| <br>Copyright by SAP AG | Generic symbol representing a Milestone. |
| <br>Copyright by SAP AG | Overview PS Text. |
| <br>Copyright by SAP AG | Overview Documents attached to an Object. |
| <br>Copyright by SAP AG | Overview Material Components (Network only). |
| <br>Copyright by SAP AG | Create a new project or an object (WBS, Activity, Milestone, etc.). |
| <br>Copyright by SAP AG | Display the current and historical System and User Statuses. |

## Project Builder Menus

The following screenshots provide a composite view of each pull-down menu in the Project Builder and will save you having to navigate online to find out where you need to go.

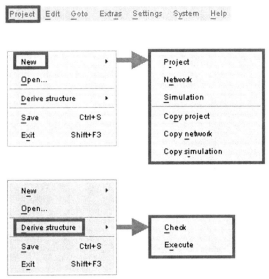

Copyright by SAP AG

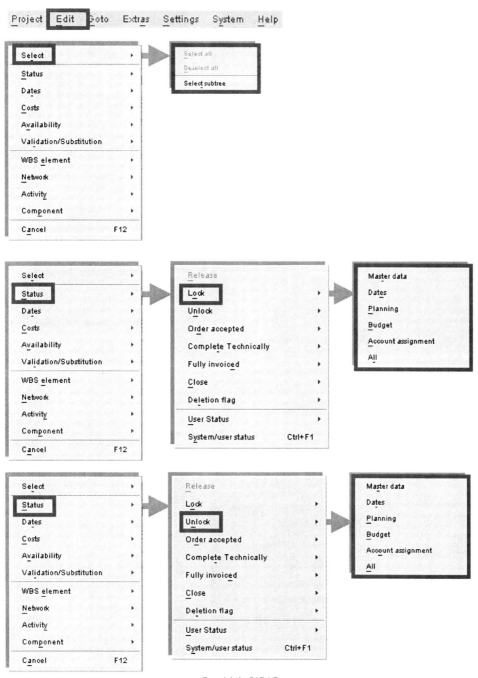

Copyright by SAP AG

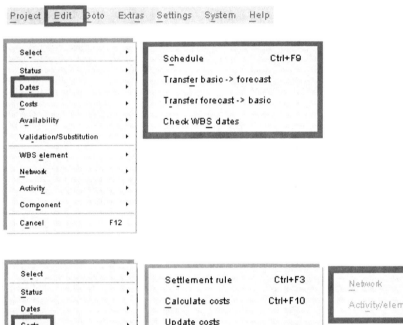

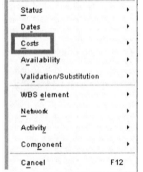

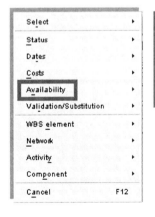

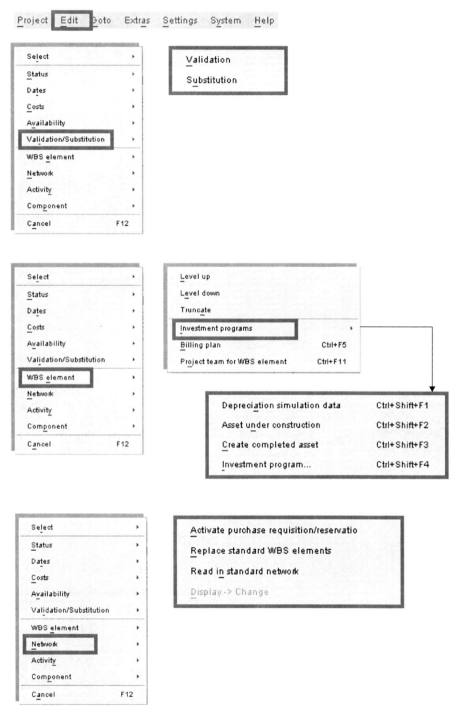

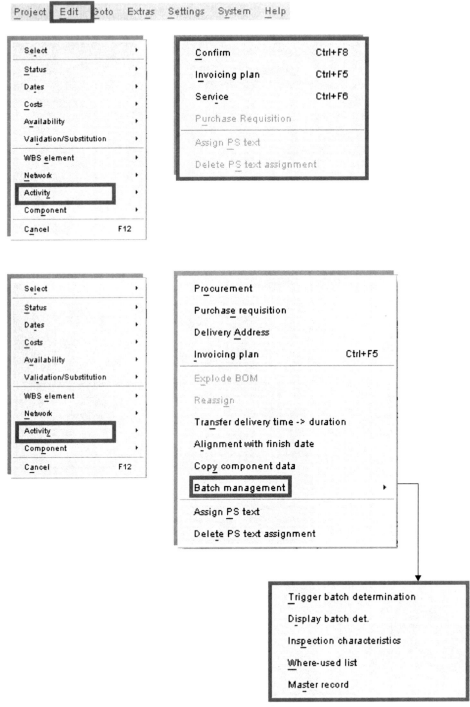

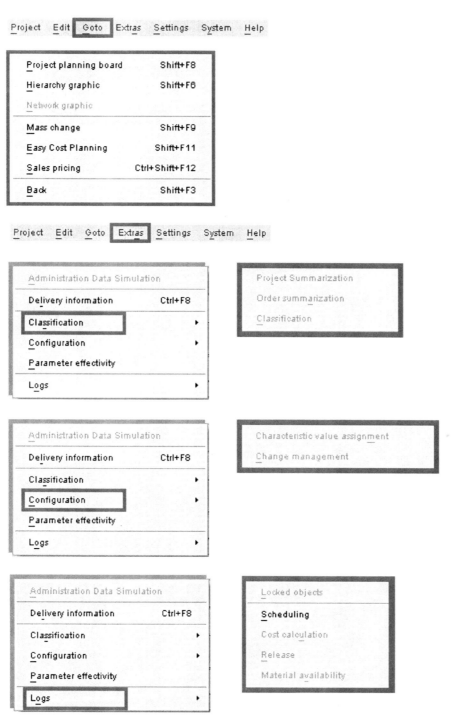

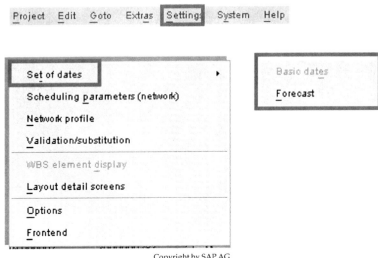

## Inside the Project Builder

This section describes the data inside a Project Definition, a WBS, a Milestone, and a Network Activity. Most of the data featured here can be automatically copied from a Standard Project (Template). Throughout this section, you will see Transaction Codes referenced within fields—these may help you determine where the original configuration comes from.

### Project Definition

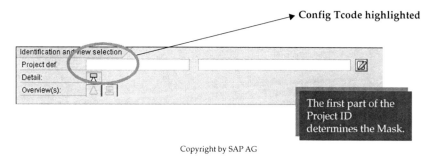

Copyright by SAP AG

### Project Definition – Basic Data tab

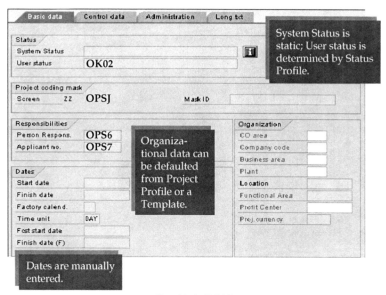

Copyright by SAP AG

### Project Definition – Control Data tab

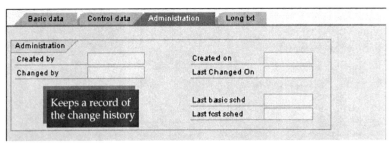

Copyright by SAP AG

### Project Definition – Administration tab

Copyright by SAP AG

### Project Definition – Long Txt tab

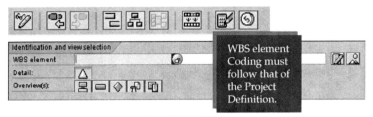

Copyright by SAP AG

### Work Breakdown Structure (WBS)

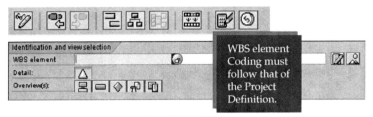

Copyright by SAP AG

## WBS – Basic Data

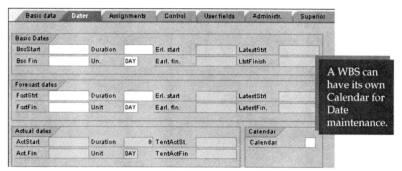

Copyright by SAP AG

## WBS – Dates

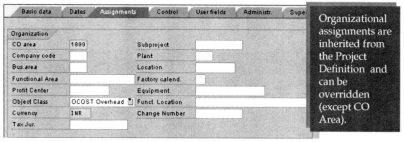

Copyright by SAP AG

## WBS – Assignments

Copyright by SAP AG

## WBS – Control

| Basic data | Dates | Assignments | Control | User fields | Administr. | Superior |
| --- | --- | --- | --- | --- | --- | --- |

Transfer to proj.def

**Accounting**

| | | | |
| --- | --- | --- | --- |
| Costing Sheet | KZS2 | Statistical | CCtr post. |
| Overhead key | OKOG | Integ. planning | |
| Interest Profile | OPIA | | |
| Investment profile | OITA | | |
| Results Analysis Key | OKG1 | | |

> If you tick Integ. planning, you cannot use Easy Cost Planning.

**Planning dates**

| | | |
| --- | --- | --- |
| Network asst | 2 | For WBS element |
| Plan.meth/basic | 2 | Bottom-up (taking da |
| Plan.meth/fcst | 2 | Bottom-up (taking da |

**Investment Management**

| | |
| --- | --- |
| Scale | |
| Investment reason | |
| Envir. investment | |

Copyright by SAP AG

## WBS – User Fields

| Basic data | Dates | Assignments | Control | User fields | Administr. | Su |
| --- | --- | --- | --- | --- | --- | --- |

| Field key | OPS1 |
| --- | --- |

**General fields**

| | |
| --- | --- |
| Text 1 | |
| Text 2 | |
| Text 3 | |
| Text 4 | |

**Numeric fields**

| | | |
| --- | --- | --- |
| Quantity 1 | | |
| Quantity 2 | | |
| Value 3 | | |
| Value 4 | | |

**Dates**

| | |
| --- | --- |
| Date 1 | |
| Date 2 | |

**Checkboxes**

| |
| --- |
| Indicator 1 |
| Indicator 2 |

> Each WBS can have its own Field Key with different UDFs – but be careful because the same table is used to carry this information.

Copyright by SAP AG

## WBS – Administration

| Basic data | Dates | Assignments | Control | User fields | Administr. |
| --- | --- | --- | --- | --- | --- |

**Administration**

| | | | |
| --- | --- | --- | --- |
| Created by | | Created on | |
| Changed by | | Changed on | |

Copyright by SAP AG

## WBS – Superior

Copyright by SAP AG

## WBS – Progress

Copyright by SAP AG

## WBS – Long Text

Copyright by SAP AG

## Milestone (WBS)

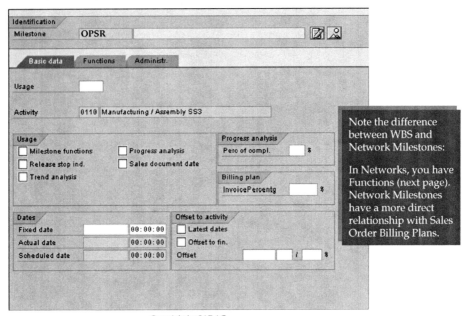

If Prog. analysis is ticked, fill in the Percentage of completion. If Sales doc. date is ticked, Billing date is determined by the Sales Order. It is optional to fill InvoicePercentg. If Trend analysis is ticked, you will need Project Versions. If Offset to fin. is ticked (milestone set to the scheduled finish date of the WBS), enter an Offset value/unit (e.g., Days) or Offset % (refers to the duration of the WBS). Normally, the Milestone date is set to the Earliest Start date of the WBS. Actual date will only be available for entry when the WBS is Released (Similarly for Activity Milestones)

Copyright by SAP AG

## Milestone (Network)

Note the difference between WBS and Network Milestones:

In Networks, you have Functions (next page). Network Milestones have a more direct relationship with Sales Order Billing Plans.

Copyright by SAP AG

## Milestone Functions (Network)

Functions allow you to perform additional steps after a Milestone has been reached. The functions are triggered based on System status. Each function must have its Parameters completed (e.g., if your function is "Create Network," you need to specify a Standard Network).

This section only appears if the Function selected requires it.

Copyright by SAP AG

## Network Header – Scheduling

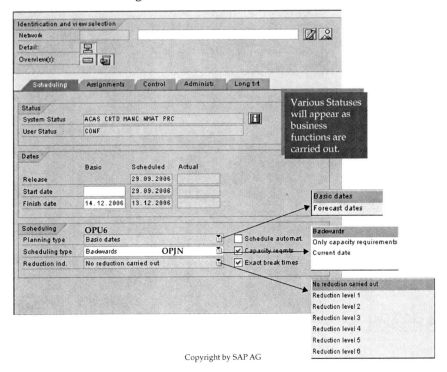

Copyright by SAP AG

## Network Header – Assignments

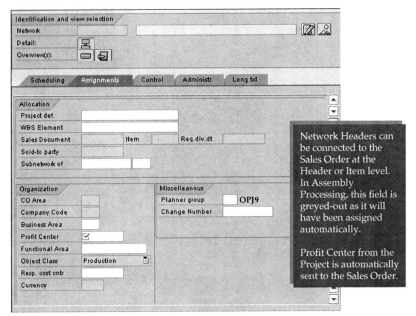

Copyright by SAP AG

## Network Header – Control

Copyright by SAP AG

## Network Header – Administration

Copyright by SAP AG

## Network Header – Long Txt

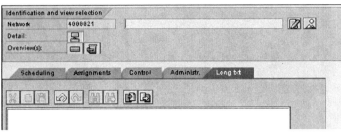

Copyright by SAP AG

## Network Activity – Internal

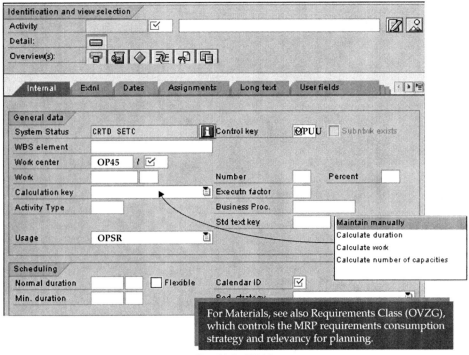

Copyright by SAP AG

## Network Activity – External

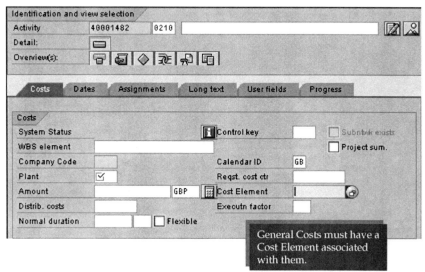

## Network Activity – General Costs

General Costs must have a Cost Element associated with them.

## Network Activity – Dates

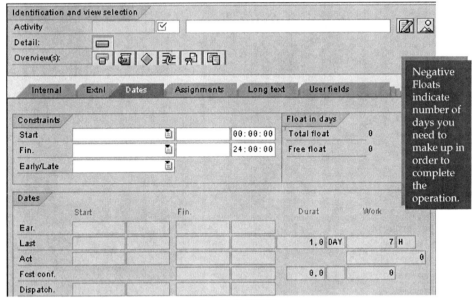

Negative Floats indicate number of days you need to make up in order to complete the operation.

## Network Activity – Assignments

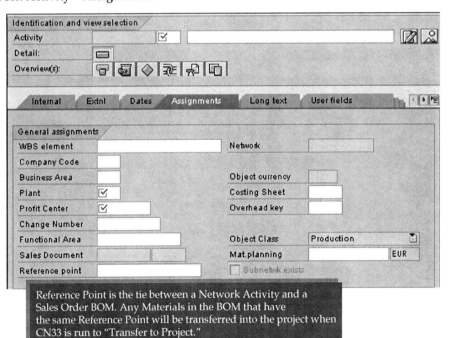

Reference Point is the tie between a Network Activity and a Sales Order BOM. Any Materials in the BOM that have the same Reference Point will be transferred into the project when CN33 is run to "Transfer to Project."

## Network Activity – User Fields

UDFs can have their names customized in OPS1.
E.g., Text 1 could be "Old Project Number."

Copyright by SAP AG

## Network Activity – Person Assignment

This screen only applies to Projects with Internal Activities that have a valid Work Center/Activity Type. The HR Master must also have persons assigned to the Work Center.

Copyright by SAP AG

## Network Activity – Additional Data

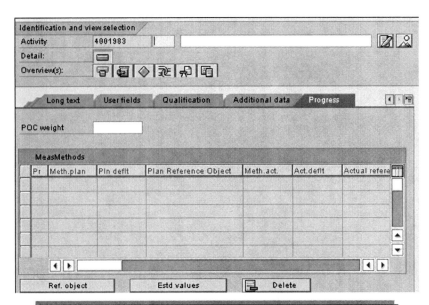

Copyright by SAP AG

## Network Activity – Progress

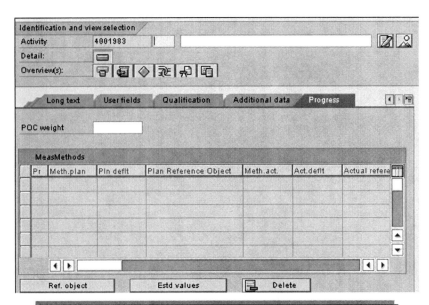

Progress Analysis requires a Progress Version to be configured against your Controlling Area and your CO Versions.

Copyright by SAP AG

## Material Component

Copyright by SAP AG

## Material Component – Processing Parameters (Proc.param)

Copyright by SAP AG

## The Planning Board

The Planning Board is used to manage your project from a graphical Planning perspective. In essence it is a Gantt Chart and has the capability of moving information about in a more graphical form. Used properly, it is an excellent tool for viewing the planning-oriented elements of your project. The Planning Board Profile can be configured to suit your needs, as shown in the IMG extract:

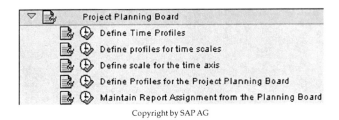

Copyright by SAP AG

The Project Planning Board is divided into two main sections:

- **Structure**   In here the structural elements of a project are shown in a Hierarchical format. Displayed fields can be easily changed. You can also double-click objects to gain access for editing.

- **Gantt Chart**   This is a graphical representation of your project from a Date and relationship point of view.

Figure 6-2 shows how the screen is structured.

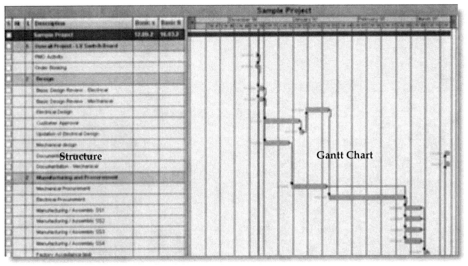

Copyright by SAP AG

FIGURE 6-2   Planning Board structure

## Planning Board Icons

The following table describes all the available icons inside the Planning Board:

| Icon | Description |
|------|-------------|
| Copyright by SAP AG | Services for Object (allows you to send a Workflow to other office users or external recipients). The pull-down gives a list; the call-out provides icons. |
| Copyright by SAP AG | Select all objects (all objects will be ticked). |
| Copyright by SAP AG | Deselect all objects (all objects will be unchecked). |
| Copyright by SAP AG | Move the object a level UP in the hierarchy. Subordinate WBSs are also affected. |
| Copyright by SAP AG | Move the object a level DOWN in the hierarchy. Subordinate WBSs are also affected. |
| Copyright by SAP AG | Cut the highlighted object (ready for Paste). |
| Copyright by SAP AG | Copy an object. |
| Copyright by SAP AG | Paste a cut or copied object. |
| Copyright by SAP AG | Undo last Cut/Paste. |
| Copyright by SAP AG | Connect Selected Activities. |
| Copyright by SAP AG | Switch to Editing Activity relationships (tabular view). |
| Copyright by SAP AG | Delete (physically remove) the highlighted object and any subordinate objects. |
| Copyright by SAP AG | Show details of selected object (same as double-click). |
| Copyright by SAP AG | Confirm selected Activity. |
| Copyright by SAP AG | Perform Scheduling for the selected object. |
| Copyright by SAP AG | Calculate Costs for selected object. |

| | |
|---|---|
| Copyright by SAP AG | Takes you straight to the Network Header. |
| Copyright by SAP AG | Overview Material Components (Network only). |
| Copyright by SAP AG | Display the current and historical System and User Statuses. |
| Copyright by SAP AG | Expand project hierarchy from highlighted object. |
| Copyright by SAP AG | Compress project hierarchy from highlighted object. |
| Copyright by SAP AG | Reveal Graphics screen for Capacity Overview (by Work Center). |
| Copyright by SAP AG | Filter the current view by selected field values (will include only selected objects). |
| Copyright by SAP AG | Group specific objects together by selected fields (will shift them). |
| Copyright by SAP AG | Sort objects into an order by selected fields. |
| Copyright by SAP AG | Highlight objects by selected fields. |
| Copyright by SAP AG | Switch on/off Connect Mode (allows you to graphically connect Activities). |
| Copyright by SAP AG | Scheduling comparison (Delete Copies, Display Original, Display Last). |
| Copyright by SAP AG | Zoom in to graphic (make entire Planning Board bigger or smaller). |
| Copyright by SAP AG | Adapt Graphics Area (fit it into the Gantt area or optimize lengths). |
| Copyright by SAP AG | Adapt time scale. |
| Copyright by SAP AG | Launch Planning Board Assistant (lets you customize how the PB looks). |
| Copyright by SAP AG | Launch the Time Scale Assistant (lets you decide if you want Days, Months, Years). |
| Copyright by SAP AG | Sets of Dates view (lets you select which dates are represented in the Bar Chart). |

| | |
|---|---|
| Copyright by SAP AG | Options—lets you view and change some of the default values for the project (Scheduling, Planning, Templates available). |
| Copyright by SAP AG | Field Selection (same as double-clicking in the fields header)—lets you select/deselect which fields are shown in the structure area of the Planning Board. |
| Copyright by SAP AG | Legend—switches the legend on/off. |
| Copyright by SAP AG | Logs/Lists—lets you display available logs and list such as Scheduling, Costs. |
| Copyright by SAP AG | Undo User Settings—lets you reset customized settings (as set in Options). |

# ProMan (Project-Oriented Procurement)

ProMan consolidates information related to procurement documents assigned to WBS Elements and Network Activities.

This includes the following:

- Purchase Requisitions
- Inquiries
- Purchase Orders
- Deliveries
- Material Documents (Goods Movements)
- Planned Orders
- Production Orders
- Maintenance Orders
- Reservations

In relation to the preceding, ProMan functionality permits you to view the following:

- Material Components
- Network Activities and Activity Elements
- Quantities
- Dates
- Deliveries from Project
- Project Stock
- Orders

And to Execute certain functions:

- Generate Purchase Requisitions from Network Activities
- Group and generate summary Purchase Requisitions

- Generate Purchase Orders from Purchase Requisitions
- Generate a Delivery Item from a Project
- Transfer Stock

## Exceptions

To personalize the view in ProMan reporting (Transaction CNMM), you can configure an Exception Profile, which is attached to a ProMan Profile. They provide you with "Traffic Lights." Exceptions are maintained in a similar fashion to Validations and Substitutions. For example: If a Material Component exists, a Green traffic light will show; but if there is no Purchase Order for that Component, a Red traffic light will show. Or, if a Purchase Order exists, a Green traffic light will show; but if the Goods Receipt has not been posted, a Red traffic light will show. The combinations are many and can be customized to suit your business environment.

## Using ProMan

Transaction CNMM—Project System->Material->Execution

This transaction provides a hierarchical view of a project structure, including Project Definition, WBS, Network Header, Network Activity/Element, and Material Components. The usual symbols for these objects apply.

In the selection screen, you specify a Project or Network plus other selection criteria to limit what you see:

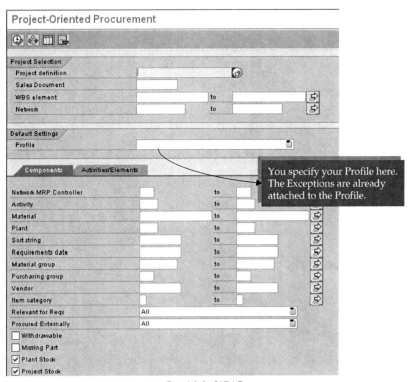

Copyright by SAP AG

The actual working screen is managed in two separate sections:

- **Structure**   In here the structural elements of a project are shown in a Hierarchical format. The Project Structure cannot be changed, but you can filter out those objects you don't want to see.

- **Detail Section**   In here you see the various documents that relate to Material activity in your project. From this point it is possible to view Documents, Dates, and Quantities. You can also perform Functions, such as Create a Purchase Req, Purchase Order, Movement, and so on.

Figure 6-3 shows how the screen is structured.

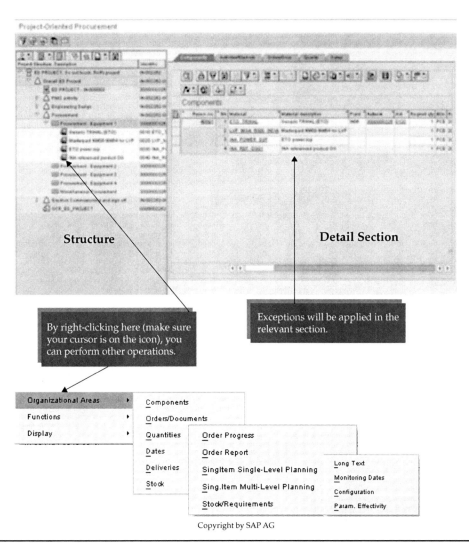

Copyright by SAP AG

**FIGURE 6-3**   ProMan

## Standard Reporting

Though it is not necessary to perform any major configuration to make standard reports work, it is usual to at least customize a DB Profile. Standard SAP provides these, which are effectively a list of objects available for reporting. Usually, when executing a report, you will see these icons:

Execute  Choose  Get Variant  Dynamic  Delete  Test Scope

In summary, these are the main elements of reporting:

**DB Profile**

A profile of the Master Data that will be available within a given report.

**PS Info Profile**

This is configured to determine the "view," which can be work breakdown structure, cost center, profit center, or project summarization.

**Status Selection Profile**

A profile containing preconfigured System/User Status values that can be selected at the time of running a report. This is the <u>only</u> way that you can select information based on a project's status.

**Selection Screens**

The primary screen into which the values of your selection master data are entered. Data entered in these screens can be saved as a Selection Version, which can be retrieved on demand.

**Dynamic Selections**

Nonkey fields, which can be used to refine your primary selections.

**Filters**

Once a report has been performed, additional filters that leave out / include data in the report.

**Drilldown**

Additional Master Data or Transactional Data that is linked to the information in your report.

**Fields**

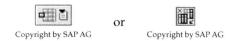

or

Additional fields that may be available for inclusion in columns of the report.

**Variants** (Sometimes you must use the Go To Menu option.)

Predefined selection information that may include all of the preceding attributes. Used for commonly selected information or when reports are run in the background.

**Export**

Export information from the report to a Spreadsheet, Word Processor, or Local file, or send it to another user as XML, HTML, or URL.

An idiosyncrasy of SAP reporting is that you can never be sure they will all have the same functionality, have the same kinds of messages or even (in some rare cases) give you the same results as the data you know to be true.

The standard reports sometimes fail to combine the type of information you are looking for (for example, Plan and Budget information is not shown in one report). The redeeming aspect of this is the use of the Report Painter, which lets you copy standard reports and modify their content. Another useful tool is Quick Viewer (SQVI), which is a very quick way of extracting information from one or many linked tables.

### Summarization, BW, and Other Means of Reporting

For years, SAP have been threatening to remove all support for this functionality. In a nutshell, it is a batch process that totals up Project data based on characteristic values (such as WBS, Network Numbers, and other values). Therefore, to gain anything useful from it, you have to perform a "summarization run."

In the end, it will be BW (Business Warehouse) that wins through because its functionality forces the business to predefine what information it wants to report on.

Another brilliant alternative is to use Crystal Reports or Cognos. These tools work a bit like BW, where you define the views you want and then perform extracts.

So, if you haven't done that or are not using BW, just get the best out of the many standard reports that are available by combing through them, making them better, and maybe using Report Painter, Report Writer, ABAP Query, or a combination of them all.

Finally, remember that you can extract information into spreadsheets quite easily.

---

**NOTE** *Some reports do not permit the selection of additional fields. The ones that do usually allow selection of fields via "Layout." This functionality permits you to not only select the fields you want, but will also let you save that layout for future use. The icon you will see is this:*

Copyright by SAP AG

Copyright by SAP AG

When this facility is available in a report, you will also see a Layout section in the main selection screen:

Copyright by SAP AG

Some reports carry these icons:

Copyright by SAP AG

which will achieve the same result but do not have the Layout shown in the Selection Screen. Reports that let you choose fields but not save the layout show this icon:

Copyright by SAP AG

Below is a table of all the Standard PS reports.

### Information System

| Structures | CN41 - Structure Overview |
|---|---|
| **Individual Overviews** | CN42N - Project Definitions |
| | CN43N - WBS Elements |
| | CN46N - Networks |
| | CN47N - Activities |
| | CN45N - Orders |
| | CN54N - Sales and Distribution Documents |
| | CN55N - Sales Document Items |
| | CN49N - Relationships |
| | CN53N - Milestones |
| | CN51N - Production Resources and Tools |
| **Enhanced Individual Overview** | CN42 - Project Definitions |
| | CN43 - WBS Elements |
| | CN44 - Planned Orders |
| | CN45 - Orders |
| | CN46 - Networks |
| | CN47 - Activities/Elements |
| | CN48 - Confirmations |
| | CN49 - Relationships |
| | CN50 - Capacity Requirements |
| | CN51 - Production Resources and Tools |
| | CN52 - Components |

| | CN53 - Milestones |
|---|---|
| | CNS54 - Sales and Distribution Documents (*DB Profile must be Sales view*) |
| | CNS55 - Sales Document Items (*DB Profile must be Sales view*) |
| **Where-Used Lists** | CA83 - Standard Networks for Work Center |
| | CA73 - Standard Networks for Production Resources and Tools |
| **Networks for Production Resources and Tools** | CF16 - For Material |
| | CF17 - For Document |
| | CF15 - For Production Resources and Tools Master |
| | CF18 - For Equipment |
| **Change Documents** | CN60 - For Project/Network |
| | CJCS - For Standard WBS |
| | CN61 - For Standard Network |
| | CNPAR - Partner Overview |
| **Claim** | CLM10 - Overview |
| | CLM11 - Hierarchy |
| **Financials** | S_ALR_87013531 - Costs/Revenues/Expenditures/Receipts |
| **Costs Plan-Based-Hierarchical** | S_ALR_87013532 - Plan/Actual/Variance |
| | S_ALR_87013533 - Plan/Actual/Commitment/Rem.Plan/Assigned |
| | |
| | S_ALR_87013534 - Plan 1/Plan 2/Actual/Commitments |
| | S_ALR_87013535 - Actual in CO Area/Object/Transaction Currency |
| | S_ALR_87013536 - Plan/Actual/Down Payment as Expense |
| | S_ALR_87013537 - Commitment Detail |
| | S_ALR_87013538 - Project Version Comparison: Actual/Plan |
| | S_ALR_87013539 - Project Version Comparison: Plan |
| | S_ALR_87013540 - Forecast |
| | S_ALR_87013541 - Project Interest: Plan/Actual |
| | S_ALR_87100185 - Actual Costs for Each Month (Current Fiscal Year) |
| | S_ALR_87100186 - Planned Costs for Each Month (Current Fiscal Year) |
| | S_ALR_87100187 - Commitments for Each Month (Current Fiscal Year) |
| | S_ALR_87100188 - Cumulated Actual Costs |

| | |
|---|---|
| | S_ALR_87100189 - Actual/Planned Time Series |
| | S_ALR_87100190 - Plan/Actual/Variance for Each Project and Person Resp. |
| **By Cost Element** | S_ALR_87013542 - Actual/Commitment/Total/Plan in CO Area Currency |
| | S_ALR_87013543 - Actual/Plan/Variance Absolute/Variance % |
| | S_ALR_87013544 - Actual/Plan Comparison: Periods |
| | S_ALR_87013545 - Period Comparison - Actual |
| | S_ALR_87013546 - Commitments: Period Comparison |
| | S_ALR_87013547 - Period Comparison - Plan |
| | S_ALR_87013548 - Statistical Key Figures/Periods |
| | S_ALR_87013549 - Act/plan compare with partner |
| | S_ALR_87013550 - Debit in Object/CO Area Currency |
| | S_ALR_87013551 - Planned Debits in Object/CO Area Currency |
| | S_ALR_87013552 - Debit/Credit, Actual |
| | S_ALR_87013553 - Debit/Credit, Plan |
| | S_ALR_87013554 - Comparison of two plan versions |
| | S_ALR_87013555 - Project Results |
| **Budget-Related** | S_ALR_87013556 - Funds Overview |
| | S_ALR_87013557 - Budget/Actual/Variance |
| | S_ALR_87013558 - Budget/Actual/Commitment/Rem Plan/Assigned |
| | S_ALR_87013559 - Budget/Distributed/Plan/Distributed |
| | S_ALR_87013560 - Budget updates |
| | S_ALR_87013561 - Availability Control |
| **Revenues and Earnings Hierarchical** | S_ALR_87013562 - Annual Overview |
| | S_ALR_87013563 - Structure |
| | S_ALR_87013564 - Plan/Actual/Variance |
| | S_ALR_87013565 - Planned Contribution Margin |
| | S_ALR_87013566 - Actual Contribution Margin |
| | S_ALR_87013567 - Quotation/Order/Plan/Actual |
| | S_ALR_87013568 - Project Results |
| | S_ALR_87013569 - Incoming Orders/Balance |
| **By Cost Element** | S_ALR_87013570 - Act/Plan/Variance Abs./ % Var. |
| | S_ALR_87013571 - Actual/Plan Comparison: Periods |
| | S_ALR_87013572 - Project Results |

| Payments | S_ALR_87100191 - Receipts/Expenditures in Fiscal Year |
|---|---|
| | S_ALR_87013573 - Receipts/Expenditures for all Fiscal Years |
| | S_ALR_87013575 - Receipts |
| | S_ALR_87013574 - Expenditures |
| Line Items | CJI3 - Actual Costs/Revenues |
| | CJI5 - Commitments |
| | CJI4 - Plan Costs/Revenues |
| | CJI9 - Hierarchical Cost/Revenue Planning |
| | CJI8 - Budget |
| | CJIA - Actual Payments/Payment Commitments |
| | CJIB - Planned Payments |
| | CJIF - Results Analysis |
| | CJID - Line Item Settlement |
| Document Display | KSB5 - Actual Costs/Revenues |
| | CJ3B - Budget |
| | CJIG - Payments |
| Summarization | S_ALR_87013576 - Overview: Project Hierarchies |
| | S_ALR_87013577 - Costs/Revenues/Expenditures/Receipts |
| Costs Plan-Based-Hierarchical | S_ALR_87013578 - Plan/Actual/Variance |
| | S_ALR_87013579 - Plan/Actual/Commitment |
| By Cost Element | S_ALR_87013580 - Actual/Plan/Variance |
| | S_ALR_87013581 - Actual/Plan/Commitment |
| | S_ALR_87013582 - Current/Cumulative/Total |
| Budget-Related | S_ALR_87013583 - Budget/Actual/Variance |
| | S_ALR_87013584 - Budget/Actual/Commitment |
| Revenues and Earnings Hierarchical | S_ALR_87013585 - Plan/Actual/Variance |
| | S_ALR_87013586 - Planned Contribution Margin |
| | S_ALR_87013587 - Actual Contribution Margin |
| By Cost Element | S_ALR_87013588 - Order Profit |
| | S_ALR_87013589 - Actual/Plan/Variance |
| | S_ALR_87013590 - Current/Cumulative/Total |
| Payments | S_ALR_87013591 - Overview |

| Execute Report | CJE0 - Hierarchy Report |
|---|---|
| | CJEB - Hierarchy Report in Background |
| | GR55 - Cost Element Report |
| **Progress** | CN48N - Confirmations |
| | ACOMPXPD - Progress Tracking Evaluations |
| **Progress Analysis** | CNE5 - Structure Overview |
| | S_ALR_87015124 - Project Hierarchy |
| | S_ALR_87015125 - Details |
| | CNMT - Milestone Trend Analysis |
| **Resources** | CN50N - Capacity Requirements |
| **Capacity Load** | CM01 - Work Center View |
| | CM07 - Variable View |
| | CMP9 - Workforce Planning |
| **Material** | CN52N - Material Components |
| | MD04 - Stock/Requirements |
| | CO24 - Missing Parts |
| | MD09 - Pegged Requirements |
| | MD4C - Order Report |
| | MB25 - Reservations |
| | CN44N - Planned Orders |
| **Purchase Requisitions** | ME5J - For Project |
| | ME5K - For Account Assignment |
| **Purchase Orders** | ME2J - For Project |
| | ME2K - For Account Assignment |
| | ME3K - Outline Agreements |
| | MBBS - Valuated Project Stock |

## Summary

There are other generic tools available for projects. Those described in this chapter are the main ones affecting PS, and you should consider learning others such as the Report Writer/Painter or ABAP Quick Query if you need to customize the standard reports or retrieve data that is not covered in standard functions. Also consider the use of simple table reviews such as SE16n, where you may review the content of tables. SE38 works well for seeing the full PS structure (PSJ).

# 7

# CHAPTER

# Technical Information

This chapter provides handy reference for Transaction Codes, Tables (Project Definition and WBS only), and the IMG itself (in its entirety). Note that Configuration Transaction Codes are covered in Chapter 5. Only Operational Transaction Codes are listed here.

## Transaction Codes (Operational)

Transaction Codes beginning with CJ are generally attributed to Project WBS Elements and associated processes.

Transaction Codes beginning with CN are generally attributed to Project Networks and associated processes.

These codes are entered in the dialogue box at the top of the SAP Easy Access screen—usually you just enter the code, press ENTER, and are presented with the process.

Note that you <u>cannot</u> just enter the transaction code when you are already in a process—you can only do that when you are at the Easy Access menu level. To achieve the loading of a new process from within another, enter the prefix /N (for example, /NCJ20N). Remember—when you do use the /N option, the old session is closed without any regard to data changes you may have made in the old session, so be careful.

To open a new session entirely (in parallel to the one you are running), enter the prefix /O (for example, /OCJ20N)—this will open a new session, leaving the old one running and accessible as a separate Windows session.

## CJ and CN Sorted by Code

| TCode | Transaction Text |
|-------|------------------|
| CJ00  | Find Digital Signatures |
| CJ01  | Create Work Breakdown Structure |
| CJ02  | Change Work Breakdown Structure |
| CJ03  | Display Work Breakdown Structure |
| CJ06  | Create Project Definition |
| CJ07  | Change Project Definition |
| CJ08  | Display Project Definition |
| CJ11  | Create WBS Element |
| CJ12  | Change WBS Element |
| CJ13  | Display WBS Element |
| CJ14  | Display WBS Element (From DMS) |
| CJ20  | Structure Planning |
| CJ20N | Project Builder |
| CJ21  | Change Basic Dates |
| CJ22  | Display Basic Dates |
| CJ23  | Change Forecast Dates |
| CJ24  | Display Forecast Dates |
| CJ25  | Change Actual Dates |
| CJ26  | Display Actual Dates |
| CJ27  | Project Planning Board |
| CJ29  | Update WBS (Forecast) |
| CJ2A  | Display Structure Planning |
| CJ2B  | Change Project Planning Board |
| CJ2C  | Display Project Planning Board |
| CJ2D  | Structure Planning |
| CJ30  | Change Project Original Budget |
| CJ31  | Display Project Original Budget |
| CJ32  | Change Project Release |
| CJ33  | Display Project Release |
| CJ34  | Project Budget Transfer |
| CJ35  | Budget Return from Project |
| CJ36  | Budget Supplement to Project |
| CJ37  | Budget Supplement in Project |
| CJ38  | Budget Return in Project |
| CJ3A  | Change Budget Document |

| TCode | Transaction Text |
|-------|------------------|
| CJ3B | Display Budget Document |
| CJ40 | Change Project Plan |
| CJ41 | Display Project Plan |
| CJ42 | Change Project Revenues |
| CJ43 | Display Project Revenues |
| CJ44 | Act. overhd: Projects, Ind. Process. |
| CJ45 | Act. ovhd: Projects, Coll. Process. |
| CJ46 | Plnd ovrhd: Projects, Ind. Process. |
| CJ47 | Pld Overhead: Projects, Coll.Procssg |
| CJ48 | Change Payment Planning: Init.Screen |
| CJ49 | Display Payment Planning: Init.Scrn |
| CJ70 | Maintain Project Settlement LIs |
| CJ72 | Project: Act. amt. line item settlmt |
| CJ74 | Project Actual Cost Line Items |
| CJ76 | Project Commitment Line Items |
| CJ7E | Plan Data Transfer: Projects |
| CJ7G | Plan Data Transfer: Projects |
| CJ7M | Project Plan Cost Line Items |
| CJ7N | Maint. DRG Inv.Projects for Retmt. |
| CJ80 | Availability Control—Overview |
| CJ81 | Update Report List |
| CJ88 | Settle Projects and Networks |
| CJ8A | Act.-Setlmt: Proj. Retirmt. from IM |
| CJ8G | Actual Settlement: Projects/Networks |
| CJ8V | Period Close for Project Selection |
| CJ91 | Create Standard WBS |
| CJ92 | Change Standard WBS |
| CJ93 | Display Standard WBS |
| CJ9B | Copy WBS Plan to Plan (Collective) |
| CJ9B_OLD | Copy Project Cost Planning (Old) |
| CJ9BS | Copy WBS Plan to Plan (Indiv.) |
| CJ9C | Copy WBS Actual to Plan (Collective) |
| CJ9C_OLD | Copy Project Revenue Planning (Old) |
| CJ9CS | Copy WBS Actual to Plan (Indiv.) |
| CJ9D | Copy Plan Versions |
| CJ9E | Plan Settlement: Projects |

| TCode | Transaction Text |
|-------|------------------|
| CJ9ECP | Project System: Easy Cost Planning |
| CJ9F | Copy Project Costing (Collective) |
| CJ9FS | Copy Project Costing (Indiv.) |
| CJ9G | Plan Settlement: Projects |
| CJ9K | Network Costing |
| CJ9L | Forecast Costs: Individual Projects |
| CJ9M | Forecast Costs: Coll.Project Proc. |
| CJ9Q | Integrated Planning for Ntwks(Coll.) |
| CJ9QS | Integrated Planning for Ntwks (Ind.) |
| CJA1 | Proj.Rel.Order Receipts: Coll.Proc. |
| CJA2 | Proj.Rel. Order Receipts: Ind.Proc. |
| CJAL | Send Project |
| CJB1 | Generate Settlmt Rule: Coll.Proc. |
| CJB2 | Generate Settlmt Rule: Indiv.Proc. |
| CJBBS1 | Planning Board Report Assignment |
| CJBBS2 | Structure Overview Report Asst |
| CJBN | Reconstruct Availability Control |
| CJBV | Activate Project Availabilty Control |
| CJBW | Deactivate Project Availabilty Cntrl |
| CJC1 | Maintenance Dialog for Stat.by Per. |
| CJC2 | Maintain Planned Status Changes |
| CJCD | Change Documents: WBS |
| CJCF | Carry Forward Project Commitments |
| CJCO | Carry Forward Project Budget |
| CJCS | Standard WBS |
| CJE0 | Run Hierarchy Report |
| CJE1 | Create Hierarchy Report |
| CJE2 | Change Hierarchy Report |
| CJE3 | Display Hierarchy Report |
| CJE4 | Create Project Report Layout |
| CJE5 | Change Project Report Layout |
| CJE6 | Display Project Report Layout |
| CJEA | Call Hierarchy Report |
| CJEB | Background Processing, Hier.Reports |
| CJEC | Maintain Project Crcy Trans.Type |
| CJEK | Copy Interfaces/Reports |

| TCode | Transaction Text |
|-------|------------------|
| CJEM | Project Reports: Test Monitor |
| CJEN | Reconstruct: Summarized Proj.Data |
| CJEO | Transport Reports |
| CJEP | Transport Forms |
| CJEQ | Import Reports from Client |
| CJET | Translation Tool—Drilldown |
| CJEV | Maintain Global Variable |
| CJEX | Reorganize Drilldown Reports |
| CJEY | Reorganize Report Data |
| CJEZ | Reorganize Forms |
| CJF1 | Create Transfer Price Agreement |
| CJF2 | Change Transfer Price Agreement |
| CJF3 | Display Transfer Price Agreement |
| CJF4 | Transfer Price Agreement List |
| CJFA | Analysis of Data Trans. into PS Cash |
| CJFN | CBM Payment Converter |
| CJG1 | Enter Transfer Price Allocation |
| CJG3 | Display Transfer Price Allocation |
| CJG4 | Enter Trsfr Price Allocation: List |
| CJG5 | Cancel Transfer Price Allocation |
| CJH1 | Reconstruct Project Inheritance |
| CJH2 | Project Inheritance Log |
| CJI1 | Project Budget Line Items |
| CJI2 | Budget Line Items: Document Chain |
| CJI3 | Project Actual Cost Line Items |
| CJI4 | Project Plan Cost Line Items |
| CJI5 | Project Commitment Line Items |
| CJI8 | Project Budget Line Items |
| CJI9 | Project Struct.Pld Costs Line Items |
| CJIA | Project Actual and Commt Paymt LIs |
| CJIB | Project Plan Payment Line Items |
| CJIC | Maintain Project Settlement LIs |
| CJID | Display Project Settlement Line Itms |
| CJIE | Projects: Retirement LI Settlement |
| CJIF | Projects: Profitability Analysis LI |
| CJIG | Display PS Cash Documents |

| TCode | Transaction Text |
|-------|------------------|
| CJJ2 | Change Statistical Key Figures |
| CJJ3 | Display Statistical Key Figures |
| CJK2 | Change Statistical Key Figures |
| CJK3 | Display Statistical Key Figures |
| CJL2 | Collective Agreement |
| CJN1 | Reval. ACT: Projects Ind.Pro. |
| CJN2 | Reval. ACT: Projects Col.Pro. |
| CJNO | Number Range Maintenance: FMCJ_BELNR |
| CJO8 | Overhead COMM: Projects Ind.Pro. |
| CJO9 | Overhead COMM: Projects Col.Pro. |
| CJP1 | Create Project Plan Adjustment |
| CJP2 | Change Project Plan Adjustment |
| CJP3 | Display Project Plan Adjustment |
| CJP4 | Delete Project Plan Adjustment |
| CJPN | Number Range Maintenance: Proj.Items |
| CJPU | Execute Project Plan Adjustment |
| CJR2 | PS: Change Plan CElem/Activ. Input |
| CJR3 | PS: Display Plan CElem/Activ. Input |
| CJR4 | PS: Change Plan Primary Cost Element |
| CJR5 | PS: Display Plan Primary Cost Element |
| CJR6 | PS: Change Activity Input Planning |
| CJR7 | PS: Display Activity Input Planning |
| CJR8 | PS: Change Revenue Type Planning |
| CJR9 | PS: Display Revenue Element Planning |
| CJS2 | PS: Change Stat. Key Figure Planning |
| CJS3 | PS: Display Stat. Key Figure Planning |
| CJS4 | PS: Change Stat. Key Figure Planning |
| CJS5 | PS: Display Stat. Key Figure Planning |
| CJSA | Data Transfer to SAP-EIS |
| CJSB | Select Key Figure and Characteristic |
| CJSG | Generate WBS Element Group |
| CJSN | Number Range Maintenance: Projects |
| CJT2 | Project Actual Payment Line Items |
| CJV1 | Create Project Version (simulation) |
| CJV2 | Change Project Version (simulation) |
| CJV3 | Display Project Version (simulation) |

| TCode | Transaction Text |
|-------|------------------|
| CJV4 | Transfer Project |
| CJV5 | Delete Simulation Version |
| CJV6 | Maintenance: Version administration |
| CJV7 | Display Transfer Log |
| CJVC | Value Category Checking Program |
| CJW1 | EURO: Adjust Project Budget |
| CJZ1 | Act. Int.Calc.: Projects Coll. Prc. |
| CJZ2 | Actual Int.Calc.: Project Indiv.Prc. |
| CJZ3 | Plan Int.Calc.: Project Indiv.Prc. |
| CJZ5 | Plan Int.Calc.: Project Coll.Prc. |
| CJZ6 | Actual Int.Calc.: Indiv.CO Order Prc |
| CJZ7 | Planned Int.Calc: Indiv.CO Ord.Prc. |
| CJZ8 | Actual Int.Calc.: Coll.CO Order Prc. |
| CJZ9 | Plan Int.Calc.: Coll.CO Order Prc. |
| CN01 | Create Standard Network |
| CN02 | Change Standard Network |
| CN03 | Display Standard Network |
| CN04 | Edit PS Text Catalog |
| CN05 | Display PS Text Catalog |
| CN06 | MPX Download: Standard Network |
| CN07 | MPX Upload: Standard Network |
| CN08 | Allocate Material -> Stand. Network |
| CN09 | Allocate Material -> Stand. Network |
| CN11 | Create Standard Milestone |
| CN12 | Change Standard Milestone |
| CN13 | Display Standard Milestone |
| CN19 | Display Activity (From DMS) |
| CN20 | Dsply Network/act.bsc data init.scrn |
| CN21 | Create Network |
| CN22 | Change Network |
| CN23 | Display Network |
| CN24 | Overall Network Scheduling |
| CN24N | Overall Network Scheduling |
| CN25 | Confirm Completions in Network |
| CN26 | Display Mat.Comp/Init: Ntwk,Acty,Itm |
| CN26N | Display Mat. Components (From DMS) |

| TCode | Transaction Text |
|-------|------------------|
| CN27 | Collective Confirm. |
| CN28 | Display Network Confirmations |
| CN29 | Cancel Network Confirmation |
| CN2X | Confirm Completions in Network |
| CN30 | Processing PDC Error Records |
| CN33 | PDM-PS Interface |
| CN34 | Maintain release table TCNRL |
| CN35 | Control Stock/Account Assignment |
| CN36 | BOM Transfer Profile |
| CN37 | BOM Allocation Field Selection |
| CN38 | Maintain Flexible Reference Point |
| CN40 | Project Overview |
| CN41 | Structure Overview |
| CN42 | Overview: Project Definitions |
| CN42N | Overview: Project Definitions |
| CN43 | Overview: WBS Elements |
| CN43N | Overview: WBS Elements |
| CN44 | Overview: Planned Orders |
| CN44N | Overview: Planned Orders |
| CN45 | Overview: Orders |
| CN45N | Overview: Orders |
| CN46 | Overview: Networks |
| CN46N | Overview: Networks |
| CN47 | Overview: Activities/Elements |
| CN47N | Overview: Activities/Elements |
| CN48 | Overview: Confirmations |
| CN48N | Overview: Confirmations |
| CN49 | Overview: Relationships |
| CN49N | Overview: Relationships |
| CN50 | Overview: Capacity Requirements |
| CN50N | Overview: Capacity Requirements |
| CN51 | Overview: PRTs |
| CN51N | Overview: PRTs |
| CN52 | Overview: Components |
| CN52N | Overview: Components |
| CN53 | Overview: Milestones |

| TCode | Transaction Text |
|-------|------------------|
| CN53N | Overview: Milestones |
| CN54N | Overview: Sales Document |
| CN55N | Overview: Sales and Dist. Doc. Items |
| CN60 | Change Documents for Projects/Netw. |
| CN61 | Standard Network |
| CN65 | Change documents Order/Network |
| CN70 | Overview: Batch Variants |
| CN71 | Create Versions |
| CN72 | Create Project Version |
| CN80 | Archiving Project Structures |
| CN81 | PS: Archiving Project—Preliminary |
| CN82 | PS: Archiving Project Structures |
| CN83 | PS: Archiving Project—Info System |
| CN84 | PS: Archiving Project—Admin. |
| CN85 | PS: Delete Operative Structures |
| CN98 | Delete Standard Networks |
| CN99 | Archiving Standard Networks |
| CNB1 | Purchase Requisitions for Project |
| CNB2 | Purchase Orders for Project |
| CNC4 | Consistency Checks for WBS |
| CNC5 | Consistency Checks Sales Order/Proj. |
| CNE1 | Project Progress (Individual Proc.) |
| CNE2 | Project Progress (Collective Proc.) |
| CNE5 | Progress Analysis |
| CNG1 | Netw./Hier.: Maintain Frame Types |
| CNG2 | Netw./Hier.: Maintain Form Def. |
| CNG3 | Netw./hier.: maintain Color Definit. |
| CNG4 | Netw./Hier.: Maintain Graph. Profile |
| CNG5 | Netw./Hier: Maintain Options Profile |
| CNG6 | Netw./hier.: Maintain Node Type |
| CNG7 | Netw./Hier.: Maintain Link Types |
| CNG8 | Netw./Hier.: Maintain Field Def. |
| CNG9 | Graph. Cust. Netw./Hierarchy Graph. |
| CNL1 | Create Delivery Information |
| CNL2 | Change Delivery Information |
| CNL3 | Display Delivery Information |

| TCode | Transaction Text |
|---|---|
| CNMASS | Mass Changes in Project System |
| CNMASSPROT | Display Log f. Mass Changes PS |
| CNMM | Project-Oriented Procurement |
| CNMT | Milestone Trend Analysis |
| CNN0 | Number Range for Library Network |
| CNN1 | Number Range Maint.: ROUTING_0 |
| CNPAR | Partner Overview |
| CNPRG | Network Progress |
| CNR1 | Create Work Center |
| CNR2 | Change Work Center |
| CNR3 | Display Work Center |
| CNS0 | Create Delivery from Project |
| CNS40 | Project Overview |
| CNS41 | Structure Overview |
| CNS42 | Overview: Project Definitions |
| CNS43 | Overview: WBS Elements |
| CNS44 | Overview: Planned Orders |
| CNS45 | Overview: Orders |
| CNS46 | Overview: Networks |
| CNS47 | Overview: Activities/Elements |
| CNS48 | Overview: Confirmations |
| CNS49 | Overview: Relationships |
| CNS50 | Overview: Capacity Requirements |
| CNS51 | Overview: PRTs |
| CNS52 | Overview: Components |
| CNS53 | Overview: Milestones |
| CNS54 | Overview: Sales Document |
| CNS55 | Overview: Sales and Dist. Doc. Items |
| CNS60 | Change Documents for Projects/Netw. |
| CNS71 | Create versions |
| CNS83 | PS: Archiving project—Info System |
| CNSE5 | Progress Analysis |
| CNVL | Variable Overviews |
| CNW1 | WWW: Confirmation |
| CNW4 | Project Documents |

## CJ and CN Sorted by Description

| Transaction Text | TCode |
|---|---|
| Act. Int Calc.: Projects Coll. Proc. | CJZ1 |
| Act. overhd: Projects, Ind. Process. | CJ44 |
| Act. ovhd: Projects, Coll. Process. | CJ45 |
| Act.-setlmt: Proj. Retirmt. from IM | CJ8A |
| Activate Project Availabilty Control | CJBV |
| Actual Int.Calc.: Coll.CO Order Prc. | CJZ8 |
| Actual Int.Calc.: Indiv.CO Order Prc | CJZ6 |
| Actual Int.Calc.: Project Indiv.Prc. | CJZ2 |
| Actual Settlement: Projects/Networks | CJ8G |
| Allocate Material -> Stand. Network | CN08 |
| Allocate Material -> Stand. Network | CN09 |
| Analysis of Data Trans. into PS Cash | CJFA |
| Archiving Project Structures | CN80 |
| Archiving Standard Networks | CN99 |
| Availability Control—Overview | CJ80 |
| Background Processing, Hier.Reports | CJEB |
| BOM Allocation Field Selection | CN37 |
| BOM Transfer Profile | CN36 |
| Budget Line Items: Document Chain | CJI2 |
| Budget Return from Project | CJ35 |
| Budget Return in Project | CJ38 |
| Budget Supplement in Project | CJ37 |
| Budget Supplement to Project | CJ36 |
| Call Hierarchy Report | CJEA |
| Cancel Network Confirmation | CN29 |
| Cancel Transfer Price Allocation | CJG5 |
| Carry Forward Project Budget | CJCO |
| Carry Forward Project Commitments | CJCF |
| CBM Payment Converter | CJFN |
| Change Actual Dates | CJ25 |
| Change Basic Dates | CJ21 |
| Change Budget Document | CJ3A |
| Change Delivery Information | CNL2 |
| Change Documents for Projects/Netw. | CN60 |
| Change Documents for Projects/Netw. | CNS60 |

| Transaction Text | TCode |
|---|---|
| Change Documents Order/Network | CN65 |
| Change Documents: WBS | CJCD |
| Change Forecast Dates | CJ23 |
| Change Hierarchy Report | CJE2 |
| Change Network | CN22 |
| Change Payment Planning: Init.Screen | CJ48 |
| Change Project Definition | CJ07 |
| Change Project Original Budget | CJ30 |
| Change Project Plan | CJ40 |
| Change Project Plan Adjustment | CJP2 |
| Change Project Planning Board | CJ2B |
| Change Project Release | CJ32 |
| Change Project Report Layout | CJE5 |
| Change Project Revenues | CJ42 |
| Change Project Version (simulation) | CJV2 |
| Change Standard Milestone | CN12 |
| Change Standard Network | CN02 |
| Change Standard WBS | CJ92 |
| Change Statistical Key Figures | CJJ2 |
| Change Statistical Key Figures | CJK2 |
| Change Transfer Price Agreement | CJF2 |
| Change WBS Element | CJ12 |
| Change Work Breakdown Structure | CJ02 |
| Change Work Center | CNR2 |
| Collective Agreement | CJL2 |
| Collective Confirm. | CN27 |
| Confirm Completions in Network | CN25 |
| Confirm Completions in Network | CN2X |
| Consistency Checks for WBS | CNC4 |
| Consistency Checks Sales Order/Proj. | CNC5 |
| Control Stock/Account Assignment | CN35 |
| Copy Interfaces/Reports | CJEK |
| Copy Plan Versions | CJ9D |
| Copy Project Cost Planning (Old) | CJ9B_OLD |
| Copy Project Costing (Collective) | CJ9F |
| Copy Project Costing (Indiv.) | CJ9FS |

| Transaction Text | TCode |
|---|---|
| Copy Project Revenue Planning (old) | CJ9C_OLD |
| Copy WBS Actual to Plan (Collective) | CJ9C |
| Copy WBS Actual to Plan (Indiv.) | CJ9CS |
| Copy WBS Plan to Plan (Collective) | CJ9B |
| Copy WBS Plan to Plan (Indiv.) | CJ9BS |
| Create Delivery from Project | CNS0 |
| Create Delivery Information | CNL1 |
| Create Hierarchy Report | CJE1 |
| Create Network | CN21 |
| Create Project Definition | CJ06 |
| Create Project Plan Adjustment | CJP1 |
| Create Project Report Layout | CJE4 |
| Create Project Version | CN72 |
| Create Project Version (simulation) | CJV1 |
| Create Standard Milestone | CN11 |
| Create Standard Network | CN01 |
| Create Standard WBS | CJ91 |
| Create Transfer Price Agreement | CJF1 |
| Create Versions | CN71 |
| Create Versions | CNS71 |
| Create WBS Element | CJ11 |
| Create Work Breakdown Structure | CJ01 |
| Create Work Center | CNR1 |
| Data Transfer to SAP-EIS | CJSA |
| Deactivate Project Availability Cntrl | CJBW |
| Delete Project Plan Adjustment | CJP4 |
| Delete Simulation Version | CJV5 |
| Delete Standard Networks | CN98 |
| Display Activity (From DMS) | CN19 |
| Display Actual Dates | CJ26 |
| Display Basic Dates | CJ22 |
| Display Budget Document | CJ3B |
| Display Delivery Information | CNL3 |
| Display Forecast Dates | CJ24 |
| Display Hierarchy Report | CJE3 |
| Display Log f. Mass Changes PS | CNMASSPROT |

| Transaction Text | TCode |
|---|---|
| Display Mat. Components (From DMS) | CN26N |
| Display Mat.Comp/Init: Ntwk,Acty,Itm | CN26 |
| Display Network | CN23 |
| Display Network Confirmations | CN28 |
| Display Payment Planning: Init.Scrn | CJ49 |
| Display Project Definition | CJ08 |
| Display Project Original Budget | CJ31 |
| Display Project Plan | CJ41 |
| Display Project Plan Adjustment | CJP3 |
| Display Project Planning Board | CJ2C |
| Display Project Release | CJ33 |
| Display Project Report Layout | CJE6 |
| Display Project Revenues | CJ43 |
| Display Project Settlement Line Itms | CJID |
| Display Project Version (simulation) | CJV3 |
| Display PS Cash Documents | CJIG |
| Display PS Text Catalog | CN05 |
| Display Standard Milestone | CN13 |
| Display Standard Network | CN03 |
| Display Standard WBS | CJ93 |
| Display Statistical Key Figures | CJJ3 |
| Display Statistical Key Figures | CJK3 |
| Display Structure Planning | CJ2A |
| Display Transfer Log | CJV7 |
| Display Transfer Price Agreement | CJF3 |
| Display Transfer Price Allocation | CJG3 |
| Display WBS Element | CJ13 |
| Display WBS Element (From DMS) | CJ14 |
| Display Work Breakdown Structure | CJ03 |
| Display Work Center | CNR3 |
| Dsply Network/act.bsc data init.scrn | CN20 |
| Edit PS Text Catalog | CN04 |
| Enter Transfer Price Allocation | CJG1 |
| Enter Trsfr Price Allocation: List | CJG4 |
| EURO: Adjust Project Budget | CJW1 |
| Execute Project Plan Adjustment | CJPU |

| Transaction Text | TCode |
|---|---|
| Find Digital Signatures | CJ00 |
| Forecast Costs: Coll.Project Proc. | CJ9M |
| Forecast Costs: Individual Projects | CJ9L |
| Generate Settlmt Rule: Coll.Proc. | CJB1 |
| Generate Settlmt Rule: Indiv.Proc. | CJB2 |
| Generate WBS Element Group | CJSG |
| Graph. Cust. Netw./Hierarchy Graph. | CNG9 |
| Import Reports from Client | CJEQ |
| Integrated Planning for Ntwks (Ind.) | CJ9QS |
| Integrated Planning for Ntwks (Coll.) | CJ9Q |
| Maint. DRG Inv.Projects for Retmt. | CJ7N |
| Maintain Flexible Reference Point | CN38 |
| Maintain Global Variable | CJEV |
| Maintain Planned Status Changes | CJC2 |
| Maintain Project Crcy Trans.Type | CJEC |
| Maintain Project Settlement LIs | CJ70 |
| Maintain Project Settlement LIs | CJIC |
| Maintain Release Table TCNRL | CN34 |
| Maintenance Dialog for Stat. by Per. | CJC1 |
| Maintenance: Version Administration | CJV6 |
| Mass Changes in Project System | CNMASS |
| Milestone Trend Analysis | CNMT |
| MPX Download: Standard Network | CN06 |
| MPX Upload: Standard Network | CN07 |
| Netw./hier.: Maintain Color Definit. | CNG3 |
| Netw./Hier.: Maintain Field Def. | CNG8 |
| Netw./Hier.: Maintain Form Def. | CNG2 |
| Netw./Hier.: Maintain Frame Types | CNG1 |
| Netw./Hier.: Maintain Graph. Profile | CNG4 |
| Netw./Hier.: Maintain Link Types | CNG7 |
| Netw./Hier.: Maintain Node Type | CNG6 |
| Netw./Hier: Maintain Options Profile | CNG5 |
| Network Costing | CJ9K |
| Network Progress | CNPRG |
| Number Range for Library Network | CNN0 |
| Number Range Maint.: ROUTING_0 | CNN1 |

| Transaction Text | TCode |
|---|---|
| Number Range Maintenance: FMCJ_BELNR | CJNO |
| Number Range Maintenance: Proj.Items | CJPN |
| Number Range Maintenance: Projects | CJSN |
| Overall Network Scheduling | CN24 |
| Overall Network Scheduling | CN24N |
| Overhead  COMM: Projects    Col.Pro. | CJO9 |
| Overhead  COMM: Projects    Ind.Pro. | CJO8 |
| Overview: Activities/Elements | CN47 |
| Overview: Activities/Elements | CN47N |
| Overview: Activities/Elements | CNS47 |
| Overview: Batch variants | CN70 |
| Overview: Capacity Requirements | CN50 |
| Overview: Capacity Requirements | CN50N |
| Overview: Capacity Requirements | CNS50 |
| Overview: Components | CN52 |
| Overview: Components | CN52N |
| Overview: Components | CNS52 |
| Overview: Confirmations | CN48 |
| Overview: Confirmations | CN48N |
| Overview: Confirmations | CNS48 |
| Overview: Milestones | CN53 |
| Overview: Milestones | CN53N |
| Overview: Milestones | CNS53 |
| Overview: Networks | CN46 |
| Overview: Networks | CN46N |
| Overview: Networks | CNS46 |
| Overview: Orders | CN45 |
| Overview: Orders | CN45N |
| Overview: Orders | CNS45 |
| Overview: Planned Orders | CN44 |
| Overview: Planned Orders | CN44N |
| Overview: Planned Orders | CNS44 |
| Overview: Project Definitions | CN42 |
| Overview: Project Definitions | CN42N |
| Overview: Project Definitions | CNS42 |
| Overview: PRTs | CN51 |

| Transaction Text | TCode |
|---|---|
| Overview: PRTs | CN51N |
| Overview: PRTs | CNS51 |
| Overview: Relationships | CN49 |
| Overview: Relationships | CN49N |
| Overview: Relationships | CNS49 |
| Overview: Sales and Dist. Doc. Items | CN55N |
| Overview: Sales and Dist. Doc. Items | CNS55 |
| Overview: Sales Document | CN54N |
| Overview: Sales Document | CNS54 |
| Overview: WBS Elements | CN43 |
| Overview: WBS Elements | CN43N |
| Overview: WBS Elements | CNS43 |
| Partner Overview | CNPAR |
| PDM-PS Interface | CN33 |
| Period Close for Project Selection | CJ8V |
| Plan Data Transfer: Projects | CJ7E |
| Plan Data Transfer: Projects | CJ7G |
| Plan Int.Calc.: Coll.CO Order Prc. | CJZ9 |
| Plan Int.Calc.: Project Coll.Prc. | CJZ5 |
| Plan Int.Calc.: Project Indiv.Prc. | CJZ3 |
| Plan Settlement: Projects | CJ9E |
| Plan Settlement: Projects | CJ9G |
| Planned Int.Calc: Indiv.CO Ord.Proc. | CJZ7 |
| Planning Board Report Assignment | CJBBS1 |
| Plnd Overhead: Projects, Coll.Process. | CJ47 |
| Plnd Overhead: Projects, Ind. Process. | CJ46 |
| Processing PDC Error Records | CN30 |
| Progress Analysis | CNE5 |
| Progress Analysis | CNSE5 |
| Proj.Rel. Order Receipts: Ind.Proc. | CJA2 |
| Proj.Rel.Order Receipts: Coll.Proc. | CJA1 |
| Project Actual and Commt Paymt LIs | CJIA |
| Project Actual Cost Line Items | CJ74 |
| Project Actual Cost Line Items | CJI3 |
| Project Actual Payment Line Items | CJT2 |
| Project Budget Line Items | CJI1 |

| Transaction Text | TCode |
|---|---|
| Project Budget Line Items | CJI8 |
| Project Budget Transfer | CJ34 |
| Project Builder | CJ20N |
| Project Commitment Line Items | CJ76 |
| Project Commitment Line Items | CJI5 |
| Project Documents | CNW4 |
| Project Inheritance Log | CJH2 |
| Project Overview | CN40 |
| Project Overview | CNS40 |
| Project Plan Cost Line Items | CJ7M |
| Project Plan Cost Line Items | CJI4 |
| Project Plan Payment Line Items | CJIB |
| Project Planning Board | CJ27 |
| Project Progress (Collective Proc.) | CNE2 |
| Project Progress (Individual Proc.) | CNE1 |
| Project Reports: Test Monitor | CJEM |
| Project Struct.Pld Costs Line Items | CJI9 |
| Project System: Easy Cost Planning | CJ9ECP |
| Project: Act. Amt. Line Item Settlmt | CJ72 |
| Project-Oriented Procurement | CNMM |
| Projects: Profitability Analysis LI | CJIF |
| Projects: Retirement LI Settlement | CJIE |
| PS: Archiving Project - Admin. | CN84 |
| PS: Archiving Project - Info System | CN83 |
| PS: Archiving Project - Info System | CNS83 |
| PS: Archiving Project - Preliminary | CN81 |
| PS: Archiving Project Structures | CN82 |
| PS: Change Activity Input Planning | CJR6 |
| PS: Change Plan CElem/Activ. Input | CJR2 |
| PS: Change Plan Primary Cost Element | CJR4 |
| PS: Change Revenue Type Planning | CJR8 |
| PS: Change Stat. Key Figure Planning | CJS2 |
| PS: Change Stat. Key Figure Planning | CJS4 |
| PS: Delete Operative Structures | CN85 |
| PS: Display Activity Input Planning | CJR7 |
| PS: Display Plan CElem/Activ. Input | CJR3 |

| Transaction Text | TCode |
|---|---|
| PS: Display Plan Primary Cost Elem. | CJR5 |
| PS: Display Revenue Element Planning | CJR9 |
| PS: Display Stat. Key Fig. Planning | CJS3 |
| PS: Display Stat. Key Fig. Planning | CJS5 |
| Purchase Orders for Project | CNB2 |
| Purchase Requisitions for Project | CNB1 |
| Reconstruct Availability Control | CJBN |
| Reconstruct Project Inheritance | CJH1 |
| Reconstruct: Summarized Proj.Data | CJEN |
| Reorganize Drilldown Reports | CJEX |
| Reorganize Forms | CJEZ |
| Reorganize Report Data | CJEY |
| Reval.   ACT: Projects   Col.Pro. | CJN2 |
| Reval.   ACT: Projects   Ind.Pro. | CJN1 |
| Run Hierarchy Report | CJE0 |
| Select Key Figure and Characteristic | CJSB |
| Send Project | CJAL |
| Settle Projects and Networks | CJ88 |
| Standard Network | CN61 |
| Standard WBS | CJCS |
| Structure Overview | CN41 |
| Structure Overview | CNS41 |
| Structure Overview Report Asst | CJBBS2 |
| Structure Planning | CJ20 |
| Structure Planning | CJ2D |
| Transfer Price Agreement List | CJF4 |
| Transfer Project | CJV4 |
| Translation Tool—Drilldown | CJET |
| Transport Forms | CJEP |
| Transport Reports | CJEO |
| Update Report List | CJ81 |
| Update WBS (Forecast) | CJ29 |
| Value Category Checking Program | CJVC |
| Variable Overviews | CNVL |
| WWW: Confirmation | CNW1 |

## Tables

Following is a list of the most commonly used Tables in PS. Displaying contents can be achieved in a few ways:

- SE36 to view in ABAP Query
- SE80 to show all table relationships
- SE11 to view a Structure
- SE16/n to view an SAP Table

## General Tables

### Master Data Tables

| PROJ | Project Definition |
|------|-------------------|
| PRPS | WBS Elements |
| PRTE | WBS Scheduling Data |
| PRHI | WBS Hierarchy |
| AUFK | Orders/Network Headers |
| AFKO | Order Header Data PP Orders |
| AFVC | Operation Within an Order |
| AFVU | DB Structure of the User Fields of the Operation |
| AFVV | DB Structure of the Quantities/Dates/Values in the Operation |
| RESB | Reservation/Dependent Requirements |
| MLST | Milestones |

### Transactional Data Tables

| RPSCO | Project Info Database: Costs, Revenues, Finances |
|-------|--------------------------------------------------|
| RPSQT | Project Info Database: Quantities |
| COSP | CO Object: Cost Totals for External Postings |
| COSS | CO Object: Cost Totals for Internal Postings |
| COSB | CO Object: Total Variances/Results Analyses |
| COBK | CO Object: Document Header |
| COEP | CO Object: Line Items (by Period) |
| COOI | Commitments Management: Line Items |
| COEJ | CO Object: Line Items (by Fiscal Year) |
| BPGE | Totals Record for Total Value Controlling obj. |
| BPJA | Totals Record for Annual Total Controlling Obj. |
| QBEW | Project Stock Valuation |
| MSPR | Project Stock |
| CATSDB | CATS Time-Sheets |

## Miscellaneous Tables

| | |
|---|---|
| CKHS | Easy Cost Planning Header |
| CKHT | Texts for CKHS |
| CKIS | Easy Cost Planning Detail |
| CKIT | Easy Cost Planning Text for CKIS |
| CKCM | Cost Model |
| CKCMC | Cost Model Characteristics |
| CKCMCT | Characteristics of a Costing Model—Texts |
| CKCMT | Name for the Costing Model |
| CKCMV | Costing Model: Model Valuation |
| KEKO | Product Costing—Header Data |
| CKHS | Header: Unit Costing (Control + Totals) |
| CKIS | Items Unit Costing/Itemization Product Costing |
| CKIT | Texts for CKIS |
| VBAK | Sales Order Header |
| VBAP | Sale Order Line Items |
| RPSCO | Structure Planning |
| DPPROFH | DIP Profiles Header |
| TKA09 | Plan Versions |
| CSLA | Activity Types |
| CSKS | Cost Centers |
| JEST | Object (Project) Current Status |
| JCDS | Status History |

## Table Fields

### Project Definition

| Description | Field | Data Element | Type | Length |
|---|---|---|---|---|
| Client | MANDT | MANDT | CLNT | 3 |
| Project Definition (Internal) | PSPNR | PS_INTNR | NUMC | 8 |
| PS: Data Portion of Project Definition Include | .INCLUDE | PROJ_INC | STRU | 0 |
| Project Definition | PSPID | PS_PSPID | CHAR | 24 |
| PS: Data Portion of Project Definition Include | .INCLUDE | PROJ2_INC | STRU | 0 |
| PS: Short Description (1st text line) | POST1 | PS_POST1 | CHAR | 40 |
| Object Number | OBJNR | J_OBJNR | CHAR | 22 |
| Name of Person Who Created the Object | ERNAM | ERNAM | CHAR | 12 |
| Date on Which the Record was Created | ERDAT | ERDAT | DATS | 8 |
| Name of Person Who Changed Object | AENAM | AENAM | CHAR | 12 |
| Date on Which Object was Last Changed | AEDAT | UPDAT | DATS | 8 |
| Selection Mask for WBS Element Short IDs | KIMSK | PS_KIMSK | CHAR | 24 |
| Automatic Value Transfer from WBS Element to Project Def. | AUTOD | PS_AUTOD | CHAR | 1 |
| Status Profile for Project Definition | STSPD | PS_STSPD | CHAR | 8 |
| Status Profile for WBS Element | STSPR | PS_STSPR | CHAR | 8 |
| Number of the Responsible Person (Project Manager) | VERNR | PS_VERNR | NUMC | 8 |
| Name of Responsible Person (Project Manager) | VERNA | PS_VERNA | CHAR | 25 |
| Applicant Number | ASTNR | PS_ASTNR | NUMC | 8 |
| Applicant | ASTNA | PS_ASTNA | CHAR | 25 |
| Company Code for the Project | VBUKR | PS_VBUKR | CHAR | 4 |
| Business Area for the Project | VGSBR | PS_VGSBR | CHAR | 4 |
| Controlling Area for the Project | VKOKR | PS_VKOKR | CHAR | 4 |
| Profit Center | PRCTR | PRCTR | CHAR | 10 |
| WBS Currency (Project Definition) | PWHIE | PS_PWHIE | CUKY | 5 |
| Network Assignment | ZUORD | PS_ZUORD | NUMC | 1 |
| Indicator: WBS Dates Detailed by Activity Dates | TRMEQ | PS_TRMEQ | CHAR | 1 |
| Project Planned Start Date | PLFAZ | PS_PLFAZ | DATS | 8 |
| Project Planned Finish Date | PLSEZ | PS_PLSEZ | DATS | 8 |
| Plant | WERKS | WERKS_D | CHAR | 4 |
| Factory Calendar Key | KALID | FABKL | CHAR | 2 |
| Planning Method for Project Basic Dates | VGPLF | PS_VGPLF | NUMC | 1 |

| Description | Field | Data Element | Type | Length |
|---|---|---|---|---|
| Planning Method for Project Forecast Dates | EWPLF | PS_EWPLF | NUMC | 1 |
| Time Unit in Time Scheduling | ZTEHT | PS_ZTEHT | UNIT | 3 |
| Indicator: Network Header Visible to End User | NZANZ | NETZOBERFL | CHAR | 1 |
| Application of the Task List | PLNAW | PLNAW | CHAR | 1 |
| Network Profile | VPROF | PROFIDNZPL | CHAR | 7 |
| Project Profile | PROFL | PROFIDPROJ | CHAR | 7 |
| Budget Profile | BPROF | BP_BPROFIL | CHAR | 6 |
| Language Key | TXTSP | SPRAS | LANG | 1 |
| Cost Center | KOSTL | KOSTL | CHAR | 10 |
| Cost Object | KTRG | KSTRG | CHAR | 12 |
| Date of Last Scheduling of the Overall Network (Basic Dates) | AEDTE | PS_AEDTE | DATS | 8 |
| Date of Last Scheduling of the Overall Network (Forecast) | AEDTP | PS_AEDTP | DATS | 8 |
| Authorization Key for Project Master Data | BERST | PS_BERST | CHAR | 16 |
| Authorization Key for Project Dates (WBS) | BERTR | PS_BERTR | CHAR | 16 |
| Authorization Key for Costs and Revenues | BERKO | PS_BERKO | CHAR | 16 |
| Authorization Key for Project Budget | BERBU | PS_BERBU | CHAR | 16 |
| Current Number for Standard Project | SPSNR | PS_ISPSP | NUMC | 8 |
| Project stock | BESTA | PS_BESTAND | CHAR | 1 |
| Object Class | SCOPE | SCOPE_CV | CHAR | 2 |
| Statistical WBS Element | XSTAT | PS_XSTAT | CHAR | 1 |
| Tax Jurisdiction | TXJCD | TXJCD | CHAR | 15 |
| Interest Profile for Project/Order Interest Calculation | ZSCHM | PS_ZSCHM | CHAR | 7 |
| Profile for WBS Scheduling | SCPRF | PS_SCHDPRF | CHAR | 12 |
| Investment Measure Profile | IMPRF | IM_PROFIL | CHAR | 6 |
| Payment Plan Profile | FMPRF | PSFM_PRF | CHAR | 6 |
| Results Analysis Key | ABGSL | ABGR_SCHL | CHAR | 6 |
| PS: Short Description (1st text line) in All Caps | POSTU | PS_POSTU | CHAR | 40 |
| Planning Profile | PPROF | BP_PPROFIL | CHAR | 6 |
| Indicator for Integrated Planning | PLINT | PLINT | CHAR | 1 |
| Deletion Indicator | LOEVM | LOEVM | CHAR | 1 |
| Indicator: Project Definition Inactive | INACT | PS_INACT | CHAR | 1 |
| Valuation of Special Stock | KZBWS | KZBWS | CHAR | 1 |
| Simulation Profile | SMPRF | SIM_PROFIL | CHAR | 7 |

| Description | Field | Data Element | Type | Length |
|---|---|---|---|---|
| Indicator: Bottom-up Calculation with Activity Dates | FLGVRG | PS_FLGVRG | CHAR | 1 |
| Indicator: Automatic Requirements Grouping | GRTOP | GRONTOP | CHAR | 1 |
| Distribution Profile | PGPRF | PGPROFID | CHAR | 6 |
| Location | STORT | PS_STORT | CHAR | 10 |
| Logical System | LOGSYSTEM | LOGSYSTEM | CHAR | 10 |
| Indicator: Project Summarization via Master Data Charact. | KZERB | PS_KZERB | CHAR | 1 |
| Partner Determination Procedure | PARGR | PARGR | CHAR | 4 |
| Functional Area | FUNC_AREA | FKBER | CHAR | 16 |
| Sales Organization | VKORG | VKORG | CHAR | 4 |
| Distribution Channel | VTWEG | VTWEG | CHAR | 2 |
| Division | SPART | SPART | CHAR | 2 |
| Dynamic Item Processor Profile | DPPPROF | AD01PROFNR | CHAR | 8 |
| Node level | VPKSTU | SEU_LEVEL | NUMC | 2 |
| Project Number (External) Edited | PSPID_EDIT | PS_PSPID_EDIT | CHAR | 24 |
| JV data: (vname,recid,etype),otype,jibcl,jibsa | .INCLUDE | GJV_DATA_3 | STRU | 0 |
| General Assignments of Application Objects | .INCLUDE | GJV_DATA_0 | STRU | 0 |
| Joint Venture | VNAME | JV_NAME | CHAR | 6 |
| Recovery Indicator | RECID | JV_RECIND | CHAR | 2 |
| Equity Type | ETYPE | JV_ETYPE | CHAR | 3 |
| Joint Venture Object Type | OTYPE | JV_OTYPE | CHAR | 4 |
| JIB/JIBE Class | JIBCL | JV_JIBCL | CHAR | 3 |
| JIB/JIBE Subclass A | JIBSA | JV_JIBSA | CHAR | 5 |
|  | .INCLUDE | CI_PROJ | STRU | 0 |
| Scheduling Scenario | SCHTYP | PS_SCHED_TYPE | CHAR | 1 |
| Forecast Start Date of Project Definition | SPROG | PS_SPROG | DATS | 8 |
| Forecast Finish Date for Project Definition | EPROG | PS_EPROG | DATS | 8 |
| Append Structure for Regulatory Reporting | .APPEND | FERC_PROJ | STRU | 0 |
| Regulatory Indicator | FERC_IND | FE_IND | CHAR | 4 |

## Work Breakdown Structure (WBS)

| Description | Field | Data Element | Type | Length |
|---|---|---|---|---|
| Client | MANDT | MANDT | CLNT | 3 |
| WBS Element | PSPNR | PS_POSNR | NUMC | 8 |
| PS: Data Portion of WBS Element Master Data Include | .INCLUDE | PRPS_INC | STRU | 0 |
| Work Breakdown Structure Element (WBS Element) | POSID | PS_POSID | CHAR | 24 |
| PS: Short Description (1st text line) | POST1 | PS_POST1 | CHAR | 40 |
| Object Number | OBJNR | J_OBJNR | CHAR | 22 |
| Current Number of the Appropriate Project | PSPHI | PS_PSPHI | NUMC | 8 |
| PS: Data Portion of WBS Element Master Data Include | .INCLUDE | PRPS2_INC | STRU | 0 |
| WBS Element Short Identification | POSKI | PS_POSKI | CHAR | 16 |
| Name of Person who Created the Object | ERNAM | ERNAM | CHAR | 12 |
| Date on Which the Record was Created | ERDAT | ERDAT | DATS | 8 |
| Name of Person who Changed Object | AENAM | AENAM | CHAR | 12 |
| Date on Which Object was Last Changed | AEDAT | UPDAT | DATS | 8 |
| Number of the Responsible Person (Project Manager) | VERNR | PS_VERNR | NUMC | 8 |
| Name of Responsible Person (Project Manager) | VERNA | PS_VERNA | CHAR | 25 |
| Applicant Number | ASTNR | PS_ASTNR | NUMC | 8 |
| Applicant | ASTNA | PS_ASTNA | CHAR | 25 |
| Company Code for WBS Element | PBUKR | PS_PBUKR | CHAR | 4 |
| Business Area for WBS Element | PGSBR | PS_PGSBR | CHAR | 4 |
| Controlling Area for WBS Element | PKOKR | PS_PKOKR | CHAR | 4 |
| Profit Center | PRCTR | PRCTR | CHAR | 10 |
| Project Type | PRART | PS_PRART | CHAR | 2 |
| Level in Project Hierarchy | STUFE | PS_STUFE | INT1 | 3 |
| Indicator: Planning Element | PLAKZ | PS_PLAKZ | CHAR | 1 |
| Indicator: Account Assignment Element | BELKZ | PS_BELKZ | CHAR | 1 |
| Indicator: Billing Element | FAKKZ | PS_FAKKZ | CHAR | 1 |
| Relationship of Network Activity to Production Order | NPFAZ | PS_NPFAR | CHAR | 1 |
| Network Assignment | ZUORD | PS_ZUORD | NUMC | 1 |
| Indicator: WBS Dates Detailed by Activity Dates | TRMEQ | PS_TRMEQ | CHAR | 1 |
| Usage of the Condition Table | KVEWE | KVEWE | CHAR | 1 |
| Application | KAPPL | KAPPL | CHAR | 2 |

| Description | Field | Data Element | Type | Length |
|---|---|---|---|---|
| Costing Sheet | KALSM | AUFKALSM | CHAR | 6 |
| Overhead Key | ZSCHL | AUFZSCHL | CHAR | 6 |
| Results Analysis Key | ABGSL | ABGR_SCHL | CHAR | 6 |
| Controlling Area of Requesting Cost Center | AKOKR | PS_AKOKR | CHAR | 4 |
| Requesting Cost Center | AKSTL | PS_AKSTL | CHAR | 10 |
| Controlling Area of Responsible Cost Center | FKOKR | PS_FKOKR | CHAR | 4 |
| Responsible Cost Center | FKSTL | PS_FKSTL | CHAR | 10 |
| Factory Calendar Key | FABKL | FABKL | CHAR | 2 |
| Priority | PSPRI | NW_PRIO | CHAR | 1 |
| Equipment Number | EQUNR | EQUNR | CHAR | 18 |
| Functional Location | TPLNR | TPLNR | CHAR | 30 |
| WBS Element Currency | PWPOS | PS_PWPOS | CUKY | 5 |
| Plant | WERKS | WERKS_D | CHAR | 4 |
| Language Key | TXTSP | SPRAS | LANG | 1 |
| Key Word ID for User-Defined Fields | SLWID | SLWID | CHAR | 7 |
| 1st User Field for 20 Characters—WBS Element | USR00 | USR00PRPS | CHAR | 20 |
| 2nd User Field 20 Digits—WBS Element | USR01 | USR01PRPS | CHAR | 20 |
| 3rd User-Defined Field 10 Digits—WBS Element | USR02 | USR02PRPS | CHAR | 10 |
| 4th User-Defined Field 10 Digits—WBS Element | USR03 | USR03PRPS | CHAR | 10 |
| 1st User Defined Field for Quantity (Length 10,3) WBS Element | USR04 | USR04PRPS | QUAN | 13 |
| 1st User Defined Field for Quantity Field Unit—WBS Element | USE04 | USE04PRPS | UNIT | 3 |
| 2nd User Field for Quantity (Length 10,3) WBS Element | USR05 | USR05PRPS | QUAN | 13 |
| 2nd User Defined Field for Quantity Field Unit—WBS Element | USE05 | USE05PRPS | UNIT | 3 |
| 1st User Field for Values (Length 10,3)—WBS Element | USR06 | USR06PRPS | CURR | 13 |
| 1st User Defined Field for Value Field Unit—WBS Element | USE06 | USE06PRPS | CUKY | 5 |
| 2nd User Field for Values (Length 10,3)—WBS Element | USR07 | USR07PRPS | CURR | 13 |
| 2nd User Defined Field for Value Field Unit—WBS Element | USE07 | USE07PRPS | CUKY | 5 |
| 1st User Field for Date—WBS Element | USR08 | USR08PRPS | DATS | 8 |
| 2nd User Field for Date—WBS Element | USR09 | USR09PRPS | DATS | 8 |
| 1st User Field for "Ind. for Evaluations" WBS Element | USR10 | USR10PRPS | CHAR | 1 |

| Description | Field | Data Element | Type | Length |
|---|---|---|---|---|
| 2nd User Field for "Indicator for eval.s" WBS Element | USR11 | USR11PRPS | CHAR | 1 |
| Cost Center to Which Costs are Actually Posted | KOSTL | PS_KOSTL | CHAR | 10 |
| Cost Object | KTRG | KSTRG | CHAR | 12 |
| Authorization Key for Project Master Data | BERST | PS_BERST | CHAR | 16 |
| Authorization Key for Project Dates (WBS) | BERTR | PS_BERTR | CHAR | 16 |
| Authorization Key for Costs and Revenues | BERKO | PS_BERKO | CHAR | 16 |
| Authorization Key for Project Budget | BERBU | PS_BERBU | CHAR | 16 |
| Indicator: WBS Element Used in Project Summarization | CLASF | PS_CLASF | CHAR | 1 |
| Std WBS: Internal Project Item Number (w/Exit on ID) | SPSNR | PS_SPSNR | NUMC | 8 |
| Object Class | SCOPE | SCOPE_CV | CHAR | 2 |
| Statistical WBS Element | XSTAT | PS_XSTAT | CHAR | 1 |
| Tax Jurisdiction | TXJCD | TXJCD | CHAR | 15 |
| Interest Profile for Project/Order Interest Calculation | ZSCHM | PS_ZSCHM | CHAR | 7 |
| Investment Measure Profile | IMPRF | IM_PROFIL | CHAR | 6 |
| Aggregation Weight for POC (PS Progress) | EVGEW | EV_WEIGHTD | DEC | 8 |
| Change Number | AENNR | AENNR | CHAR | 12 |
| Sub-project in Work Breakdown Structure | SUBPR | PS_SUBPR | CHAR | 12 |
| PS: Short Description (1st text line) in All Caps | POSTU | PS_POSTU | CHAR | 40 |
| Indicator for Integrated Planning | PLINT | PLINT | CHAR | 1 |
| Deletion Indicator | LOEVM | LOEVM | CHAR | 1 |
| Valuation of Special Stock | KZBWS | KZBWS | CHAR | 1 |
| Billing Plan Number/Invoicing Plan Number | FPLNR | FPLNR | CHAR | 10 |
| Technically Complete Date | TADAT | TABGDAT | DATS | 8 |
| Reason for Investment | IZWEK | IZWEK | CHAR | 2 |
| Scale of Investment Objects | ISIZE | IM_SIZECL | CHAR | 2 |
| Reason for Environmental Investment | IUMKZ | AM_UMWKZ | CHAR | 5 |
| Requesting Company Code | ABUKR | IM_ABUKRS | CHAR | 4 |
| Indicator: Grouping WBS Element | GRPKZ | GRPSPKZ | CHAR | 1 |
| Distribution Profile | PGPRF | PGPROFID | CHAR | 6 |
| Logical System | LOGSYSTEM | LOGSYSTEM | CHAR | 10 |
| Numeric Field Length 8 | PSPNR_LOGS | NUM08 | NUMC | 8 |
| Location | STORT | PS_STORT | CHAR | 10 |
| Functional Area | FUNC_AREA | FKBER | CHAR | 16 |

| Description | Field | Data Element | Type | Length |
|---|---|---|---|---|
| Costing Variant | KLVAR | CK_KLVAR | CHAR | 4 |
| Cost Estimate Number for Cost Est. w/o Qty Structure | KALNR | CK_KALNR | NUMC | 12 |
| Work Breakdown Structure Element (WBS Element) Edited | POSID_EDIT | PS_POSID_EDIT | CHAR | 24 |
| PLP: Data Part—Include Production Lot Master Data | .INCLUDE | PLP_DATA_INC | STRU | 0 |
| Indicator: WBS Element for Production Lot | PSPKZ | PL_PSPKZ | CHAR | 1 |
| Material Number | MATNR | MATNR | CHAR | 18 |
| WBS: Reference Work Breakdown Structure Element | VLPSP | PL_PSP_PNR | NUMC | 8 |
| Indicator: Reference WBS Element for Production Lot | VLPKZ | PL_VLPKZ | CHAR | 1 |
| Sort String 1 for Production Lot | SORT1 | PL_SORT1 | CHAR | 10 |
| Sort String 2 for Production Lot | SORT2 | PL_SORT2 | CHAR | 10 |
| Sort String 3 for Production Lot | SORT3 | PL_SORT3 | CHAR | 10 |
| JV Data: (vname,recid,etype),otype,jibcl,jibsa | .INCLUDE | GJV_DATA_3 | STRU | 0 |
| General Assignments of Application Objects | .INCLUDE | GJV_DATA_0 | STRU | 0 |
| Joint Venture | VNAME | JV_NAME | CHAR | 6 |
| Recovery Indicator | RECID | JV_RECIND | CHAR | 2 |
| Equity Type | ETYPE | JV_ETYPE | CHAR | 3 |
| Joint Venture Object Type | OTYPE | JV_OTYPE | CHAR | 4 |
| JIB/JIBE Class | JIBCL | JV_JIBCL | CHAR | 3 |
| JIB/JIBE Subclass A | JIBSA | JV_JIBSA | CHAR | 5 |
| Generic Project Planning: Assignment to WBS Element | .INCLUDE | CGPL_PRPS | STRU | 0 |
| Generic Project Planning: GUID from External R/3 System | CGPL_GUID16 | CGPL_GUID16_R3 | RAW | 16 |
| Generic Project Planning: Log. System for CGPL_GUID16_R3 | CGPL_LOGSYS | CGPL_LOGSYS | CHAR | 10 |
| Generic Project Planning: Object Type from Ext. R/3 System | CGPL_OBJTYPE | CGPL_OBJECT_TYPE_R3 | CHAR | 3 |
| Reference Element PM/PS | ADPSP | ADDCOMPARE_CORE | CHAR | 40 |
| | .INCLUDE | CI_PRPS | STRU | 0 |
| Append Structure for Regulatory Reporting | .APPEND | FERC_ | | |
| Regulatory Indicator | FERC_IND | FE_IND | CHAR | 4 |

## Logical Databases

The logical database PSJ is used throughout the Project System in selecting data from the physical database. The logical database also provides the data for customer-specific reports. Basically, PSJ provides you with the relationship that project-related tables have with each other.

You can access it via transaction SE36.

| Node name | Table / Type | Node type | Short text |
|---|---|---|---|
| ARKOPF | ARKOPF | Table | Archiving run header data |
| VSKOPF | VSKOPF | Table | Version: Header    - general data for a |
| RSTHIE | RSTHIE | Table | BRST structure of the hierarchy table |
| PSDYRH | PSDYRH | Table | LDB PSJ: Dummy structure under RSTHIE |
| PROJ | PROJ | Table | Project definition |
| PSDYPD | PSDYPD | Table | LDB PSJ: Dummy structure under PROJ |
| VBAK | VBAK | Table | Sales Document: Header Data |
| VBUK | VBUK | Table | Sales Doc.: Header Status and Administrative Data |
| VBKD | VBKD | Table | Sales Document: Business Data |
| VBAP | VBAP | Table | Sales Document: Item Data |
| VBUP | VBUP | Table | Sales Document: Item Status |
| VBKDPO | VBKDPO | Table | Sales document: Business item data (POSNR > 0) |
| FPLA | FPLA | Table | Billing plan |
| FPLT | FPLT | Table | Billing Plan: Dates |
| PSDYVB | PSDYVB | Table | LDB PSJ: Dummy structure under VBAP |
| PSDYVK | PSDYVK | Table | LDB PSJ: Dummy structure under VBAK |
| PRPS_R | PRPS_R | Table | Project Hierarchy Reporting Structure |
| PRTE | PRTE | Table | Scheduling Data for Project Item |
| PSMLST | PSMLST | Table | Milestone I/O Table |
| PSTX | PSTX | Table | PS Texts (Header) |
| PLAF | PLAF | Table | Planned order |
| KBED04 | KBED04 | Table | Capacity Requirement Recs for Planned Orders (LDB) |
| RESB04 | RESB04 | Table | Reservation/dependent reqs for plan order (LDB) |
| PSMERK_PRPS | PSMERK | DDICType | Characteristics for Summarization for WBS Elements |
| PSDYPR | PSDYPR | Table | LDB PSJ: Dummy structure under PRPS_R |
| AUFK | AUFK | Table | Order master data |
| AFKO | AFKO | Table | Header Data in PP Orders |
| AFPO | AFPO | Table | Order Item |
| AFFL | AFFL | Table | Work order sequence |
| ACT01 | ACT01 | Table | Activity for LDB 01 |
| AFAB01 | AFAB01 | Table | Network Relationship (for LDB) - 01 |
| MLSTD | MLSTD | Table | Milestone I/O Table |
| PSTX1 | PSTX1 | Table | PS Texts (Header) for Activity (1) |
| AFFH01 | AFFH01 | Table | Order PRT Data (for LDB) - 01 |
| KBED01 | KBED01 | Table | Capacity Requirement Records (for LDB) - 01 |
| KBEZ | KBEZ | Table | Additional data for table KBED (for ind.req/split) |
| KPER | KPER | Table | Additional data for KBEZ (person split in days) |
| AFRU02 | AFRU02 | Table | Order Confirmations (for LDB) -02 |
| RESB01 | RESB01 | Table | Reservation/Dependent Requirement for LDB-01 |
| PSDYOK | PSDYOK | Table | LDB PSJ: Dummy structure under RESB01 |
| AFRU01 | AFRU01 | Table | Order Confirmations (for LDB) - 01 |
| PSMERK_ACT | PSMERK | DDICType | Characteristics for Summarization for Activity |
| PSDYNV | PSDYNV | Table | LDB PSJ: Dummy structure under ACT01 |
| AFIH | AFIH | Table | Maintenance order header |
| PSDYNP | PSDYNP | Table | LDB PSJ: Dummy structure under AUFK |
| IMTP | IMTP | Table | Investment programs |
| IMPR | IMPR | Table | Investment Program Positions |
| PSDYIP | PSDYIP | Table | LDB PSJ: Dummy structure under IMPR |
| PSDYPG | PSDYPG | Table | LDB PSJ: Dummy structure under IMTP |
| PEGOB | PEGOB | Table | Peg (master data of the CO object) |

Copyright by SAP AG

| Node name | Table / Type | Node type | Short text |
|---|---|---|---|
| PEGQTY | PEGQTY | Table | Assigned pegging object quantities |
| PSDYPEG | PSDYPEG | Table | LDB PSJ: Dummy Structure Under PEGOB |
| ELM_PS | ELM_PS | Table | Additional data for hierarchy nodes (LDB PSJ) |
| JSTO | JSTO | Table | Status object information |
| PSTAT | PSTAT | Table | Condensed status display |
| JCDO | JCDO | Table | Change Documents for Status Object (Table JSTO) |
| JEST | JEST | Table | Individual Status per Object |
| JCDS | JCDS | Table | Change docs. for system/user status (table JEST) |
| ONR00 | ONR00 | Table | General Object Number |
| RPSCO1 | RPSCO1 | Table | Summarization Table for Project Reporting |
| RPSQT | RPSQT | Table | Summarization table for project reporting (quants) |
| EV_PARAM | EVOP | DDICType | Object parameters for earned value analysis |
| EV_POC | EVPOC_RPS... | DDICType | Earned value analysis: percentage of completion |
| EV_VAL | EVVA_RPSCO | DDICType | Earned value analysis: earned value |
| COBRA | COBRA | Table | Settlement Rule for Order Settlement |
| COBRB | COBRB | Table | Distribution rules for sett. rule for order sett. |
| BPHI1 | BPHI1 | Table | Cross-hierarchy data                     Control |
| BPTR1 | BPTR1 | Table | Object Data                              Control |
| BPGE1 | BPGE1 | Table | Totals record total value                Control |
| BPVG1 | BPVG1 | Table | Table Generated for View BPVG1 |
| BKHS1 | BKHS1 | Table | Header - Unit Costing (Control + Totals) |
| HEAD10 | HEAD10 | Table | SAPscript: Text Header |
| LINE10 | LINE10 | Table | SAPscript: Text Lines |
| BKHT1 | BKHT1 | Table | Texts for CKHS |
| BKIS1 | BKIS1 | Table | Individual calculation/verification item gen. |
| BKIT1 | BKIT1 | Table | Texts for CKIS |
| BKIP1 | BKIP1 | Table | Periodic Values for Unit Costing Item |
| BPJA1 | BPJA1 | Table | Totals record for total year value       Control |
| BPVJ1 | BPVJ1 | Table | Table Generated for View BPVJ1 |
| BKHS2 | BKHS2 | Table | Header - Unit Costing (Control + Totals) |
| HEAD20 | HEAD20 | Table | SAPscript: Text Header |
| LINE20 | LINE20 | Table | SAPscript: Text Lines |
| BKHT2 | BKHT2 | Table | Texts for CKHS |
| BKIS2 | BKIS2 | Table | Individual calculation/verification item gen. |
| BKIT2 | BKIT2 | Table | Texts for CKIS |
| BKIP2 | BKIP2 | Table | Periodic Values for Unit Costing Item |
| BPPE1 | BPPE1 | Table | Totals Record for Period Values          Control |
| BPVP1 | BPVP1 | Table | Table Generated for View BPVP1 |
| BPIG1 | BPIG1 | Table | Budget Object Index (Overall Budget) |
| BPIJ1 | BPIJ1 | Table | Budget Object Index (Annual Budget) |
| COKA1 | COKA1 | Table | CO Object: Cost Element Control Data |
| COKP1 | COKP1 | Table | CO Object: Primary Planning Control Data |
| HEAD11 | HEAD11 | Table | SAPscript: Text Header |
| LINE11 | LINE11 | Table | SAPscript: Text Lines |
| CKHS1 | CKHS1 | Table | Header - Unit Costing (Control + Totals) |
| CKHT1 | CKHT1 | Table | Texts for CKHS |
| HEAD12 | HEAD12 | Table | SAPscript: Text Header |
| LINE12 | LINE12 | Table | SAPscript: Text Lines |
| CKIS1 | CKIS1 | Table | Individual calculation/verification item gen. |
| CKIT1 | CKIT1 | Table | Texts for CKIS |
| CKIP1 | CKIP1 | Table | Periodic Values for Unit Costing Item |

Copyright by SAP AG

| Node name | Table / Type | Node type | Short text |
|---|---|---|---|
| ▽ COSP1 | COSP1 | Table | CO Object: Cost Totals for External Postings |
| ▽ COVP11 | COVP11 | Table | CO object: Line items with doc. header (by period) |
| ▽ COEPD11 | COEPD11 | Table | CO object: Unvaluated ln. item settlement w/status |
| COEPBR11 | COEPBR11 | Table | CO Object: Valuated Line Item Settlement |
| COVJ11 | COVJ11 | Table | CO object: Line items with doc header (by year) |
| COVO1 | COVO1 | Table | CO Object: Open Items for Line Items (w/o doc.Hdr) |
| COSPD1 | COSPD1 | Table | CO object: External cost totals - calculated |
| COSPP | COSPP | Table | Transfer of Order in the COSP Table to the Project |
| ▽ COKS1 | COKS1 | Table | CO Object: Control Data for Secondary Planning |
| ▽ HEAD13 | HEAD13 | Table | SAPscript: Text Header |
| LINE13 | LINE13 | Table | SAPscript: Text Lines |
| ▽ COSS1 | COSS1 | Table | CO Object: Cost Totals for Internal Postings |
| ▽ COVP12 | COVP12 | Table | CO object: Line items with doc. header (by period) |
| ▽ COEPD12 | COEPD12 | Table | CO object: Unvaluated ln. item settlement w/status |
| COEPBR12 | COEPBR12 | Table | CO Object: Valuated Line Item Settlement |
| COVJ12 | COVJ12 | Table | CO object: Line items with doc header (by year) |
| COVO12 | COVO12 | Table | CO object: Fxd price agreement commitment ln items |
| COSSD1 | COSSD1 | Table | CO object: Internal cost totals - calculated |
| COSSP | COSSP | Table | Transfer of the Order COSS Table to the Project |
| ▽ COKR1 | COKR1 | Table | CO Object: Control Data for Statistical Key Figs |
| ▽ HEAD14 | HEAD14 | Table | SAPscript: Text Header |
| LINE14 | LINE14 | Table | SAPscript: Text Lines |
| ▽ COSR1 | COSR1 | Table | CO Object: Statistical Key Figure Totals |
| COVPR1 | COVPR1 | Table | CO object: Stat. key figure line items by period |
| COVJR1 | COVJR1 | Table | CO object: Line items stat. key figures (by year) |
| ▽ COSL1 | COSL1 | Table | CO Object: Activity Type Totals |
| COVPL1 | COVPL1 | Table | CO object: Activity type line items by period |
| COVJL1 | COVJL1 | Table | CO object: Line items for acty types (by year) |
| COSLD | COSLD | Table | CO object: Activity type sums - calculated |
| ▽ COSB1 | COSB1 | Table | CO Object: Total Variances/Results Analyses |
| COVPB1 | COVPB1 | Table | CO object: Variance/accrual line items by period |
| COSBD1 | COSBD1 | Table | CO object: Sums of variance/accrual - calculated |
| ▽ ANIA1 | ANIA1 | Table | Depr. simulation for invest. projects |
| ANIE1 | ANIB1 | Table | Invest. projects: Depr. simulation analysis report |
| ANLI1 | ANLI1 | Table | Link table for capital investment measure -> AuC |
| ▽ FMSU1 | FMSU1 | Table | FM totals records for financial data |
| COVFP1 | COVFP1 | Table | CO object: Financial data line items with doc. hdr |
| TPI031 | TPI031 | Table | CO Objects: Date of Last Interest Run |
| ▽ EKKO | EKKO | Table | Purchasing Document Header |
| ▽ EKPO | EKPO | Table | Purchasing Document Item |
| EKET | EKET | Table | Scheduling Agreement Schedule Lines |
| EKKN | EKKN | Table | Account Assignment in Purchasing Document |
| EKBE | EKBE | Table | Purchasing Document History |
| ▽ EBAN | EBAN | Table | Purchase requisition |
| EBKN | EBKN | Table | Purchase Requisition Account Assignment |
| ▽ FPLAPS | FPLA | DDICType | Billing plan for PSP network plan |
| FPLTPS | FPLT | DDICType | Billing plan for PSP/network (dates) |
| ▽ LIKP | LIKP | Table | SD Document: Delivery Header Data |
| LIPS | LIPS | Table | SD document: Delivery: Item data |
| PSMERK | PSMERK | Table | Characteristics for summarization wo. classificatn |
| DRAD | DRAD | Table | Document object link |

## The Complete IMG

Included here is the compete IMG as shown in transaction SPRO.

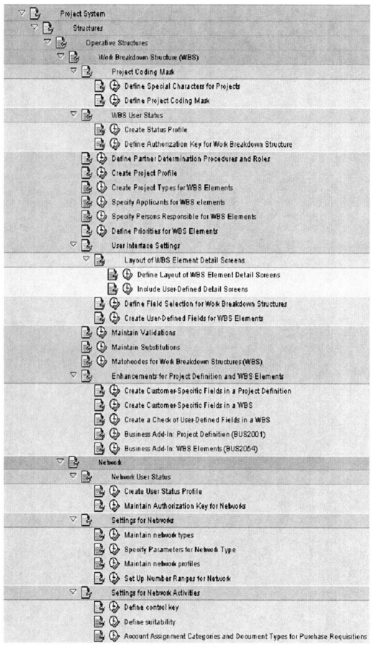

Copyright by SAP AG

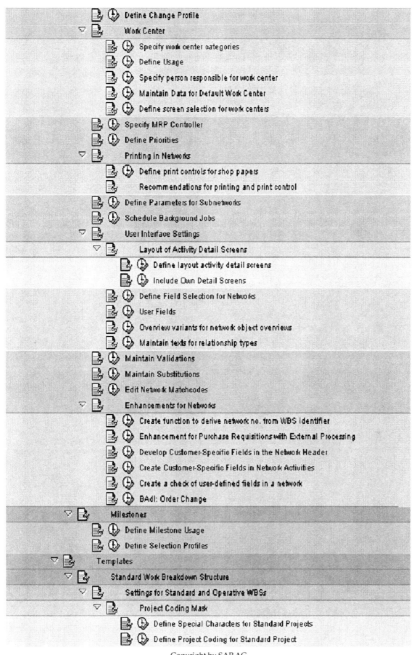

Define Change Profile

Work Center

   Specify work center categories

   Define Usage

   Specify person responsible for work center

   Maintain Data for Default Work Center

   Define screen selection for work centers

Specify MRP Controller

Define Priorities

Printing in Networks

   Define print controls for shop papers

   Recommendations for printing and print control

Define Parameters for Subnetworks

Schedule Background Jobs

User Interface Settings

   Layout of Activity Detail Screens

      Define layout activity detail screens

      Include Own Detail Screens

   Define Field Selection for Networks

   User Fields

   Overview variants for network object overviews

   Maintain texts for relationship types

Maintain Validations

Maintain Substitutions

Edit Network Matchcodes

Enhancements for Networks

   Create function to derive network no. from WBS identifier

   Enhancement for Purchase Requisitions with External Processing

   Develop Customer-Specific Fields in the Network Header

   Create Customer-Specific Fields in Network Activities

   Create a check of user-defined fields in a network

   BAdI: Order Change

Milestones

Define Milestone Usage

Define Selection Profiles

Templates

Standard Work Breakdown Structure

Settings for Standard and Operative WBSs

   Project Coding Mask

      Define Special Characters for Standard Projects

      Define Project Coding for Standard Project

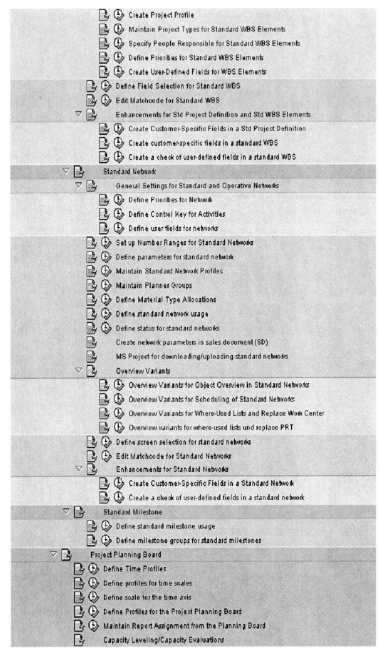

Create Project Profile

Maintain Project Types for Standard WBS Elements

Specify People Responsible for Standard WBS Elements

Define Priorities for Standard WBS Elements

Create User-Defined Fields for WBS Elements

Define Field Selection for Standard WBS

Edit Matchcode for Standard WBS

Enhancements for Std Project Definition and Std WBS Elements

Create Customer-Specific Fields in a Std Project Definition

Create customer-specific fields in a standard WBS

Create a check of user-defined fields in a standard WBS

Standard Network

General Settings for Standard and Operative Networks

Define Priorities for Network

Define Control Key for Activities

Define user fields for networks

Set up Number Ranges for Standard Networks

Define parameters for standard network

Maintain Standard Network Profiles

Maintain Planner Groups

Define Material Type Allocations

Define standard network usage

Define status for standard networks

Create network parameters in sales document (SD)

MS Project for downloading/uploading standard networks

Overview Variants

Overview Variants for Object Overview in Standard Networks

Overview Variants for Scheduling of Standard Networks

Overview Variants for Where-Used Lists and Replace Work Center

Overview variants for where-used lists und replace PRT

Define screen selection for standard networks

Edit Matchcode for Standard Networks

Enhancements for Standard Networks

Create Customer-Specific Fields in a Standard Network

Create a check of user-defined fields in a standard network

Standard Milestone

Define standard milestone usage

Define milestone groups for standard milestones

Project Planning Board

Define Time Profiles

Define profiles for time scales

Define scale for the time axis

Define Profiles for the Project Planning Board

Maintain Report Assignment from the Planning Board

Capacity Leveling/Capacity Evaluations

- ▽ Documents
  - Define Text Types for PS Texts
  - ▽ Document Search in the WWW
    - Maintain Search Server Relation
    - Set Up Search Engine Index
    - Start Processing for Documents
- ▽ Collaboration
  - Define Field Selection
  - Define CEP profile
  - Define Life Cycle Profile
  - Define Workflow
  - Administration of CEP Documents
  - ▽ Enhancements for Collaboration
    - Check User Authorization for Folders
- ▽ Claim
  - ▽ Notification - Claim
    - Overview of Notification Type
    - ▽ Notification Creation
      - ▽ Notification Type
        - Define Notification Types
        - Define Number Ranges
        - Define Screen Templates
        - Define Transaction Start Values
        - Allowed Change of Notification Type
      - ▽ Notification Contents
        - Maintain Catalogs
        - Define Catalog Profiles
        - Catalogs and Catalog Profiles for Notification Type
      - ▽ Partner
        - Define Partner Determination Procedures
        - Define Fields for Partner Lists
        - Define Standard Messages to Partners
    - ▽ Notification Processing
      - ▽ Response Control
        - Define Priorities
        - Define Response Monitoring
      - ▽ Additional Notification Functions
        - Define Action Box
        - Define Follow-Up Actions for Tasks
      - ▽ Print Control
        - Define Shop Papers, Forms, Print Programs
        - Define Printer

- Status Management
  - Define Status Profile
  - Define Selection Profiles
- Define List Variants
- Activate Workflow Template and Assign Processor
- Determine Costing Variant
- Notification Processing on the Intranet
  - Define Scenarios
  - Settings for Cost-Generating Scenarios
    - Settings for Template Transport
    - Define Settings for Execution Services
- Settings for Claims
  - Field selection
  - Codes for Detailed Long Texts
  - Activate Workflows and Assign Personnel
  - Controlling Scenario for Claims
  - Assignment of Controlling Scenario for Notification Type
  - Business Add-In: Customer-Specific Check Before Creating Cost Collector
  - Business Add-In: Data Change in 'Claim Overview' Report
  - Business Add-In: Data Change in 'Claim Hierarchy' Report
- Production Resources and Tools
  - General Data
    - Define PRT Authorization Group
    - Define PRT Status
    - Define Usage
    - Define PRT Group Key
  - Assignment of Production Resources/Tools
    - Define PRT Control Key
    - Define Formula Parameters
    - Maintain Formula Definitions
  - Costs
    - Activate Project Management in Controlling Area
    - Create CO Versions
    - Maintain Currency Exchange Rates
    - Object Class Default Values
      - Specify Default for Project Definition Object Class
      - Specify Default for Network Header Object Class
    - Value Categories
      - Maintain Value Categories
      - Assign Cost Elements to Value Categories
      - Check Consistency of Value Category Assignment

Copyright by SAP AG

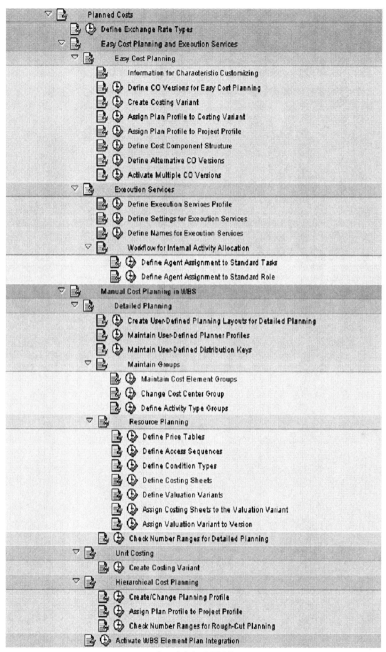

- Planned Costs
  - Define Exchange Rate Types
  - Easy Cost Planning and Execution Services
    - Easy Cost Planning
      - Information for Characteristic Customizing
      - Define CO Versions for Easy Cost Planning
      - Create Costing Variant
      - Assign Plan Profile to Costing Variant
      - Assign Plan Profile to Project Profile
      - Define Cost Component Structure
      - Define Alternative CO Versions
      - Activate Multiple CO Versions
    - Execution Services
      - Define Execution Services Profile
      - Define Settings for Execution Services
      - Define Names for Execution Services
      - Workflow for Internal Activity Allocation
        - Define Agent Assignment to Standard Tasks
        - Define Agent Assignment to Standard Role
  - Manual Cost Planning in WBS
    - Detailed Planning
      - Create User-Defined Planning Layouts for Detailed Planning
      - Maintain User-Defined Planner Profiles
      - Maintain User-Defined Distribution Keys
      - Maintain Groups
        - Maintain Cost Element Groups
        - Change Cost Center Group
        - Define Activity Type Groups
      - Resource Planning
        - Define Price Tables
        - Define Access Sequences
        - Define Condition Types
        - Define Costing Sheets
        - Define Valuation Variants
        - Assign Costing Sheets to the Valuation Variant
        - Assign Valuation Variant to Version
      - Check Number Ranges for Detailed Planning
    - Unit Costing
      - Create Costing Variant
    - Hierarchical Cost Planning
      - Create/Change Planning Profile
      - Assign Plan Profile to Project Profile
      - Check Number Ranges for Rough-Cut Planning
    - Activate WBS Element Plan Integration

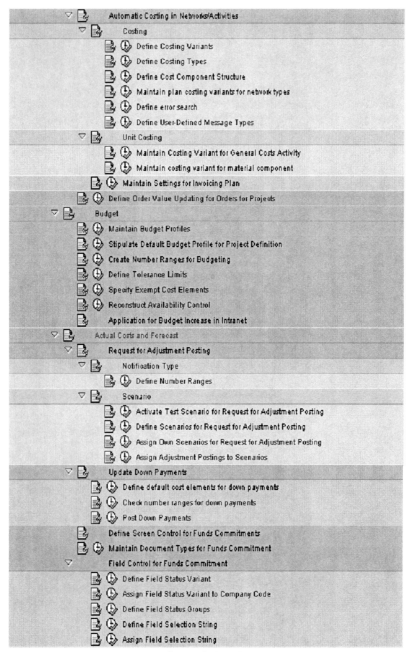

Copyright by SAP AG

- ▽ Number Ranges
  - Check Number Ranges for CO Postings
  - Check Number Ranges for Funds Commitments
  - User-Defined Screen Variants for Postings in Controlling
- ▷ Automatic and Periodic Allocations
- ▽ Revenues and Earnings
  - Create CO Versions
  - Maintain Currency Exchange Rates
  - ▽ Value Categories
    - Maintain Value Categories
    - Assign Value Categories to Revenue Elements
    - Check Consistency of Value Category Assignment
  - ▽ Planned Revenues
    - Define Exchange Rate Types
    - ▽ Manual Revenue Planning
      - ▽ Detailed Planning
        - Create User-Defined Planning Layouts for Revenue Element Planning
        - Maintain User-Defined Planner Profiles
        - Maintain User-Defined Distribution Keys
        - Maintain Cost Element Group
        - Check Number Ranges for Detailed Planning
      - ▽ Structure Planning
        - Maintain Planning Profiles
        - Specify Default Plan Profiles for Project Definitions
        - Create Number Ranges for Planning
      - Activate WBS Element Plan Integration
    - ▽ Automatic Plan Revenue Calculation
      - Maintain Billing Plan Settings
      - Specify Revenue Plan Update from Sales Document
  - ▽ Actual Revenues and Forecast
    - Check CO Posting Number Ranges
    - User-Defined Screen Variants for Postings in Controlling
  - ▽ Automatic and Periodic Allocations
    - Define Interest Relevance for Revenue Value Categories
    - ▽ Results Analysis
      - Edit results analysis cost elements
      - ▽ Edit Results Analysis Keys and Version
        - Maintain results analysis keys
        - Maintain results analysis versions
        - Define Valuation Methods for Results Analysis
        - Define line IDs
        - Define assignments for results analysis
        - Define Update for Results Analysis
        - Define Posting Rules for Settlement to Accounting

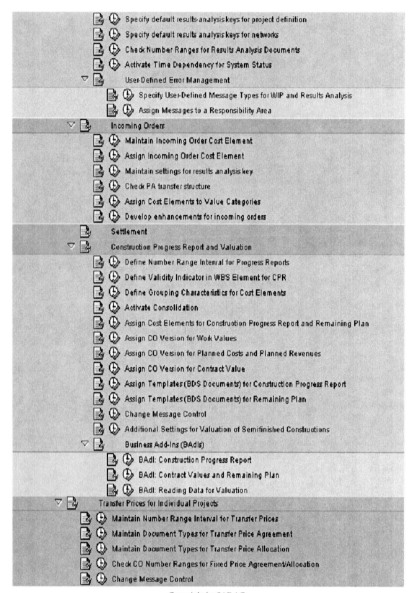

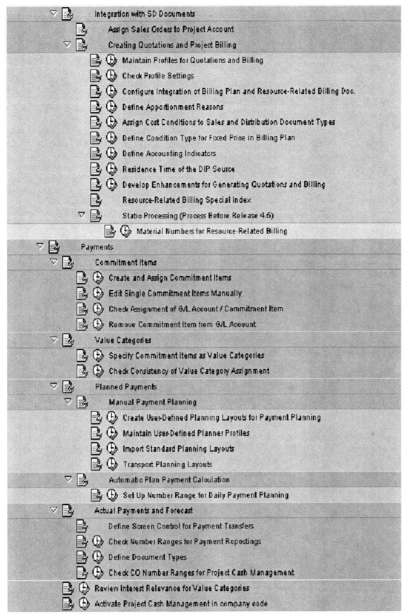

Integration with SD Documents
Assign Sales Orders to Project Account
Creating Quotations and Project Billing
Maintain Profiles for Quotations and Billing
Check Profile Settings
Configure Integration of Billing Plan and Resource-Related Billing Doc.
Define Apportionment Reasons
Assign Cost Conditions to Sales and Distribution Document Types
Define Condition Type for Fixed Price in Billing Plan
Define Accounting Indicators
Residence Time of the DIP Source
Develop Enhancements for Generating Quotations and Billing
Resource-Related Billing Special Index
Static Processing (Process Before Release 4.6)
Material Numbers for Resource-Related Billing
Payments
Commitment Items
Create and Assign Commitment Items
Edit Single Commitment Items Manually
Check Assignment of G/L Account / Commitment Item
Remove Commitment Item from G/L Account
Value Categories
Specify Commitment Items as Value Categories
Check Consistency of Value Category Assignment
Planned Payments
Manual Payment Planning
Create User-Defined Planning Layouts for Payment Planning
Maintain User-Defined Planner Profiles
Import Standard Planning Layouts
Transport Planning Layouts
Automatic Plan Payment Calculation
Set Up Number Range for Daily Payment Planning
Actual Payments and Forecast
Define Screen Control for Payment Transfers
Check Number Ranges for Payment Repostings
Define Document Types
Check CO Number Ranges for Project Cash Management
Review Interest Relevance for Value Categories
Activate Project Cash Management in company code

- ▽ Prepare for Going Live
  - ▽ Delete Test Data
    - Delete Actual Data
    - Delete Planning Data
    - Delete Master Data
  - ▽ Data Transfer
    - Post documents from Materials Management
    - ▽ Post Documents from Financial Accounting
      - Successive Document Transfer
      - Complete Document Transfer
    - Post Payment Transfers
- ▽ Dates
  - ▽ Scheduling
    - Define Scheduling Types
    - Define Time Units
    - Define Reduction Strategies
    - Specify Parameters for Network Scheduling
    - Define Levels for Networks
    - BAdI: Overall Network Scheduling with Selection Option
  - ▽ Date Planning in WBS
    - Define Parameters for WBS Scheduling
    - Specify Graphics Profile for WBS Date Planning
    - Overview Variants for Schedule and Capacity Overviews
- ▽ Resources
  - ▽ Work Center
    - Specify work center categories
    - Define Usage
    - Specify person responsible for work center
    - Maintain Data for Default Work Center
    - Define screen selection for work centers
  - Define Capacity Categories
  - Define Capacity Planners
  - Define Key for Performance Efficiency Rate
  - Define Shift Sequences
  - Maintain Control Parameters for the Availability Check
  - Define Profiles for Workforce Planning
  - ▽ Formulas
    - Define Formula Parameters
    - Maintain Formula Definitions
  - ▽ Distribution
    - Define Distribution Functions
    - Define Distribution Strategies
    - Define Requirements Distribution

Copyright by SAP AG

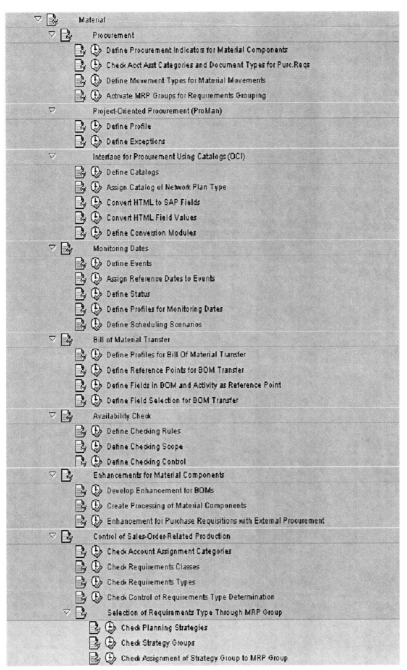

Material
  Procurement
    Define Procurement Indicators for Material Components
    Check Acct Asst Categories and Document Types for Purc.Reqs
    Define Movement Types for Material Movements
    Activate MRP Groups for Requirements Grouping
  Project-Oriented Procurement (ProMan)
    Define Profile
    Define Exceptions
  Interface for Procurement Using Catalogs (OCI)
    Define Catalogs
    Assign Catalog of Network Plan Type
    Convert HTML to SAP Fields
    Convert HTML Field Values
    Define Conversion Modules
  Monitoring Dates
    Define Events
    Assign Reference Dates to Events
    Define Status
    Define Profiles for Monitoring Dates
    Define Scheduling Scenarios
  Bill of Material Transfer
    Define Profiles for Bill Of Material Transfer
    Define Reference Points for BOM Transfer
    Define Fields in BOM and Activity as Reference Point
    Define Field Selection for BOM Transfer
  Availability Check
    Define Checking Rules
    Define Checking Scope
    Define Checking Control
  Enhancements for Material Components
    Develop Enhancement for BOMs
    Create Processing of Material Components
    Enhancement for Purchase Requisitions with External Procurement
  Control of Sales-Order-Related Production
    Check Account Assignment Categories
    Check Requirements Classes
    Check Requirements Types
    Check Control of Requirements Type Determination
    Selection of Requirements Type Through MRP Group
      Check Planning Strategies
      Check Strategy Groups
      Check Assignment of Strategy Group to MRP Group

- ▽ Selection of Requirements Type Through SD Item Category
  - Check Item Categories
  - Check Item Category Groups
  - Check Assignment of Item Categories
- ▽ Confirmation
  - Stipulate Time for Confirmation Processing
  - Define Paralleling Type for Confirmation Processes
  - Schedule Background Jobs Confirmation Processes
  - Define Confirmation Parameters
  - Define Causes for Variances
  - Define Field Selection for Confirmation
  - ▽ Enhancements for Confirmation
    - Develop the Determination of Cust.-Specific Default Values
    - Develop Customer-Specific Input Checks (1)
    - Develop Customer-Specific Check after Activity Selection
    - Develop Customer-Specific Input Checks (2)
    - Develop Customer-Specific Enhancements for Saving
- ▽ Simulation
  - Stipulate Version Keys for the Simulation
  - Stipulate Simulation Profiles
- ▽ Project Versions
  - Create Profile for Project Version
- ▽ Progress
  - ▽ Progress Analysis
    - Maintain Progress Version
    - Define Statistical Key Figure for Percentage of Completion
    - Define Measurement Methods
    - Define Measurement Method as Default Value
    - Enter Measurement Methods for Order Type
    - Maintain Assignment of Cost Element Group
    - Develop Measurement Technique Enhancement
    - Evaluation in Information System
  - ▽ Progress Tracking
    - Define Standard Events
    - Define Event Scenarios
    - Maintain Relationships Between Events in a Scenario
    - Assign Default Scenario to Material Group
    - Maintain Priorities for an Event
    - Define Progress Tracking Profile
    - Define Status Info Types
    - Number Range Status Information
    - User-Defined Evaluation

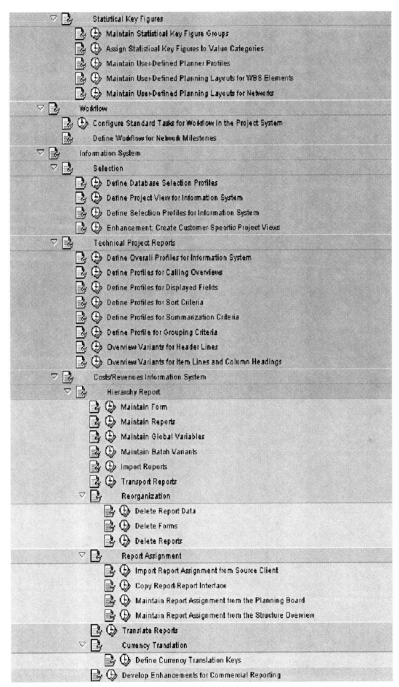

Statistical Key Figures
- Maintain Statistical Key Figure Groups
- Assign Statistical Key Figures to Value Categories
- Maintain User-Defined Planner Profiles
- Maintain User-Defined Planning Layouts for WBS Elements
- Maintain User-Defined Planning Layouts for Networks

Workflow
- Configure Standard Tasks for Workflow in the Project System
- Define Workflow for Network Milestones

Information System
- Selection
  - Define Database Selection Profiles
  - Define Project View for Information System
  - Define Selection Profiles for Information System
  - Enhancement: Create Customer-Specific Project Views
- Technical Project Reports
  - Define Overall Profiles for Information System
  - Define Profiles for Calling Overviews
  - Define Profiles for Displayed Fields
  - Define Profiles for Sort Criteria
  - Define Profiles for Summarization Criteria
  - Define Profile for Grouping Criteria
  - Overview Variants for Header Lines
  - Overview Variants for Item Lines and Column Headings
- Costs/Revenues Information System
  - Hierarchy Report
    - Maintain Form
    - Maintain Reports
    - Maintain Global Variables
    - Maintain Batch Variants
    - Import Reports
    - Transport Reports
    - Reorganization
      - Delete Report Data
      - Delete Forms
      - Delete Reports
    - Report Assignment
      - Import Report Assignment from Source Client
      - Copy Report-Report Interface
      - Maintain Report Assignment from the Planning Board
      - Maintain Report Assignment from the Structure Overview
    - Translate Reports
    - Currency Translation
      - Define Currency Translation Keys
      - Develop Enhancements for Commercial Reporting

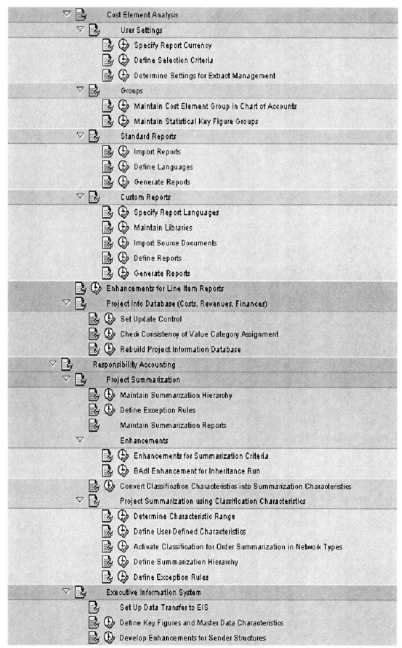

Copyright by SAP AG

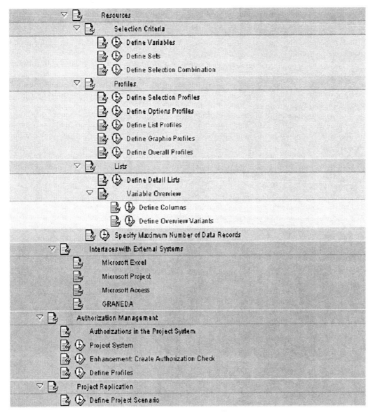

Copyright by SAP AG

---

## Summary

The Technical elements of PS are many and far-reaching. This book does not cover the ABAP (SAP's 4GL coding language) side of PS. Its objectives are to show both novices and professionals the functional elements of PS. The technical elements covered in this chapter provide you with the basic tables and fields you may need to help write functional specifications with some technical knowledge.

# Tips and Tricks

T his chapter provides you with tips and tricks that may be useful in the world of PS. Some of the subjects here have been briefly covered in earlier chapters.

## Design Tips

In your design (whether it be for simple cost-collecting, customer, asset, or any other specific purpose) certain subtleties need to be understood to work around some of SAP's behaviour. Sometimes it's hard to find out exactly what the system is doing (and why) without combing through thousands of pages of help text, or indeed looking for SAP Notes to cure certain behaviour. The following design tips can help you work with SAP.

### Projects with Sales Documents

Normally, customer projects have a WBS linked to a line item on a sales order (or quotation). This linkage can be performed manually or automatically. In Assembly Processing, the sales order line-item is automatically account-assigned to the Billing WBS. However, when viewed from the project (and when Networks are used), it is the Network Header that shows a link to the sales order line-item (seen via the Assignments tab of the header).

Because Assembly Processing requires a Billing WBS to perform this link, there may be instances where you have more than one billing element. If they are at the same level, SAP will not know which one to use and will issue a dialogue box for you to decide. This is because you have one Network Header and it is that to which the link is primarily made. To overcome this, nest your billing elements, as shown in Figure 8-1. This is SAP Best Practice for designs where you may have a "Front" and a "Back" office and need to segregate their postings.

Also, remember that the "delivery Plant" in the sales order line-item must point to a WBS that has a valid Company Code (to which the Plant is assigned). This particular problem arises when you have multiple Company Codes in your project. To further provide a structure that suits cross-company scenarios, you can separate your network header from its activities by clever use of assignments in the standard Network, as shown in Figure 8-2.

FIGURE 8-1
Nesting of billing
elements

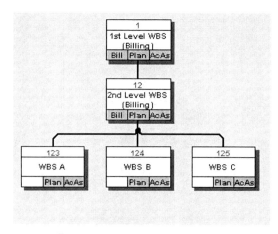

Project with Multiple Billing Elements

Copyright by SAP AG

Point Network Header to the 1st
Level WBS.

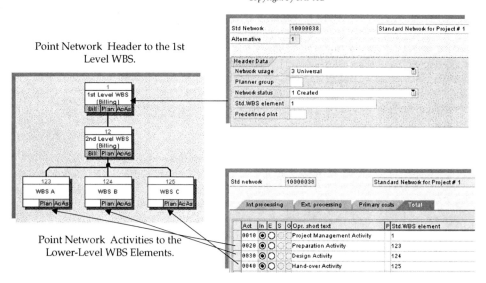

Point Network Activities to the
Lower-Level WBS Elements.

Resulting in an operative project that
looks like this, which enables you to
point the Top Level Billing Element to
the Sales Order line-item, but plan and
post costs at the lower levels.

Note that this technique may be used
when you have special Results Analysis
and Settlement rules for both Billing
Elements.

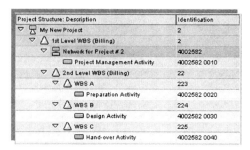

Copyright by SAP AG

FIGURE 8-2   Separation of network header

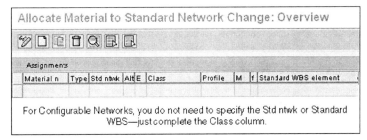

Copyright by SAP AG

FIGURE 8-3   Class Assignment

## Classes and Characteristics

If you want to be flexible about which standard network is used in Assembly Processing, you can use a "characteristic class." The class will feature characteristics that automatically select the correct standard network "alternative." Additionally, the relevant class is attached to the configurable material you specify on your sales order line-item. In cases like this, transaction CN08 (Material Assignment) will have both the standard WBS and standard Network left blank, but will have the Class column filled in, as shown in Figure 8-3.

Then, when your project is created, the correct standard network alternative will be selected by the system. Following are the steps required to achieve this:

| Transaction | Purpose |
|---|---|
| 1. CLO4 | Create your characteristics CHR_PLANT (this can also be done in CLO2, next). |
| 2. CLO2 | Create a new Class MYCLASS using Class Type "Standard Network Class" and add characteristic CHR_PLANT. |
| 3. CU42 | Assign Class MYCLASS to the Configuration Profile for your Material. |
| 4. CU50 a. Select the Material/Plant and set radio buttons Sales/Distribution and BOM. b. Select Menu option Value Assignments->Interface Design->Characteristic grouping to group the characteristic. c. Create a "Plant" tab. d. Assign the CHR_PLANT Characteristics to the tab. | Assign the CHR_PLANT characteristics the Configurable Material and create a "Plant" tab. (Note: If step 2 on the left has the menu option greyed-out, go back to CU42 and make sure the "Configuration Design" field has been completed.) |
| 5. CN01/CN02 a. For each alternative, select menu path Extras->Classification. b. Add the Class. c. Add the characteristics. | Create Std Network with some Activities. |
| 6. VA01/VA02 | Create a Sales Order with a line item specifying the configurable material to which you added your characteristics. Go to the Plant tab and enter a value. |

## Object Dependencies

In addition to performing the preceding, you can pass data from a configurable material to the project using a characteristic. Let's say you want to automate the entry of a General Cost Activity. All you have to do is follow the same steps as earlier, but create an additional Tab for Costs in step 4 and add your characteristic (for instance, CHR_COST). Then, in step 5, instead of adding the Class and the characteristics to the Alternative, go to your previously created General Cost Activities in CN02 and follow the Extras->Object Dependencies-> Assignments menu path. Create a new entry and enter "CHR_COST specified."

This means that if a value was placed against the characteristic CHR_COST in the Sales Order, it will be transferred to the network activity without the user having to edit the project at all. Needless to say, the characteristic names you use will depend on your own naming conventions.

Following are the steps required to achieve this:

| Transaction | Purpose |
|---|---|
| 1. CL04 | Create your characteristics CHR_COST (this can also be done in CL02, following). If you want to specify different costs to reflect the various Cost Elements, just give them a meaningful name, like CHR_INSURANCE_COST or CHR_HOTEL_COST. |
| 2. CL02 | Create a new Class MYCLASS using Class Type "Standard Network Class" and add characteristic CHR_COST (you can use an existing class if you want). You can add the other cost characteristics here as well. |
| 3. CU42 | Assign Class MYCLASS to the Configuration Profile for your Material. |
| 4. CU50<br>a. Select the Material/Plant and set radio buttons Sales/Distribution and BOM.<br>b. Select Menu option Value Assignments->Interface Design->Characteristic grouping to group the characteristic.<br>c. Create a "Plant" tab.<br>d. Assign the CHR_PLANT Characteristics to the tab. | Assign the CHR_COST characteristics the Configurable Material and create a "Costs" tab or some other meaningful name.<br>(Note: If step 2 on the left has the menu option greyed-out, go back to CU42 and make sure the "Configuration Design" field has been completed.) |
| 5. CN01/CN02<br>a. For each General Cost Activity, follow the menu path Extras->Object Dependencies->Assignments.<br>b. Create a new entry and enter "CHR_COST specified." | Create Std Network with some General Cost Activities. |
| 6. VA01/VA02 | Create Sales Order with a line item specifying the configurable material to which you added your characteristics. Go to the Costs tab and enter a value. |

When your sales order is saved, the values will be passed to the project.

This method of using characteristics to move information between SD and PS is only a simple example—the possibilities are endless.

## Validations and Substitutions

### Prerequisites

Sometimes it's easy to forget that "prerequisites" use normal logic and "checks" use reverse-logic. That is:

- In Validations: If the prerequisite is met, but the check is not, the validation has failed and a message will be issued.
- In Substitutions: If the prerequisite is met, the substitution will take place.

Have you ever wanted to stop a Standard WBS from executing a validation rule? It's annoying when the rule you want to apply is only relevant for an Operative project (remember, the Validation Rule itself is placed within your Project Profile and usually has the "automatic" box ticked so it validates when you save your project). Due to the nature of Validation Rules (and Substitutions for that matter), they apply to both Standard and Operative projects—there is no distinction, so it will be applied to both.

There are many examples of a scenario for this. For instance, say you have a rule that validates if the Person Responsible is between a certain range when the Project Type is equal to a certain value. If you don't want this done in the Standard project, but do want it done in the project that is created from it, then in your Validation Prerequisite, enter the value shown in Figure 8-4 along with your other prerequisites.

What this does is check to see if the project was derived from a standard project and save you from having to worry about other prerequisites such as "is the Person Responsible equal to blank." This technique is most useful in Substitutions, because your standard projects are created once (and may not need the substitution), but operative projects are more dynamic and usually have some of their default or null values manually changed from whatever was in the template.

If you want to avoid performing a validation/substitution when a project is created from an outside source, you need only have a prerequisite that looks at the "Created By" field, as shown in Figure 8-5 using its technical field name.

This works because the Created By field is not actually recorded until the project is saved.

---

**FIGURE 8-4**
Standard WBS, in prerequisite using its technical field name

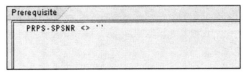

Prerequisite

PRPS-SPSNR <> ''

**Figure 8-5**
Created By, in
prerequisite

Two more points:

- Projects created from external sources will have their substitutions performed <u>before</u> the project is saved.

- In contrast, manually created projects have their Validations/Substitutions performed when you save the project. And/or, they can have their Validations/Substitutions performed manually, by triggering the event via the menu path Edit-> Validation/Substitution.

## Project Progress

SAP's Project Progress includes Progress Analysis, Milestone Trend Analysis, and Cost Forecast:

- Progress analysis determines and compares planned and actual project progress values and Expected Progress. It evaluates Earned value Analysis where comparisons are made against Time and Cost combined relevance.

- Milestone Trend Analysis tracks a milestone's schedule trends against a baseline.

- Cost forecast performs a forecast "estimate-at-completion" based on plan and actuals to date and calculates cost-to-complete.

### Progress Analysis

One of the most fundamental aspects of PS is the need to analyze the progress of a project. This does not necessarily apply to all projects—particularly those where dates and milestones don't matter and scheduling of work does not apply. However, projects that are time and cost critical have at their disposal a few ways of analyzing their progress.

### CO Versions

Before you start, there are a few prerequisites: In the IMG, you must define Progress Versions that are CO (Controlling) Version for exclusive Use in Progress Analysis for projects. Here, the system records the progress analysis data that you can evaluate at any time. Apart from forming the basis for determining Earned Value (Cost Plan or Budget), they also determine:

- **POC Weightage**   Based on Cost Plan, Budget, or Work
- **Planning type**   Basic or Forecast
- **Set of dates**   Early or Late Dates
- **Reference**   Default Method for Plan and Actual

If you work with statistical key figures, that is, you want to calculate the POC (Percentage of Completion) on a quantity-proportion basis, you must make the following settings in the IMG:

- The statistical key figures where you want the POCs to be recorded. You assign the statistical key figures to Value Categories so that the system can display them.
- The Default Cost Elements or Groups against which values will be recorded.
- For Progress Analysis Config: Go to the Implementation Guide of the *Project System* and choose *Progress → Progress Analysis*.

The POC calculation requires a measurement method:

- Use one of the measurement methods prescribed by SAP.
- Define default measurement methods per object in customizing.

### Steps to Perform Progress Analysis

1. Create your project structures, say, using transaction CJ20N.
2. Enter a measurement method for the WBS element, activity, or activity element.
3. Enter the planned data for the project (Cost Element Costs, dates, milestones, and so on).
4. Enter/post the actual data for the project.
5. Determine the progress of your project (CNE1/CNE2). Determine Plan and Actual POC.
6. Calculate the BCWP and BCWS based on the reference factor (planned costs, budget).
7. Evaluate your project's progress in the information system.

### Glossary of Terms

- **Planned POC (planned progress in percentage of the overall work)**   Weightage factor (normally proportional to planned cost)
- **BCWS (Budgeted Cost of Work Scheduled)**   Value of planned work/services = Planned POC × overall budget *or* POC × overall planned cost (as set in IMG)
- **BCWP (Budgeted Cost of Work Performed)**   Value of actual work performed/earned value = Actual POC × Overall Budget *or* POC × Overall planned cost (per IMG)
- **ACWP (Actual Cost of Work Performed)**   Actual cost incurred
- SV (Schedule Variance) = BCWP – BCWS
- CV (Cost Variance) = BCWP – ACWP
- CPI (Cost Performance Index) = BCWP/ACWP (Cost efficiency indicator)

- SPI (Schedule Performance Indicator) = BCWP/BCWS (Schedule efficiency indicator)
- EAC (Estimated Cost at Completion = Total Planned Costs/CPI

Example:

| Example: | Period-> | Dec-06 | Jan-07 | Feb-07 | Mar-07 | Apr-07 | May-07 | Month-Ends |
|---|---|---|---|---|---|---|---|---|
| (Cumulative values in $) | BCWP | 0 | 80 | 100 | 180 | 300 | 350 | Budgeted Cost of Work Performed |
| (Cumulative values in $) | BCWS | 0 | 100 | 160 | 250 | 380 | 420 | Budgeted Cost of Work Scheduled |
| (Cumulative values in $) | ACWP | 0 | 120 | 200 | 300 | 480 | 540 | Actual Cost of Work Performed |

See Figure 8-6 for a typical EVA graph, as produced in SAP.

### POC (Percentage of Completion) Measurement Methods

In the measurement method, you determine how the system calculates the POC for an object WBS, Activity, or Activity Element.

The following table shows where you maintain the measurement methods for the various objects:

| Object | Maintaining the Measurement Method |
|---|---|
| Projects in structure planning | *Details → General*, then *Progress* tab page |
| Projects in the project planning board | *Details → Detailed information on object*, then *Progress* tab page |
| WBS element | *Details → General*, then *Progress* tab page |
| Activities or activity elements | *Details → Activity/Element → General*, then *Progress* tab page |
| Assigned orders | In Project System customizing, under *Progress → Progress analysis* |

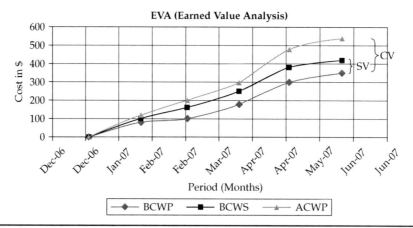

**FIGURE 8-6**   Earned Value Analysis

## Measurement Techniques

The measurement technique determines how the system uses the available data to determine the POC. In the SAP system, the following measurement techniques are available:

- **Start-Finish Rule** Based on scheduling, the Start and Finish (Basic/Actual) for the Percentage of Confirmation; applying the 20-80 Rule would mean POC = 20% on Start of the Activity and remaining 80% POC only on completion.

- **Milestone Technique** Set Indicator for Progress Analysis & Actual Cumulative POC on milestones.

- **Estimates** Manually maintain plan/actual POC for WBS/activity for each period; in IMG set max POC.

- **Time Proportionality** System determines POC in proportion to the total project duration.

- **Degree of Processing** Degree of Processing entered on activity confirmation is the POC.

- **Quantity Proportionality** Use SKF, Planned Qty, Actual Qty, and Total Qty for calculating POCs.

- **Secondary Proportionality** POC of a WBS/Act is dependant on POC of another WBS/Activity.

- **Cost Proportionality** Use Planned Cost, Actual Costs, and Overall Costs to calculate POC.

SAP recommend the POC methods listed as follows:

| Object | Plan | Actual | Comments |
|---|---|---|---|
| Internally processed activity | Milestone technique, cost proportional | Milestone technique, degree of processing | |
| Externally processed activity | Cost proportional, time proportional | Cost proportional, time proportional | |
| General costs activities | Cost proportional, milestone, estimate, start-finish | Cost proportional, milestone, estimate, start-finish | |
| Production order for project | Cost proportional | Cost proportional | The system uses a suitable weighting to aggregate the POC for the order in the activity. |
| WBS element | Milestone Quantity proportional Start finish Estimates Time proportional Cost proportional | Milestone Quantity proportional Start finish Estimates Time proportional Cost proportional | If activities are assigned to the WBS element, the POC should be calculated in the activity. The system uses a suitable weighting to aggregate the POC for the activities in the WBS element. |

Define a default measurement method for each object type by entering this setting in the Project System IMG: Progress-Progress Analysis-Define Measurement Method as Default Value.

Progress Determination is performed using CNE1 (Indiv) or CNE2 (Collective). The system calculates EV = POC × Overall Costs and records the values.

### Evaluating Project Progress

1. Use Structure Report CNE5
2. S_ALR_87015124
3. S_ALR_87015125

You can also call a Graphical Report by choosing menu option Goto->Graphic->Progress Analysis Workbench: Logistics->Project System->Progress-Progress Analysis->Workbench. Customizing for the Project System is found under Confirmation->Enhancements for Confirmation->Develop Customer-Specific Confirmations for the Progress Analysis Workbench.

### Milestone Trend Analysis (MTA)

In the Project Builder, CJ20N or other maintenance transactions such as CJ2B, create/modify the milestones for WBS/Activities and set the Trend analysis indicator in the Usage section.

Create Project Versions by accessing Project Information System menu path Structure->Structure Overview or in Project Execution menu path Period-End closing->Project Versions. Set the MTA relevant indicator while saving the project version with a version key, the version group, and if required a description of the version.

Reschedule if you want to use data from the operative project or a simulation version and update this data.

Milestone Trend Analysis can be accessed via menu path Project System->Information System->Progress->Milestone Trend Analysis or in the project planning board. Both Graphic and Tabular forms are available. Either basic dates or forecast dates are used. The System takes previous schedule dates milestones from project versions and compares them with current milestone schedule dates.

In MTA, it is possible to choose either Historical curve or Historical Milestones for reporting on Milestones with the MTA indicator set for current period or earlier (but not set in current) respectively.

Example:

| Example | | | | | | Jan-07 | Feb-07 | Mar-07 | Apr-07 | <-- X axis: Status Month-Ends |
|---------|---|---|---|---|---|--------|--------|--------|--------|---|
| Milestone | Descp | ProjDefn | WBS | Network | Act | Release | Proj Ver 1 | Proj Ver 2 | Proj Ver 3 | : <-- Are Project Versions |
| 27296 | Design - Complete | 16261 | 16261.10.30 | 5020674 | 0030 | 5/4/2007 | 5/10/2007 | 5/16/2007 | 5/22/2007 | <-- Y axis: Schedule Dates on Milestones of the Project per project versions |
| 27300 | Build - Complete | 16261 | 16261.10.30 | 5020674 | 0130 | 7/1/2007 | 7/1/2007 | 7/1/2007 | 7/1/2007 | |
| 27304 | Testing Complete | 16261 | 16261.10.30 | 5020674 | 0290 | 8/25/2007 | 8/15/2007 | 8/1/2007 | 8/1/2007 | |

**Figure 8-7**
Milestone Trend
Analysis

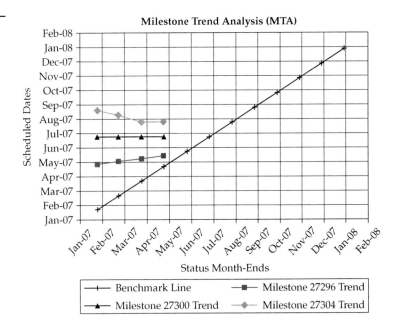

See Figure 8-7 for a typical MTA graph, as produced in SAP.

The MTA graph generated by SAP does not show a Triangle lower than the Benchmarking 45-degree line. If the trend line dips, then the Milestone is ahead of schedule; if the trend line is horizontal, then the Milestone is on schedule. If the trend line inclines upwards, then the Milestone is delayed. If the trend line hits the 45-degree benchmarking line, then it means the milestone is completed (actual date).

## Project Cost Forecast

With project progress, variances occur between the original planned cost and the actual cost. Therefore, it is necessary to check and update the figures for the remaining costs during the whole of a project's life cycle. The system determines cost to complete and evaluates remaining activities on the basis of the plan, forecast, and actual values in the network. The resulting figure is arrived at by adding the actual and commitment costs already incurred in the project to the updated cost to complete.

This forecast is detailed in Figure 8-8.

You can carry out the cost forecast at any time for one or more projects. To this end, the system copies the updated costs to complete (along with the actual and commitment values) into a separate forecast version, which you can then evaluate in the information system. If required, you can manage more than one forecast version in parallel. The standard version is CO version 110 for exclusive use of forecast costs.

The system determines cost to complete only for activity-assigned networks that are both appended and apportioned. Preliminary planning networks are not included.

1. Before accessing the cost forecast, Reschedule the project and Calculate overhead on actual and commitment values.

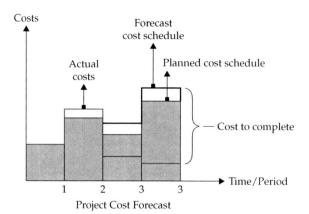

**FIGURE 8-8**
Project Cost
Forecast

2. Use menu path Financials->Period-End Closing->Single Functions to access the cost forecast. You can run the cost forecast in individual or collective processing.

3. Based on planned, actual, and commitment values, the system determines the remaining costs in network activities. It includes all actual and commitment values in the project, plan values for network activities in CO Version 0, and Forecast values from confirmations. However, it does not consider WBS element plan values or Network preliminary planning values or Plan costs for material components in valuated project stock.

4. Based on planned, actual, and commitment costs, the system determines what is still to be done in network activities and costs this again. The system records the value so determined as cost to complete, by period, in a forecast version for Internally processed activities, Externally processed activities, General costs activities, and Material components not managed as part of project stock (whether valued or not).

5. If an activity is marked as complete or there is a final confirmation for it, the system sets the cost to complete to zero. The system copies the cost to complete to the forecast version, along with the actual and commitment values for the project, which it reads from the database. Commitment values from periods before the period of the cost forecast key date are recorded in the forecast version as of the period of the key date (default: current period).

As mentioned before, the standard system offers forecast version 110. Forecast versions are CO versions that can only be used to handle forecast costs. You can define additional forecast versions in the Project System IMG.

Cost forecasts are normally performed as part of periodic processing. Use Project Information System to report Forecast values, Cost to complete, Actual, and Commitment values at the time of the cost forecast. You can use hierarchy reports and cost element reports to evaluate the data. With the standard system, SAP delivers hierarchy report Forecast 12CTC1.

---

**NOTE** *It is not possible to carry out Cost Forecast for Simulation Versions.*

# Other Useful Information

- Use transaction BS23 to get a <u>list of Project Status</u>.

- Use transaction CMOD to <u>manage User Exits</u>.

- Use transaction SM12 to <u>unlock tables</u> that may have gotten locked.

- Use transaction OKKS to <u>set Controlling Area</u> from any point.

- Use transaction SU53 to <u>check if you have an Authorizations problem</u> when a function does not appear to work.

- Use transaction GS01 to <u>maintain Sets</u> (which are like Groups). Useful if you want to create them outside of maintaining things like DIP Profile sets.

- Use transaction CT04 to <u>maintain characteristics</u> where you want to specify Additional Data (Table names and Fields).

- Use transaction OKSS at any time to <u>set the Controlling Area</u> (in another session, so use the /o prefix if you don't want to lose data from your current session).

- To see what possible <u>IMG Customization</u> is available for tables that are used in Projects, use transaction SM30 and select Customization (continue "without project" to see all IMG points). It is unlikely you will have a maintenance dialogue box for PROJ and PRPS, so don't bother with these tables.

- If you want to start a <u>new session using the /N option,</u> changes that you may have made in the current transaction will be immediately lost, without warning.

- Use transaction CN41 to get a good <u>structural overview</u> for a range of Projects. In this transaction, you can perform additional processes such as Mass Change. If you are not using "Status Selection Profiles," you can display all projects and then set a Filter (or Exception) to highlight projects with a specific status by placing a value in the Status Indicator under General Data.

- <u>Persons Responsible and Applicants</u> are featured in Configuration and are transportable. However, they can be directly edited in transactions OPS6 and OPS7 respectively via the Easy Access Menu in Current Settings.

- When using DIP Profiles to <u>generate Debit Memo Requests</u>, remember to tick the Document Number characteristic if you want every posting associated with an object to be selected. Otherwise, you will only get a summary.

- In CJ20N (Project Builder), you can <u>change the "Display Sequence"</u> from Description - identification to Identification - name by right-clicking in the blank area (below the structure) on the left side of the screen.

- Press CTRL-Y to mark blocks of text in any transaction, CTRL-C to copy that text, and CTRL-V to paste that text into the same transaction in a different session. These <u>key combinations</u> are useful particularly when creating Standard Projects and Network activities from other projects. You can also copy blocks of text from spreadsheets using the standard copy/paste methods, as long as the columns are spaced relatively.

## Known Limitations

- If you are using Easy Cost Planning with DIP Profiles for generating <u>Sales Order Simulations</u>, you may wonder why sometimes the calculations don't change even though you have added some costs. Try Deleting the pricing you did before and repeat the creation of pricing. This is done by selecting the menu path "Sales Pricing->Delete" when you are actually in the simulation screen.

- If you have modified a DIP Profile, it sometimes does not work in <u>Simulated Sales Pricing</u> if you used that DIP before. It issues an error message stating there were no costs found. If the problem persists, the best way to overcome it is to make a copy of the project in its entirety and start again. To avoid the problem, always delete the Sales Pricing before you change a DIP Profile.

- When in the <u>Project Builder</u> (CJ20N), the left side of the screen is used to position the object you see on the right side. If you are positioned on an object somewhere down the hierarchy and you select the Display/Change icon whilst in Change mode, all objects will be dimmed. However, if your cursor remains on that object and you re-press the Display/Change icon, that object will now appear at the top of the screen and you will lose sight of all objects above the one you were on. You can only get them back by starting CJ20N again.

- You cannot automatically set System Status REL (Release) for a Project. You can, however, automatically set a <u>User Status that simulates Release</u> by applying a User Status Profile that is set to Initial and "Allows" all Business Transactions. It's not ideal, but can be done. You can also simulate the other System Statuses. Projects automatically replicated from CRM are released, however.

- <u>Asynchronous Project Costing</u> (CJ9K) does not take into account modified values from a Sales Order BOM. This is not really an oversight on SAP's part—the transaction is designed to take both a Standard BOM and a WBS BOM into account.

- <u>Deleting an Operative project</u> is not easy. Normally, you have to set the status to CLSD (Closed) at the Project Definition level. Then you have to set the status to DLFL (Deletion Flag). Next use transaction CN80 (Archiving) and set the Deletion Indicator using a Variant for the range of projects. It is also possible to set the status DLFL here (not a wise choice unless your variant only selects specific projects), but you must set the Deletion Indicator here in order for the Archiving run to store the project(s) offline. Be aware of the Residence Time—this is determined for Networks in the Network Type under the Reorganization tab. For detailed information on this, see "Network Types" in Chapter 5.

## Summary

There are many ways of navigating and maintaining PS and trying to document them all would be impossible. What you have seen here are just some of the tips and tricks available to you. In future editions of this book, the list will grow. There are many forums around that also help you to find better ways of solving problems.

# Index

Breinigsville, PA USA
20 December 2010
251768BV00002B/23/P